Creating Schools That Heal

Real-Life Solutions

Creating Schools That Heal

Real-Life Solutions

Lesley Koplow

Teachers College, Columbia University
New York and London

To my sweetest girl, Yoela

Published by Teachers College Press, 1234 Amsterdam Avenue,
New York, NY 10027

Library of Congress Cataloging-in-Publication Data

Koplow, Lesley.
   Creating schools that heal: real-life solutions / Lesley Koplow.
      p.   cm.
   Includes bibliographical references and index.
   ISBN 0-8077-4268-6 (pbk.) — ISBN 0-8077-4269-4 (cloth)
      1. Early childhood education—Social aspects—United States.   2. School environment—Social aspects—United States.   3. Child development—United States.   I. Title.
LB1139.25 .K65 2002
372.21—dc21   2002021141

ISBN 0-8077-4268-6   (paper)
ISBN 0-8077-4269-4   (cloth)

Printed on acid-free paper
Manufactured in the United States of America

09   08   07   8   7   6   5   4   3

Contents

PART IV
A Challenge for Policymakers
∼ 161 ∼

∼ Handouts ∼

Acknowledgments

I GRATEFULLY ACKNOWLEDGE the contributions of all the fine practitioners I have had the privilege to observe in the process of their daily struggle to create healing environments for children in the school settings. I offer special thanks to Eleanor Greig Ukoli, Laurel O. Fraser, Lillian Burke, Tina Volpe, and Jean McPadden for their vision and dedication to the emotional health of young children. I would like to thank Jackie Lewis, Felice Wagman, Claire Dougherty, Tim Lightman, and Elizabeth McLaughlin for allowing me to observe best practices in classroom life, as well as the many public school teachers, paraprofessionals, administrators, and school-based clinicians whose work has helped to inform the ideas developed here. In addition, I would like to thank Sarah Carlson for assisting me in the preparation of the manuscript.

PART I

First Things First: Understanding Children's Social and Emotional Needs

CHILDREN MUST LEARN *the "basics" in order to succeed in school. We often hear this statement from politicians who are pledging to reform low-performing schools. Children must, indeed, learn the "basics" in order to do well in school, but in Part I of this book, the basics are redefined to include the social and emotional milestones that constitute a foundation for learning. The "basics" of teacher education are also redefined here to include understanding the "personhood" of young children and actively nurturing that emerging personhood as an essential element of early-grade education.*

When children don't have the opportunity to resolve social and emotional developmental milestones that underlie emotional well-being, they may be distracted and difficult to manage in the classroom. Part I orients early-childhood professionals to reading signs of emotional distress in young schoolchildren so that staff can be responsive to unresolved social and emotional issues during this critical period. Early-grade classrooms are in the position to invite children to work on those developmental issues because they can do so in a way that is compatible with sound early-childhood educational practice.

1

When educators learn how to read and address signs of emotional distress in early childhood, they integrate preventive mental health intervention into the public school experience, thus protecting children from risk as they go into the upper-school grades and move toward adolescence.

The final chapter of Part I emphasizes the importance of allowing kindergarten children to express genuine affects in school. Kindergarten teachers must encourage children to engage in open-ended play, drawing, work with expressive arts materials, and building in order to promote emotional well-being and enhance ultimate learning potential. When five-year-olds are forced into academically prescriptive curriculums, they are deprived of expressive outlets and social opportunities that increase their ability to cope with stressors and protect them from feelings of isolation and distractibility. The long-term learning potential of young children is enhanced when the agenda of the kindergarten teacher supports the social and emotional agenda of the group.

CHAPTER 1

The Development of Personhood

CHILDREN ENTERING public school for the first time come into their classrooms wide-eyed, struck by the "bigness" of the environment, the variety of materials for exploration, and the din of voices of so many other children their age. The high ceilings, huge windows, and echoing hallways seem cavernous, and many children hold the hand of the adults who brought them more tightly, occasionally eyeing the teacher's face for signs of trustworthiness. The child has a daunting task ahead of him. He must become comfortable in this big, new world. He must find experiences of intimacy to embrace him so he will not be lost in the crowd. He must find a way to communicate so his voice will not be lost in the muddle of voices. He must find a way to continue his developmental journey toward personhood while taking in and being receptive to new learning.

The teacher receiving children entering public school for the first time has an equally daunting task. She must find a way to make the environment intimate, inviting, and emotionally safe. She must become attuned to these new voices so that she can respond to each one in a personal way. She must gradually discover the level of receptivity that each child has and the avenues of learning that are the most accessible. She must find a way to become a partner in development to each of the twenty-five children in her room or risk leaving those children alone with the overwhelming assignment of moving toward personhood without a partner for the six or more hours that they are at school.

Teachers who have mastered addressing these essential tasks in the early grades find that they know a lot about the children in their classrooms. If they teach 5-year-olds for more than a few years, they come to know a lot about their developmental issues. They begin to understand what motivates 5-year-olds, what excites them, and what makes them cry. Over time, these teachers begin to learn about each child's life experience. This happens as the teacher watches the child's unfolding themes in the dramatic play area, as parents confide in the teacher during conferences, and as the child himself or herself begins to communicate experiences. The teacher sees the interaction between development and experience within each child and finds a way to interact with the child that supports the integration of those two processes, encourages the expression of a joyful and confident sense of 5-year-old self, and provides positive imagery for future growth and evolution. All masterly teachers know that a 5-year-old desperately needs to believe that, if he cannot do something now because it is too difficult, he will have the power to do it when he is older.

The Risk

Teachers who have chosen to become partners in their students' developmental journeys often have done so without invitation. They have done so because it has "felt right" to them. When questioned about their style of teaching, such teachers say such things as, "How can I teach them if I don't really know them?" For them, teaching is by definition about personal involvement. When asked whether an emphasis on the child as a whole person was present in their particular school or school district, or whether it was explored and taught in the teacher-education program that prepared them to teach, many of these teachers say that these concerns sometimes get lip service in their programs, but the techniques taught and the pressures to use prescriptive programs often contradict rather than support their commitment to children's well-being and emotional health in the classroom.

If teachers in the early grades can choose to practice as partners in development to the children in their classrooms, and can also choose not to practice this way, then there are many children who remain partnerless during the six or more hours a day that they attend school. If some teachers express a desire to practice in a way that heightens their opportunities for relationships with children but feel that this runs counter to the desires of the system for which they work, they will often surrender the desire to avoid conflict. Their students may never know that the teacher sees them as individuals who are worthy of being known in a deep way. Some children may have partnerships at home or in other arenas of their lives that can help compensate for this. Many children do not. By not making the emotional well-being of children at school an institutional priority, we run great risks: that many children's journeys toward personhood will become clouded; that many children will spend hours each day feeling isolated and lonely; that many children will not be able to connect to the peer group in healthy ways and will become outcasts or members of anti-social peer group. Some of these children will act out as a cry for help, causing their teachers grief in elementary school. Many will not find avenues of expression for their pain until adolescence, when the developmental and physiological changes that occur may disturb their equilibrium and cause eruption. Most such children will not cause the kind of pain to others that makes the newspapers, but they may always be in pain themselves. Many will be distracted by this pain and will become poor achievers as a result.

Emotional Well-Being: Whose Responsibility?

Who is responsible for the emotional well-being of schoolchildren? Is it the parent? The teacher? The principal? The school social worker? Is it possible that all of these people are responsible? If so, what are the implications of this conclusion? If an institutional commitment were made to accompanying children on their developmental journey toward becoming the people that they are in the process of becoming, there would need to be an awareness of, and a knowledge about, developmental process among school personnel. The development of personhood would need to be the subject of a required course for teachers and administrators in training; it would also have to be an ongoing topic in staff development for veteran teachers.

Many schools of education require that educators complete at least one course in child development, yet the course may not emphasize bringing about an understanding of the development of "personhood." Personhood is not a very scientific term; I use it here to refer to the emergent sense of a self that is separate, distinctive, related to others, empathic to others, and capable of generating shared symbols to communicate those states of being. Anyone who visits the teachers' lounge in a large public elementary school will eventually hear teachers complain that certain children are not "human" enough. "They act like animals!" is a frequent remark that overwhelmed teachers make. The incidents of violence that have occurred in the nation's middle and high schools have often been hideous, and it is difficult to think that young people are capable of committing such acts. How, then, does a child grow to become "human enough" to know himself, express his likes and dislikes appropriately, become connected to the teacher and to his peers, turn away from violence, and feel empathy when this is called for? How do young children grow to become "human enough" to use language, art, and play to express their inner lives and to say something about how they make sense of their experiences at home and in school? How does this level of personhood, once achieved, enable conceptual development and learning?

Personhood from a Developmental Perspective

There is no more crucial time for a strong partnership between parent and child than the period of infancy and toddlerhood. Indeed, babies will not survive physically unless their physical needs are met by an adult, and they will not do well emotionally unless their physical needs are met by an adult who is caring, consistent, and attached. Attachment is the cornerstone of the unfolding developmental process for infants (Bowlby, 2000). The infant's cry for nurture and the attuned adult's consistent response sets the stage for an attachment relationship that becomes more intense as baby and parent get to know each other. The adult attachment figure becomes the baby's partner in the developmental process. The partner helps facilitate changes of state that would otherwise result in overwhelming discomfort and cause the baby to shut down or become overstimulated. With the help of the adult, the baby can go from a tired state to a sleeping state; from a hungry state to a full state; from a full state to a comfortable state. The intensity and intimacy of the attachment can filter out noxious experiences that would overwhelm the baby's delicate system if the baby were on his own. For example, the infant wrapped in a warm blanket is less likely to be tuned in to street noises and to feel the cold wind and more likely to be comforted by the rhythm of the mother's walking, the close hold, and the breathing of his or her attachment figure. The intimacy serves as protection from the intrusive world. Conversely, what the baby or developing toddler takes in from the outside comes through the lens of the attachment relationship.

The attuned, attached adult responds to the baby's distress in a timely manner, knowing that infants feel lost in time and cannot anticipate what comes next. Through a timely response and supportive manner, the attached adult communicates empathy for the infant's distress and does not allow him to become overwhelmed by discomfort.

The growing baby enjoys playing with toys by exploring them visually and tactilely and by banging them and putting them in his mouth. The 10-month-old who gleefully holds his rattle outside his crib, then tosses it to the floor, giggles with delight when the attentive parent retrieves it and hands it back to him, only to repeat this play sequence moments later. The adult becomes bored long before the baby tires of this game. Although it is a simple and repetitive play sequence, it is a brilliant way for the baby to give his partner in development the job of helping him experience the viability of items outside his sensory field. Infants do not seek lost objects. Between 9 months and 12 months of age, infants become capable of generating images of objects outside their moment-to-moment contact with them. This developmental milestone, called object permanence, is achieved when babies can imagine the object without seeing it, hearing it, or sensing it in other ways. The "mommy-get-the-toy" game helps children to experience their world as stable and dependable and to experience losses as recoverable.

Once babies have achieved object permanence, many important ego functions begin to unfold. A baby who knows that the items that interest him in his environment exist as entities separate from himself—and, in fact, exist even outside his sensory field—becomes curious about the names and function of objects. If this isn't me, what is this? After achieving object permanence, young toddlers begin to point, ask for, and often repeat labels of objects. It is an exciting time for toddlers and for their parents, who often hear the toddler's first words as clear evidence of personhood. The labels learned and words jointly invented to code items in the intimate environment are born within the attachment relationship, and the world becomes endowed with language and meaning that is shared by parent and child. The well-attached toddler will not leave his parents out of his exploration process; rather, he will engage his parents to point out and share discoveries (Stern, 1985).

When toddlers begin to point and label, they often are also starting to toddle. Between 12 months and 18 months of age, most children are on their feet, experiencing an increasing mobility that makes their world bigger and their dilemmas more intense. The young toddler is elated by her ability to go forth. She is empowered by her abilities to explore at a level, to reach new things, and to get herself onto more interesting ground. Between 15 months and 18 months of age, however, the toddler begins to feel ambivalence: Going forth is exciting and wonderful but often results in moving away from the attachment figure, who is the source of security. Children work at resolving this conflict in different ways throughout toddlerhood. The young toddler who has experienced the elation of going forth often spends much time making a bridge between parent and the environment. She moves away from the parent, finds something interesting to explore, and brings the item to the parent's lap. Parent and child connect, label, and explore the function of the treasure, then the toddler goes off to retrieve something else. The parent's job is to stay put so that the child can practice creating a psychological home base, somewhere that she can go from and return to without getting lost in the wide world (Mahler, Pine, & Bergman, 2000). By going away from the parent, coming back and connecting, and going away again, the toddler finds a way to remain oriented in the environment, taking initiative and exploring without becoming disconnected from her source of security.

Eventually, the need for frequent refueling becomes too confining, and the developing toddler needs more freedom to forge a relationship to the world. She often accomplishes this by creating a transitional object, such as a blanket or soft toy that is part of her intimate environment, as a symbol for the attachment relationship (Winnicott & Winnicott, 1982). With this blanket or other symbol, the toddler can feel the comfort of being with the attached parent even though the parent may be in another room or at work. The invention of a transitional object is important, because it shows not only that the child has a primary attachment but also that she has the cognitive capacity to be representational in thinking. The transitional object can also provide true comfort when a separation experience has become too frightening for a toddler or preschooler. This is essential for children who must be separated from their parents for many hours of the day, because the ability to imagine the attached adult who is out of sight comes later than the ability to recall lost items. Children typically achieve object permanence between 9 months and 12 months of age, but object constancy—the ability to carry the image of important people—is not in place until toddlers are 28 months to 36 months old. Separation anxiety can become overwhelming for children before object constancy is achieved, and the use of transitional objects may ameliorate the anxiety by providing physical and psychological evidence of mother.

Object Constancy and the Development of Personhood

A 2½-year-old who has achieved object permanence and object constancy knows a lot about her world and a lot about herself. She knows what is around her, what to call things, how to explore objects' use, and how to share her discoveries with others. If her grandmother is in another room doing the laundry, for example, 2½-year-old knows that grandma will come back when the laundry is in the machine, and if grandma is needed sooner, the child can call her or think about her. If adversity strikes while grandma is gone—say, the neighbor's dog begins to growl—the child will quickly seek proximity to her grandmother by going into the other room, or she will use the neighbor as a surrogate and seek protection. Because she knows that she has someone who is on her side in life, the 2½-year-old expects other adults also to be on her side and uses them as a resource. If grandma, who is usually pleasant and composed, becomes upset or angry when she returns and hears about the dog, the child may become hyperalert to the change of affect but will still recognize that her grandmother loves her, even if that feeling is temporarily expressed through anger. The achievement of object constancy demands that toddlers integrate both positive and negative affects expressed by the adult and integrate positive and negative experiences that they have had with the adult to make a whole image of the person. As long as the scales balance on the side of the positive experiences, object constancy can occur.

As toddlers integrate adults' expressions of positive and negative affects, they must also find a way to integrate their own positive and negative affects. The same toddler who is sunny and pleasant while digging in the sandbox at one moment may throw an intense tantrum the next because someone has touched her bucket. When the tantrum has passed, she may quickly resume happy play. The caregiver may watch incredulously, wondering what is possessing the child so completely during the tantrum and where all the rage has gone when it is over. The older toddler has the developmental task of getting to know both parts of herself and putting those parts together to create a sense of self. The older toddler must know that she is one girl who is sometimes happy, sometimes sad, sometimes angry, and sometimes frightened. When she looks in the mirror, she must recognize what is constant and develop an identity around what she sees about the person in the mirror. During toddlerhood, this person may be just as likely to express negative as positive affects. To develop a sense of self separate from her parents, the developing toddler thus goes through an oppositional period, saying "No!" to assert her autonomy and to feel different from the adults to whom she is so attached. By feeling different and separate, the toddler individuates from her attachment figure enough to feel confident when the caregiver is not with her (Mahler et al., 2000). If her primary adults can survive this negativity by remaining positive but firm, and by allowing the toddler to separate but remain connected, the toddler will feel that her mission to be different has been accomplished. She will be able to move away from the oppositional stance over time.

Partner as Mirror

How does a young child accomplish so much so early? These developmental tasks seem too profound for a very young child to accomplish alone. Indeed, these milestones are impossible to reach without a partner. No one can develop a sense of self-constancy without the help of a "personal mirror." The parent or primary attachment figure functions as such a mirror for the infant, toddler, and young child. The parent mirrors the affects of the infant to communicate understanding and empathy and verbally reflects the feeling states of the toddler and young child to help children clarify and express what they feel. The parent looks at the child with love and adoration, awe, respect, amazement, pride, and many other heartfelt emotions. The developing child looks into this personal or parental mirror and comes to see himself the way that significant others see him. Therefore, to support the developing toddler's process of integration, the adult must see the toddler as one child with special qualities but many different feeling states and affects. The parent must experience the child as likable and lovable in order for the child to like and love himself and to present himself as a likable, lovable person. Through the parental mirror—the eyes of his attachment figures—the young child sees the reflection of the person he is becoming and feels either valuable or worthless.

Children who have had good personal mirrors go to preschool with positive regard for themselves and for others. They view the teacher as a positive surrogate source of nurture and the preschool classroom as an arena for exploration. They initially devote their energy to discovering cause-and-effect relationships and are organized around adults' reactions of approval or displeasure and around their own activities and explorations. When children turn 4 years old, they begin to be organized by the approval of their peers, as well. The pre-kindergarten teacher lives with the paradox that, although 4-year-olds do not know what friendship really is, they do know that they desperately need it. Four-year-olds will cry if the answer to their question, "Will you be my friend?" is "No," because the peer group has begun to function as another source of feedback about self-worth. Children who are 3 do not care if other 3-year-olds like them. Four-year-olds find it hard to like themselves if other 4-year-olds do not like them. Vulnerability to the "peer group mirror" begins in pre-kindergarten and intensifies throughout a child's school years.

Life Experience and the Development of Personhood

The evolution of personhood in the young child is a developmental process, but it is also a process that depends in part on experience in order to unfold. When infants, toddlers, and preschool children lack a partner to support the process, or when traumatic and disruptive experiences occur during this important time, the development of personhood can be compromised (Karr-Morse & Wiley, 1997).

Research has shown that high amounts of stress in the lives of infants and toddlers can affect their brain chemistry and arrest their emotional and social development (Karr-Morse & Wiley, 1997). Specifically, infants and toddlers who are constantly overstimulated by a stressful environment, and who are not sufficiently protected by highly stressed adults, produce a high level of adrenaline. This causes the children to maintain a hyperaroused and hypervigilant state in which they attempt to ensure their own survival. When children spend large amounts of time in this state, they become unable to relax, even when the stressors are not present. The developmental consequences of staying on high alert are manifold. Although children on high alert may be able to make food for themselves, button their clothes, and manipulate door locks before most other children their age, they are also likely to lack self and object constancy, trust in adults, the ability to acquire frustration tolerance for age-appropriate challenges, the capacity to connect to and express a range of feeling, the ability to engage in secondary processes such as language and symbolic play, and the ability to feel empathy (Koplow, 1996). In other words, such children are likely to lack many of the developmental precursors, or building blocks, for identifying personhood. In addition, stressed children often experience benign irritations as potentially threatening: Even slightly adverse stimuli may set off the high-adrenaline fight-or-flight response, causing them to become highly charged and provoking extreme aggression or withdrawal (Karr-Morse & Wiley, 1997).

Stressed young children are often being cared for by stressed adults. Parents who are overwhelmed with multiple sources of stress tend to be less attuned to their children's needs, and less able to participate as active partners in their children's development, than their less-stressed counterparts. Parents who are deeply attached to their children but unable to protect them from the stressors in their lives because of poverty, domestic or societal violence, or other insidious factors, often feel overwhelming guilt and helplessness and experience depression. Infants and toddlers are known to synchronize their moods to those of their attachment figures in order to feel connected to them; thus, they often become depressed, as well (Figuerido, 1996; Pickens & Fields, 1993). Depression in adults often manifests in sad affect and low motivation, as well as in sleeplessness, loss of appetite, and so on. Depression in infants or toddlers may mimic a lack of alertness, hypo- or hyperactivity, and a lack of engagement with the environment, giving the impression of overall developmental delay. Depressed parents have difficulty acting as positive mirrors for their young children, because they see their children through a lens clouded by their own feelings of hopelessness. If children see hopelessness in the parental mirror, their own self-images can become often clouded, as well.

The disruption of a young child's primary attachment relationship through loss from death or abandonment can also have severe developmental and psychological consequences: Such loss can remove the partner for, and consequently arrest, the child's essential developmental processes. Children who lose the attachment relationship must find another primary adult who can not only help them grieve for their losses but also become a true partner in development. Well-nurtured, well-attached children who suffer such loss will be able to reconnect over time if there is someone else to love. Children who have had multiple losses or multiple disruptions in early life, and thus who have had few or no opportunities for stable attachment relationships, have less capacity to respond to later opportunities for attachment (Karen, 1998). Children who have undifferentiated relationships to others—or those diagnosed with Reactive Attachment Disorder—are at risk for difficult, disruptive, or aggressive behavior as they grow up, because their rage is not held by a containing parental relationship and there is a lack of superego to help inhibit destructive impulses.

Abuse and the Threat to Personhood

Teachers who are worried about poor academic performance or communication or socialization problems often single out children with histories of abuse and request that they be evaluated as a precursor to obtaining additional support for the child. Although public-school systems' evaluation processes almost always involve taking a psychosocial history, the focus is most often on the results of performance evaluations rather than on the threats to personhood contained in the story of the child's life experience. Thus, the child may receive many academic support services as a result of the evaluation, but the issues that threaten to undermine the child's emotional well-being—and thus the well-being of those around him—may go unaddressed. Many children in foster care show symptoms of, or are at risk for developing, Reactive Attachment Disorder. Almost every child in the foster-care system is there because of serious abuse or neglect. What are the developmental consequences of a history of abuse in the early school years?

Children who have been abused or seriously neglected are often unable to achieve a typical degree of object constancy (Koplow, 1996). All young children face the developmental task of integrating the positive and negative experiences that they have with primary adults; children who are being abused or extremely neglected, however, have experiences with adults that are essentially impossible to integrate. Therefore, the young child who has been repeatedly abused may use defenses of denial, dissociation, splitting, or identification with the aggressor to survive the ordeal. She may deny her parents' abusive behavior, dissociate her feelings from her body while the abuse is taking place, develop amnesia about the event and about events surrounding the experience of abuse, or identify with the parent's or parents' aggressive stance in order to feel powerful. If someone who has observed the child being roughly treated asks about it, the child may describe being punished "because I was bad." Although she may carry around an idealized or wished-for image of her parent, and refer to the goodness of her idealization, she often splits off the negative feelings and actions that belong to the parent and projects them onto other, less primary adults in her world. That is, instead of attributing the abuse to the primary adults who are actually hurting her, she may feel abused by the bus matron or by a school aide or teacher. Although the child may dissociate herself from the pain while actual abuse is occurring, she may scream, "Stop! You're hurting me! You're hurting me!" at an assistant teacher who escorts her out of the room because of disruptive behavior. In addition to difficulty retaining school lessons, the child may show other symptoms of post-traumatic stress disorder, such as vulnerability to dissociated states, sleep disturbance, hypervigilance, preoccupied state, and a tendency to experience benign events as terrifying.

Children who enter school with poor object constancy are most often difficult to contain in the classroom. Because they have not experienced consistent, nurturing adults and have not been able to integrate positive and negative experiences with adults, they do not expect teachers to be adults on whom they can count. Rather, teachers are likely to be seen as a potential threat, at best. At worst, during times of adversity, the child is likely to be oblivious to the fact that the teacher is even in the room. Children who cannot carry a positive image of an adult feel as though they are alone, and when adversity strikes, they tend to act as though they alone are responsible for their survival. Although another child's taking a cracker from a traumatized child's tray may not seem to be a life or death situation to the teacher, the child who must fend for himself at home may feel that it is, and may react as though it is. His extremely aggressive response will probably be seen as a worse offense than the taking of the cracker. In response, the adult will probably get angry, as is warranted, but may also communicate something negative about the traumatized child's self-worth or potential for personhood, thus becoming another negative mirror and further undermining the child's developmental process.

Learning about Personhood at School

Some children enter school knowing something about who they are and feeling hopeful about who they can become. But many children enter public school without that knowledge and without that hope. Can children learn about personhood in the school environment? Can they begin to feel hopeful about themselves during their early years in school? If the answer is yes, what techniques and curriculums will help bring this about?

To address some of these issues, many public-school systems now use something called "character education." This approach often employs literature and follow-up discussion about honesty, good citizenship, and positive values to help engage children in a process that may help improve their socialization and the tone of the community. Character education may be positive for some children, but is unlikely to be sufficient for children who have serious problems with emotional well-being, because it seeks to circumvent rather than address developmental issues that make social and emotional integrity difficult for stressed children. To make use of character education, the children must be "at age level" in their cognitive and emotional development so that thinking about values and identifying with the concepts presented on an abstract level is developmentally possible. Highly stressed children in the early grades often lack the ability to integrate material presented in this way. They may give all the right answers about "right and wrong" yet continue to behave in a way that contradicts their verbal conclusions.

An alternative to character education is to use early-grade curriculums, teacher–child relationships, and environments to foster emotional well-being and the evolution of personhood in the school setting. The approach advocated here is one that considers the school to be an appropriate and essential arena for addressing the development of personhood in young children by allowing for and nurturing personhood at school.

Fostering the emotional well-being of children in public schools requires teachers, administrators, paraprofessional staff, and school-based mental-health professionals to learn about the development of personhood in children and to commit to supporting their emotional well-being at school. The commitment has to be as strong and well organized as the current commitment to promoting literacy in young children. Indeed, an organized effort toward enhancing emotional well-being in young schoolchildren would provide a stronger foundation on which to build the literacy program, because enhancing children's emotional well-being is likely to increase their receptivity and create a stronger basis for developing of symbolic processes.

The commitment to creating school environments that promote emotional well-being requires many departures from business as usual in the early grades of our nation's schools. These departures would affect school regulations, policies, and routines; administrator–child relationships; teacher–child relationships; family–school interaction; and the early-grade curriculum itself. Such a shift from focusing solely on cognitive goals to creating environments that acknowledge and value emotional life might require some expansion of mental-health services within school buildings, the primary interventions would be schoolwide and would not necessarily require more funds than any other high-priority venture. Rather, what is required is a fundamental change in attitude about the value of personhood. If we value the children who attend our elementary schools and want to be realistically hopeful about the people they will become as they move through middle school and high school toward young adulthood, we can no longer leave their emotional well-being to chance.

CHAPTER 2

Teaching Ourselves to Read in the Early Years

Recognizing Signs of Distress and Addressing Psychosocial History

AN ENORMOUS AMOUNT of energy has been invested recently in assessing the academic status of children in the early grades. Determining young children's reading ability has been a special focus of this attention: Many programs have been put in place to pinpoint a child's reading level immediately on entering school so that he or she can be stimulated accordingly. Indeed, a remedial program called Reading Recovery has been created for children as young as 6—an age at which children are often emerging as readers. But from what can very young children who do not seem ready for academics be "recovering"?

Our interest in and enthusiasm for assessment in the early grades may be misplaced. We are attempting to assess academic capacity in 4- to 7-year-olds instead of assessing the social and emotional underpinnings of that capacity. Along the road to personhood, many children face enormous challenges that they cannot overcome alone. Sometimes these challenges are known, because they are described in a psychosocial history that has come from a caseworker or agency involved with the family. Most often we regard this history as a harmful agent and put it in a locked file cabinet, without informing the teacher about its content. Sometimes we know nothing about the challenges that a child has faced before coming to school, but we are soon living with the results of those challenges, which create havoc or paralysis in the classroom. Yet we have been slow to learn to read the signs of internal havoc as communication about the emotional distress that a young child may be experiencing. We have been hesitant to open the file drawer in search of information that might give context to a young child's mystifying behavior. If schools are to become emotionally responsive to children in the early grades, we need to teach ourselves to read the signs of emotional distress from young children who are struggling to become joyful people and empowered learners.

How do young children express distress in school? Can we learn to read the signs of psychological distress in young children? And if we learn to read those signs, how can teachers and administrators respond to promote healing? Most important, how can school professionals move away from a rote approach to negative behavior toward reading the meaning that the behavior is communicating? When teachers learn to read the meaning of behavior, they become more likely to employ responses that will be effective and empowering for both teacher and student.

Certainly, there have always been teachers who are attuned to expressions of psychological distress in their students, and many school systems have school-based clinicians who can be called on when teachers are concerned. Yet many early-grade teachers report that the school-based clinicians do not have the time or expertise to provide services to young children and that they usually have their hands full with the more overt needs of older children in the school. Administrators are often unresponsive to teachers' requests for more social-work services, implying that early-grade teachers should be able to handle things by themselves. Resistance to acknowledging young children's emotional distress is often systemwide, because once such problems have been acknowledged, the district becomes obliged to address them, and administrators fear that they will lack the resources to do that.

In schools that heal, everyone takes responsibility for playing a role in promoting the emotional well-being of children. When clinicians are regarded as a valuable resource, but not as the only resource, schools can afford to examine children's issues more closely. When teachers, administrators, and clinicians do not close their eyes to children's communications of distress and begin to examine the behavior that they are seeing in light of children's actual experiences, the results are often illuminating and can inform professional practice.

Attending to History

It is impossible to assess young children's abilities and behavior accurately outside the context of their actual life experiences. When teachers are worried about children, they often contact parents to discuss their concerns. The teacher may want to make the parent aware of the child's difficulties in the hope that the parent will exert positive influence on the situation. Or the teacher may hope that the parent will provide context for understanding what is occurring in the classroom. Take, for instance, a kindergarten child who shrieks inconsolably whenever the classroom lights are turned off. This behavior can be annoying, as it is often necessary to turn off lights—for rest time, to watch movies, for birthday parties, during calls for quiet, and so on. However, the teacher's feelings can turn to empathy when the child's parents explain that the behavior stems from a terrifying incident in which the child's drug-addicted cousin stormed into his bedroom while he was sleeping and became abusive. Once the teacher understands the context, she is empowered to address the situation more effectively: She lets the child know that she knows that something scary happened to him in the dark and invites him to stay next to her before she turns out the light. The child's disruptive behavior diminishes.

A 6-year-old boy in a class for children with developmental delays has not spoken a word at school, even though he has received speech therapy during his two years in the classroom. He is minimally responsive to directions and often does not participate on any level. He sits and smiles or lets other children lead him around as a prop in their play. His school evaluation reports indicate that the paucity of language is due to retarded intellectual development, and a more restrictive environment is recommended for the next school year. The boy then begins to attend an after-school program that has a therapeutic play program. After wandering around the playroom in silence for 30-minute periods each day for three weeks, he suddenly picks up a toy telephone and shouts, "You asshole! You stink!" His subsequent telephone conversations are complex but disturbing and lead the playroom therapist to work on building an alliance with the boy's overwhelmed mother, who eventually reveals that, from 18 months to 28 months old, the child had been tied up daily by a sadistic babysitter. The playroom therapist attends the child's evaluation and placement review with tape recordings of his verbal abilities and an amended psychosocial history. The recommendations are changed so that the boy is placed with other children who have intellectual potential but need emotional support.

Typically, we devote professional energy to taking psychosocial histories as part the evaluation process if concern exists about the child's developmental status or academic performance. Although we acknowledge the value of taking such histories, however, we rarely acknowledge the value of using them. The results of performance and psychological evaluations are read as if they exist independently of a child's life story. The history is put into the file, while the results of the performance evaluations determine whether and what kind of interventions are recommended. This system of relegating history to the back burner plays itself out as institutional neglect for thousands of children. Take, for example, the child who is in foster care because his father stabbed his mother in his presence when he was 2¹/₂ years old. The child has a sparse vocabulary and is not reading at age 7. He is often inattentive in class. He occasionally becomes enraged suddenly and hurts other children. After the evaluation is complete, speech therapy and resource-room work on reading skills are recommended. The child is referred to the foster-care agency's pediatrician for a prescription for Ritalin to treat the inattentiveness. No recommendation is made to attend to the traumatic experiences that preoccupy this little boy and motivate his behavior. Therefore, his difficulties persist, and his academic performance continues to be low. This child who has such a traumatic life becomes a victim of institutional neglect. Although both his behavior and his history present important information about his needs, the school does not address them.

In schools that heal, the child's history is read, and practice is informed by considering its content. Thus, a weekly visit with the school psychologist or social worker or participation in a weekly group for children who have had traumatic losses is recommended for the boy. The principal make a point of saying hello to him in the morning and acknowledges something about his learning potential. The teacher in the classroom uses the information that the history provides to help bridge the worlds of school and out-of-school life for the boy. She can say such things as, "I know it's hard to pay attention if you are thinking about other things. Sometimes kids who have had scary things happen to them think about those scary things instead of paying attention at school. Tell me if that is happening to you."

Exposure to Drugs versus Exposure to Life

Regardless of whether school personnel have access to psychosocial histories, many community-based school programs have employees who live in the school's neighborhood and know a great deal about the children's lives. In such cases, it is extremely important for paraprofessional staff to be trained to understand the positive value of psychosocial history and the need for confidentiality during casual conversation. For instance, school personnel who have heard that a child's parents are known to their neighbors as drug users or as having a history of drug abuse may be quick to attribute a child's difficulties to prenatal drug exposure. In reality, the results of research on the effects of drug exposure in utero are varied and are specific to the agent ingested and the period of time and frequency of use. Even considering these contributing factors, outcome studies vary: For crack cocaine, for example, profoundly debilitating effects have been noted for a small minority of children and some residual effects are associated with other children, but for the majority of children, no long-term effects have been reported (Karr-Morse & Wiley, 1997; Phelps, Wallace, & Bontrager, 1997). Recent studies indicate that alcohol may be the most toxic agent to developing fetuses and may have the longest-term and most insidious effects if it penetrates the placenta (Mack, 1995).

Outcome studies for children exposed to drugs in utero are inconclusive, but clinical studies of children who are cared for by drug- or alcohol-abusing parents are not. These studies show conclusively that children raised in drug-abusing environments have a range of developmental, psychological, and school-performance problems, which are associated with inconsistent parenting, inconsistent routines and lifestyles, abrupt changes in parental affects, unsafe home environments, neglect, exposure to violence, poverty, and other correlates of drug use (Administration for Children and Families, 1999). The most significant finding about babies and toddlers growing up in chaotic environments in which the parent's ability to offer adequate protection is compromised concerns the babies' physiological reaction to being chronically overstimulated by a potentially threatening environment. Such children become hypervigilant in order to survive. Their nervous systems become accustomed to a chronically high level of adrenaline, and they maintain a high-alert level of readiness to defend or flee that persists even when the particular threat has subsided. This chronic hypervigilance leaves the babies unable to attend to neutral stimuli, to concentrate on their own activity, and to trust the environment in order to devote energy to play, ultimately constituting a great barrier to learning. It also leaves them too quick to respond impulsively or destructively to adverse circumstances, as their survival instincts take over and short-circuit more sophisticated problem-solving thought processes (Karr-Morse & Wiley, 1997). How do such children present in the early grades? Often with abnormally high activity levels; inability to pay attention to academic material and overattentiveness to external stimulation; high levels of impulsivity; overly concrete thinking, with poor symbolic abilities; unelaborate play, stories, writing, and so on; difficulty with peer relationships; difficulty with respecting adults' authority; and difficulty with transitions.

Reading the Signs of Traumatic History

Young children who have been traumatized may come to traumatize their teachers and classmates by acting in ways that are confusing and disturbing. Young children who have been physically abused or have experienced violence may show symptoms such as those described earlier. In addition, they may have show signs specific to children suffering from post-traumatic stress disorder. Children with post-traumatic stress often seem to be in a *preoccupied state*. This means that the traumatic event is so disturbing that it stays on their mind most of the time, leaving little room for them to take in anything new. Children in a preoccupied state may look dreamy and inattentive. They often have a serious, faraway look. They may appear to have difficulty retaining in school, and indeed, retention may be impossible for them because they may not have been taking in the information when it was being imparted. Trauma has an insidious effect on memory function in both children and adults (Terr, 1992). Children who have had adequate care and suffer a sudden trauma may become preoccupied with the trauma in a way that takes up all of their mental space and deters taking in and recalling new information. Children who have been traumatized repeatedly, as in child-abuse cases, often develop a defensive amnesia for the incident of abuse as well as for events that happen before and after the event. Therefore, a child who suffers sexual abuse after school may not only repress aspects (or all) of the trauma but also may not remember anything that happened during that school day (Terr, 1992).

When children have a history of abuse, their teachers are likely to have concerns about their classroom functioning. Children who have been abused over time use defenses to survive the abuse that become overgeneralized and detrimental to them in the classroom. When abuse happens repeatedly, children tend to try to separate themselves from their abusive experience as it is happening. They *dissociate* themselves from their experience to avoid emotional pain. Thus, they become fragmented in an attempt to protect themselves from mental distress. At times, seemingly benign events in the classroom may evoke a dissociated state in an abused child. For example, being in the bathroom may bring on a dissociated state in a child who has been abused in a bathroom. She may appear disoriented, far away, out of contact with others and with herself, and very anxious. If other children notice, they may become frightened or worried. Teachers may suspect seizure activity or another physiological event.

When severely abused children protect themselves by employing dissociation, they often keep themselves disconnected from the reality that someone they love is hurting them. They *split off* the abusive experiences that belong to the parent–child relationship (or the relationship with another close family member) and instead attach the resulting negative effects to a relationship with a teacher, assistant, bus driver, or other adult. What ensues can be a very confusing and trying pattern in which the child provokes adults at school, then seems to experience the resulting disciplinary response as abusive. Take, for example, a 7-year-old boy who repeatedly grabs the bus matron's pencil and threatens to poke other children on the bus with it. When the matron must restrain the boy to retrieve the pencil and protect the other children, the boy bursts into tears and screams, "You're hurting me! You're hurting me!" Frequently, abused children relate to one school adult as "all bad" and another as "all good." Some children switch allegiances midweek—or even midday—but usually keep someone as the savior and cast the other as having malevolent intentions toward them.

Traumatized children may be hypervigilant and overly active, as children who are underprotected often are. They may be overly reactive to environmental stimuli that they see as having threatening potential—for example, loud noises such as school bells and fire alarms. They may seem to lack age-appropriate reality-testing abilities and be confused about what is safe and what is dangerous. Sometimes such children act as though they are moving targets, moving as fast as they can to avoid falling victim to danger. At such times, traumatized children may appear hyperactive and motor-driven. At other times, they may freeze in response to perceived danger—for example, by acting in apparently irrational ways during fire drills, field trips, or group walks.

Traumatized children may seem driven to test an adult's ability to keep them safe. They often do things that are dangerous in a way that seems provocative. They also sometimes seem to lack age-appropriate judgment about what is safe and what is dangerous. Toddlers do not know the difference between real and pretend and thus need high levels of supervision to avoid putting themselves in dangerous situations; preschool children struggle to make boundaries between reality and fantasy. By age 7, however, children should have the conceptual ability to draw firm lines. Children who have been underprotected and intruded on tend to have more difficulty distinguishing between reality and fantasy and less ability to predict cause-and-effect relationships (Koplow, 1996). This has tremendous consequences for large public-school systems that are serving a number of children with traumatic histories, because it implies that those children may have a greater need for supervision than other children their age.

Schoolchildren with traumatic histories may have flashbacks or panic attacks in the school setting. Children who are having flashbacks may suddenly start acting as if something that happened in the past is happening in the here and now. Take, for example, a child who begins to tremble and scream when the class approaches a swimming pool during a field trip: He starts shouting about not pushing him under although no one is near him. The teacher tries to calm him, but he is difficult to reach. The teacher later investigates and is told by the child's caseworker that the child's older brother tried to drown him before the child was removed from the home.

Another child seems to have frequent tantrums, but the teacher begins to notice that these "tantrums" are different from anything that she has experienced with other children. Most young tantrum-throwers are interested in maintaining visual contact with and physical proximity to the adult during the tantrum, but this girl seems to lose contact with the adult and enter her own tortured world during the attack. Although she may scream and cry as other children do, she also trembles, hyperventilates, wets herself, or throws up. Her affect may start out angry, demanding, or upset, but it eventually becomes panicky, as well. The school clinician suggests that the child is actually having a panic attack. The attack may come in response to a seemingly benign event (such as running out of snack-time cookies) but sets off a panic reaction that is probably a response to a related event that completely overwhelmed the child at another time. By becoming acquainted with the girl's psychosocial history, the teacher discovers that she was in

Sarajevo during her infancy, where her family almost starved. The panic response becomes understandable to the teacher, who must "bear witness" to the little girl's experience of starvation (Lifton & Lindy, 2001).

Play and the Traumatized Child

When traumatized children play, they often re-create traumatic events, re-enacting the sequence of the actual event and capturing the traumatic affects that were part of the event. Other children may feel uncomfortable with the intensity of the play, which is often grim, businesslike, and disconnected from the content offered by other children who are playing. The teacher may perceive that most of the children in the classroom play joyfully, in contrast to the seemingly driven *traumatic play* generated by the children with traumatic histories. Traumatic play is a clear indication that a child needs help: Its repetitive nature reveals that playing about the event alone does not help to integrate the experience and points to the necessity of a therapeutic partner.

The trauma of abuse, of witnessing violence, and of living in wartorn countries are conceptually familiar to most teachers. Less well recognized is that children with medical histories that included painful and intrusive procedures at early ages may also show symptoms of post-traumatic stress as they grow. A sample of such children whose difficulties were severe enough to necessitate therapeutic nursery placement during their preschool years showed a pattern of a very low tolerance for psychic pain and a tendency to discharge negative feelings by causing others to feel physical pain (Koplow, 2001).

Developmental regression is the name given to the most potentially harmful result of early trauma in older children and adults; for young children, this result must be called developmental arrest. A 9-year-old who is traumatized may temporarily lose some ground in the developmental process: Reading that was once effortless may become laborious; sleeping may become disturbed in a child who has always slept well. If an 18-month-old is traumatized, however, there is a risk of developmental arrest at the place in development touched by trauma: Language may not proceed, resulting in communication difficulties as the child approaches age 2; object constancy may not be achieved before the child goes to school; the ability to orient to the environment and to focus may not evolve. The young traumatized child often appears to be *developmentally arrested*. Therefore, it is extremely important to look for trauma in a child's history before assuming that any delay is organically determined. Attending to the trauma could allow the developmental process to progress and make age-appropriate learning possible.

Reading the Signs of Depression

Young children may seem to have endless amounts of energy. Teachers in the early grades may occasionally have a couple of children, often little girls, who appear sad, withdrawn, listless, and depressed, but most of the children appear anything but depressed. Early-grade teachers talk more about children who have excessive energy and whose need for action can be disruptive and difficult to accommodate.

Although some children show depression in low activity levels, sleepiness, lack of interest and motivation and sad affects similar to a depressive picture of an adult, most children who are depressed present a different constellation of symptoms. These may include teasing and provocative behavior, hyperactivity, evidence of low self-worth, isolation from peers, performance anxiety, aggression, irritability, intolerance of others, encopresis, selective mutism, reckless behavior, and suicidal and homicidal ideation expressed in the form of fantasy. It is helpful for teachers to be able to read these behaviors and understand their implications for the emotional well-being of the children who exhibit them as symptoms. Reading the signs of depression in young children will help teachers, administrators, and school-based clinicians respond better to the unmet emotional needs of children in the early grades; it will also help prevent depression from becoming an underlying threat to the well-being of schoolchildren as they grow. Recently, researchers have identified isolation from peers; being a target of teasing, bullying, and rejection; and having homicidal ideation as characteristic of school shooters (Council on Children and Families, 2000). Less attention has been paid, however, to the clinical status of the children who are involved in teasing and humiliating their vulnerable peers. Clearly, we must consider the possibility that these children engage in teasing and provocative behavior and show intolerance of others as compensation for low self-worth—signs of depression that often express themselves in the early grades but may go unattended, with catastrophic results.

The Dynamics of Teasing and Intolerance

All young children do some teasing as part of their repertoire of peer interaction before they are able to consider the long-term effect that their behavior may have on others. This kind of teasing may require intervention by teachers or parents, who may have to point out the consequences of the behavior and model appropriate expressions. However, teasing that occurs as a pervasive interaction pattern beyond age 7 or 8 may speak to a child's inability to integrate the positive and negative feelings that he has about himself as a person. He may split off characteristics that he dislikes in himself and project them onto other children or groups of children whom he perceives as more vulnerable, thus making himself feel powerful. This defense can become extremely dangerous, because it both masks the child's own vulnerability and depressive state and stresses his already socially vulnerable victim beyond his or her ability to cope. Whereas preschool and kindergarten teachers are made aware of the emotional devastation that rejection can bring to their students—4- and 5-year-olds frequently burst into tears when they are teased—in later grades, the teasing is usually more subtle and carried out when the teacher is out of earshot. Further, older victims may hesitate to express their hurt because they fear additional ridicule. Teachers and other school staff members may fail to recognize a peer-interaction dynamic that has become pervasive and may feel that peer interaction is beyond their purview. Yet if pervasive patterns of teasing and peer rejection are not read as signs of depression in the children who engage in such behavior and as a potential cause of depression for those who are targeted in the teasing, the outcome may be serious for both victims and perpetrators.

Irritability, Oversensitivity, Hyperactivity, and Aggression

Depressed children are often extremely irritable and extremely sensitive to what they feel are physical or emotional assaults on their well-being. For depressed children, maintaining an even keel is difficult and seems to demand all of their emotional energy. Any bump, push, shove, or other small transgression from other children appears to cause emotional disequilibrium. Depressed children may respond to the frequent intrusive experiences inherent in group life by becoming despondent and needy of adult reassurance or by becoming aggressive in what they perceive to be self-defense. Teachers often complain about groups of children who cannot tolerate sitting together on a rug for a discussion, because small, unintentional intrusions into one another's space cause major aggressive responses.

Although the dynamics of depression involve the turning inward of anger, children often cannot tolerate this depressive stance and attempt to fend it off by discharging their anger through aggression and locating the underlying sadness, despair, and rage that threaten to overwhelm them in their victims instead of in themselves. These children often have difficulty tolerating periods of low activity, such as rest time, needing to move as much as possible to stimulate themselves as an antidote to depressive internal states (Koplow, 1996). Many teachers comment on the sad, fearful affects of hyperactive children when they are denied the defense of hyperactivity and are made to sit during morning meeting or library time.

Performance Anxiety, Feeling Dispensable, Suicidal and Homicidal Fantasy

Some children cannot risk failing at a task because the failure becomes too big a threat to their self-esteem. Therefore, they refuse to try to do work that they fear will be too hard for them, or they become extremely anxious about the quality of their work or how it will be seen by the teacher. Children who seem to feel helpless when confronted with age-appropriate tasks need teachers who try to understand the factors that may be contributing to their feelings of helplessness. Clearly, a learning problem would engender a feeling of helplessness in a child who is unable to understand or carry out what is required. In contrast, a child who has had to accomplish tasks that are beyond his or her developmental level but are necessary for survival may manage to complete what is required but feel awash in feelings of helplessness and inadequacy, feelings that may then be evoked when any task—even an age-appropriate one—is required. Feeling helpless and unable to perform should be considered an indicator of risk, as these feelings may cause a depressed child to feel dispensable. Statements such as "This class would win the spelling bee if it weren't for me" or "The team would be better if I weren't on it" should be red flags for teachers. They express a child's conviction that his social group would benefit from his absence, a belief that underlies suicidal ideation in some children.

All children have some violent dreams and fantasies, especially during the Oedipal period. Many children have morbid fantasies in early adolescence, and many young children fantasize about joining departed loved ones in heaven as they struggle to come to terms with the meaning of death. Both early-childhood populations and middle-school and early-high-school populations struggle with conflicts about feeling powerful and fears of being powerless, and they may generate play and fantasies featuring themselves as conquerors to address these conflicts. However, when suicidal or homicidal fantasies preoccupy children, are voiced, and begin to generate ideas or plans for actualization, teachers and other school adults need to take them very seriously. The reasons for exercising caution and taking precautions are obvious, given the many incidents in schools across the nation that have resulted in the shooting deaths of children and teachers by schoolchildren. The reasons for increasing our understanding of the dynamics and expression of childhood depression include prevention of tragedy of the magnitude of Columbine as well as the prevention of more private tragedies of individual suicide or tortured and lonely childhoods. In the United States, suicide ranks sixth as the cause of death among 5- to 14-year-olds (U.S Department of Health and Human Services, 1998).

Reading the signs of depression in schoolchildren is complex because depression may be masked or may coexist with other symptoms. But the risks that come from leaving children alone in depressed states are great. To evaluate these risks properly, teachers and other school personnel must take into account that children's conceptual development is still in process throughout childhood and adolescence. In addition, a child's ability to differentiate reality from fantasy is incremental. Lines are not clearly drawn in early childhood; although well-supported and well-protected children become more certain about those lines during the latency years, differentiation becomes clouded episodically during adolescence (Siegler, 1998). Therefore, a 5-year-old who has recently lost her mother in a pedestrian–car accident may dash into the street in an attempt to re-create the condition that led to her mother's disappearance, and in the hope that she will then be reunited with her. A 6-year-old may stick his baby sister's finger into a light socket so she will "light up" like a character in a cartoon he has been watching. A depressed middle-school child who has endured weeks of peer rejection and ridicule and has spent the afternoon in an arcade playing violent video games may emerge with fantasies of his school-mates as targets in a game whose background is the school playground. If this child is well supported, well supervised, and well protected at home, he can use family support or professional help as a source of self-esteem to balance the peer assaults, and he will not have access to destructive means to actualize his fantasies. If he is not adequately supervised and is left alone in his depression—left to his own devices to augment his poor self-esteem and given access to destructive means—he is at risk for actualizing his fantasies.

It is age-appropriate for young adolescents to want a lot of privacy and to keep things from their parents and teachers; thus, it can be dif-ficult to gain insight into their thoughts and fantasies. But teachers do have access to the signs showing that conditions are ripe for depres-sion. Peer alienation, feelings of dispensability and depressiveness, and violent themes in written school assignments may be indicators of risk that are worth bringing to the attention of parents, school-based men-tal-health professionals, and administrators.

More troubling are the direct statements of despair that are made daily by young children in our nations schools and are routinely ignored. The statement "I want to die" coming form a 4-year-old needs to be heard and evaluated seriously, whether the child has told the teacher, bus driver, or guidance counselor. Young children do not fol-low protocol when they express their feelings. The expressions are often spontaneous and made in unlikely situations. School personnel must be trained to listen for these communications and to take them seriously enough to report them to school clinicians and administra-tors. Even if a determination is made that the child has no plan to carry out suicide, the suicidal ideation is an indicator of depression and despair with which no 4-year-old should have to cope alone. If the inci-dent is determined not to be an emergency, and the despair is then ignored, the probability of emergency increases as times goes on.

Selective Mutism, Encopresis, Hypoactivity

Children who refuse to participate in interactive routines over time may be depressed and manifesting this in a particular constellation of symptoms or syndromes that are considered depressive equivalents. Children who "won't" do things are usually very frustrating to teach-ers, who find themselves in power struggles with them. Selectively mute children are children who are capable of talking but will not talk in certain situations, and often will not talk at school. They control language output to such a degree that they eventually lose access to the ability to make words come out spontaneously in the school environment, even when they wish to speak. Encopretic children over-control their bowels and often refuse to use the bathroom. They then lose control over themselves and soil their pants. Selective mutism and encopresis may be depressive equivalents, as both involve struggling to feel powerful by withholding instead of taking action. Both syndromes can indicate unresolved separation issues, as well, and conflict about dependency.

Although soiling and withholding speech may be considered developmental regressions for children entering a new situation, and may be transient symptoms indicating a heightened need for support, persistent symptoms beyond the transitional period should be regarded as serious and requiring clinical attention. Selectively mute children often forgo pleasurable experience if talking is required in order to participate and thus may become more depressed and isolated as the other children participate in their routines joyfully and with a sense of camaraderie. Selectively mute children may also lack ways to express their intelligence and demonstrate their competence, and other children may see them as babies who need to be taken care of, further contributing to the development of a distorted self-image.

Encopretic children are often subject to peer ridicule, rejection, and humiliation. They may also be dealt with punitively by adults who are not knowledgeable about encopresis, further contributing to issues of negative self-image and poor self-worth.

Hypoactive children are often overlooked, because they are not disturbing anyone else and are willing to participate, although in a marginally contributing way. Teachers should monitor hypoactive children, conferring with the school nurse or the child's pediatrician to evaluate overall health, sleeping patterns, and so on. They should also watch for other signs of depression that may coexist with the hypoactivity.

Recognizing Early Signs of Mental Illness

Children who show early signs of mental illness often go undetected for years in the school setting if acting out is not one of their major symptoms. Although it would not be possible to describe all possible presentations of mental illness in children in this chapter, it is important to look at the whole child when assessing children and making determinations about their educational needs. Often one encounters children who present with developmental delays in areas, and for whom special attention is required in order to progress to age level. These children are generally well served by evaluation teams and on-site school services. Other children, however, show symptoms that are not commensurate with the diagnosis of developmental delay because they are not reminiscent of an earlier level of development. Rather, they show symptoms of developmental differences or disorder and require a special level of expertise for effective treatment. Children who are unrelated; who cannot generate meaningful language but simply repeat what they have heard; or who cannot engage in symbolic play, although they may be able to assemble puzzles and decode written words, need intervention, even if their academic level is precocious. Children who have extreme mood swings or frequent unprovoked outbursts, who cannot recover from adverse incidents, who are often disoriented, who seem to be overly identified with fantasy figures, who frequently offer verbal responses that are tangential in nature and difficult to decipher, and whose affects seem not to resonate with actual emotional experience are all in need of clinical attention. Such children often have trouble learning because they are distracted, internally preoccupied, or unable to sort fantasy from reality. Many of the children classified as having learning disabilities are in need of psychiatric evaluation and treatment and ongoing mental-health services in addition to the learning remediation that they may receive.

Readers All

If teachers and administrators teach themselves how to read the signs of emotional distress in the early years, schools can organize themselves around providing environments that help to promote emotional well-being and address difficulties. If we do this, we enable children not only as learners, but also as human beings growing up in a complex social world. It is not enough for the school-based clinician assigned to a building to be well versed in the signs of psychological distress in early-grade children. All of the adults who interact with children during the school day must enable themselves to read these signs, as well, if our children are going to be well cared for in public school.

CHAPTER 3

Saving Kindergarten

KINDERGARTEN—or in some cases, public pre-kindergarten—is a young child's port of entry into the public-school system. Historically, we have recognized the value of making this entry a gentle transition, giving children the opportunity to adjust to the school environment without the pressure to achieve academically. Instead, kindergarten has provided an opportunity for socialization and an introduction to the routines of the school day. Developmentally appropriate kindergartens have provided children with opportunities for open-ended play, structured group experiences, and exposure to material that invites exploration and mastery. The successful kindergarten child has been one who delights in this process of exploration, connects to his or her peers, and communicates discoveries to the teacher. The successful kindergarten teacher has been warm and nurturing and aware that interactions with the students and the ability to provide inherently satisfying challenges for them helps to create the disposition for learning that will motivate the children throughout their school years and beyond (Katz, 1993).

Today, we are creating kindergartens that depart from this rich tradition of early childhood education. These kindergartens demand that the successful child sit and attend for long periods, limit opportunities for play and open-ended exploration, limit outdoor play time, and forgo an afternoon rest. The successful child is under enormous pressure to learn to read and write almost from the beginning of the kindergarten year. And kindergarten teachers are under enormous pressure to track each child's progress by assessing individual performance in reading and writing, leaving little time for more personal interchanges. In an effort to promote early literacy among our schoolchildren, many school systems have dismantled kindergarten programs that create the foundation for literacy to take hold (Calkins, 2000). In her recent book *The Art of Teaching Reading,* the literacy expert Lucy Calkins reminds us that young children need the rich personal experiences that constitute the foundation for literacy. Yet when one asks a teacher or administrator about the academic emphasis in the kindergarten program, the response is often given in terms of the school's literacy goals. Children must learn to read in kindergarten, we are told, in order to meet higher standards down the road. If a visitor asks to see a copy of the city or state's standards for preschool and kindergarten classrooms, he or she often finds that the standards are developmentally appropriate and do not support the "academics-only" kindergarten in the next room.

For years the National Association for the Education of the Young Child has provided professions with guidelines for Developmentally Appropriate Practice for children in pre-school through third grade. These guidelines are based on theory and research about how children learn and develop, and they make recommendations for what is appropriate curriculum for young children and when material is best learned (NAEYC, 1997). Yet, although the guidelines apply to pre-k; kindergarten; first, second, and third grade, it is rare to find these practice guidelines being applied in programs for school-aged children.

Why have our expectations of kindergarten children changed so dramatically? Perhaps one reason is that large numbers of children in the United States attend early-childhood programs before entering kindergarten. Studies show that 55–60% of young American children have attended an early-childhood program before starting kindergarten (U.S. Department of Commerce, 2000). Head Start, day care, private preschool, and now public pre-kindergarten programs are often the young child's introduction to school routines. The perception is that early-childhood programs before kindergarten have already allowed children to acquire socialization experience and adjust to routines. Indeed, many educators look toward including pre-kindergarten in their school buildings with an eager eye, envisioning an environment in which children can be introduced to academic pursuits even earlier than kindergarten.

What are the dangers of redefining kindergarten? For those children who have already had experience in early-childhood programs, why not focus the kindergarten year on academics? If children enter kindergarten ready to learn, why not create environments in which expectations for performance are high?

Crossing the Bridge

Five is an important age, as any child about to blow out five candles on a birthday cake will proudly tell you. At 5 years old, children are building a bridge between the sense of self that they consolidated within their families in toddlerhood and the emerging sense of themselves as bigger, more competent kids who are part of a community as well as a family. This bridge allows the 5-year-old to venture forth ahead of himself when he feels inspired to try new, bigger-kid challenges. The bridge also lets him run back to the opposite end, where he can make contact with the younger, more familiar version of himself and express those dependency needs that still need to have a voice.

As 5-year-olds begin to cross the bridge, they feel competitive. They are in touch with their relative powerlessness in the world of adults and want the power that they see adults as having. They seek to compensate for these feelings of relative inadequacy by being the best, being first, being the fastest, and being identified with powerful figures. Erik Erikson saw 5-year-olds as struggling with the developmental conflict of "initiative versus guilt"—needing to be competitive and assertive without being overwhelmed by guilt about taking power and "glory" away from the grown-ups (Erikson, 1963). Resolving this conflict favorably is a precursor to the next developmental conflict, "industry versus inferiority." The positive resolution of this conflict, which is typically a marker of latency, is crucial to the child's motivation, confidence, and risk-taking ability as a successful learner in middle- and upper-elementary school.

Developmentally appropriate kindergartens supports 5-year-olds' need to feel competent by allowing children to build bridges, then slowly cross the bridges at their own pace. Developmentally appropriate programs assume that there will be a dance that takes children back and forth across the continuum of self many times. The bridge building is supported by opportunities for open-ended exploration that allows children to find their interests and discover their competencies and by inviting symbolic expression in dramatic play and play with blocks, paints, drawing, and clay in the classroom. These symbolic means become an avenue for the positive resolution of conflicts and ambivalence that kindergartners feel as they cross the bridge toward latency. In developmentally appropriate kindergartens, 5-year-olds discover that their issues of ambivalence and their conflicts about competition are common ground. They can communicate about them through play and language and are thus not isolated with them, increasing the possibility for positive outcomes.

Academically driven, fast-paced kindergartens typically do not support bridge building, because they in effect catapult many children ahead of themselves before they feel ready. When children are catapulted this way and do not feel ready, they tend to freeze in their tracks and cease their own, more gradual explorations or run back to the young end of the developmental bridge for safety. Although educators who work in academically driven kindergartens typically have the children's best interests at heart and feel that they are giving the children opportunities by challenging them at a young age, the result is often paradoxical: Because 4- and 5-year-olds are very vulnerable to feelings of inadequacy and have little ability to tolerate those feelings, many become disabled instead of enabled by material that is, in effect, over their heads. A structured learning situation that a child experiences as beyond his or her level may cause the child to feel—and, perhaps, act—out of control, because the child feels powerless to organize an effective response. Feelings of extreme inadequacy may overwhelm the kindergarten child with a sense of helplessness. If this happens repeatedly, the feelings may become associated with structured learning situations and decrease receptivity to learning.

A child may manifest feelings of inadequacy in several ways, including through difficult or frenzied behavior, a high level of anxiety about performance, avoidance of academic material, or extreme regression in structured learning situations. Some children may manage to perform much of what is required on a rote level, without much connection to or comprehension of the material. They may use tremendous amounts of energy to appear as if they are keeping up but feel little sense of accomplishment. The contradiction between external credibility and internal confusion may produce anxiety for children who begin to fear that their inadequacy will be found out. Other children may learn to relate to schoolwork as something that must be done but is mechanical and devoid of meaning.

A recent study compared outcomes of children who attended academically driven, performance-oriented kindergartens in the public schools of Newark, New Jersey, with outcomes of children who attended developmentally oriented public kindergarten. The children in the kindergartens using a developmentally appropriate practice model learned through actual experiences and had no exposure to rote teaching. The researchers found that children in the developmentally oriented kindergartens performed significantly higher on standardized reading and math measures and had better attendance than the children in the traditional kindergartens. These children all lived in poverty and had significant numbers of risk factors that might have impaired learning (Kopacsi & Onsongo, 2001). The study points out the false assumption that introducing children to academics early through structured curricula with high expectations for performance will give them an advantage in school.

Self-Esteem: Our Favorite Phrase

The messages that we give children in kindergarten in academically driven settings often contain fundamental contradictions. The first message is that we value academic performance above all; the second is that we want the children to feel good about what they can do, about who they are. That equation is sound when what we want children to do in kindergarten is developmentally appropriate, because then the children's "performance" is internally gratifying and externally validated. However, if we want children to do academic tasks that feel stressful and elicit feelings of inadequacy, the children probably will not always feel good about what they can accomplish. To compensate for this, many school systems take an approach to raising children's self-esteem that seems to function independently of the learning experience that the school provides. This approach consists of giving children positive messages about their potential and their importance. These messages are written on banners that decorate school offices, hallways, and classroom bulletin boards. Slogans such as, "We are all winners!" "Children come first!" "Every child can learn!" "Our children demonstrate excellence!" and "Everyone is special!" are commonplace in public schools, intending to advertise to the community the school's positive regard for children. Teachers say, "Let's clap for ourselves for doing such a good job," "We are all best friends in our classroom," and "We are all excellent readers in our classroom," many times a day. Children in kindergarten often initially undertake an "All About Me" curriculum, in which they are invited to write and draw about things that make them unique.

What is wrong with this picture? Do these positive messages enhance self-esteem in children? How do children acquire self-esteem, and what are the implications of positive or negative self-esteem for 5-year-olds who are crossing the bridge toward a more developed sense of self?

Directing positive messages to children can certainly be an important part of communicating their value and worthiness, but this can be effective only when the positive messages are true. One need only read the banners, then walk into the kindergarten classroom, to evaluate whether any of what is expressed so enthusiastically in written form is borne out by the children's experience. If the teacher's well-meaning comments about doing a good job, being best friends, and being an excellent reader feel empty to the distracted child who cannot yet read and is often rejected by his peers, the positive words may fuel his feelings of alienation. An All About Me curriculum may be motivating enough in the moment, but it will reveal itself to be a deceptive gesture if the ongoing curriculum and daily routines in kindergarten have little to do with appreciating the individual needs of the children in the group.

Young children feel esteemed when they are understood and valued (Katz, 1999). When young children are valued, the daily school routines, curriculum, and teacher–child interactions work together to support their sense of worthiness. For example, a 5-year-old who is esteemed by his or her teachers and administrators will have his or her basic needs for nurture met in the kindergarten setting: He or she will be able to nap when fatigued in the afternoon; will be given lunch in a contained and relatively quiet place so that the experience is not overwhelming and anxiety-inducing; and will have access to the bathroom when needed and will be supported if use of the bathroom at school initially causes distress. A 5-year-old who is esteemed will be given the opportunity for open-ended play with others, because 5-year-olds demonstrate high interest and a sense of competence when engaged in this type of play interaction. Rather than an All About Me curriculum, the entire ongoing curriculum for the esteemed child is all about him or her in the world, because it capitalizes on the child's interests and talents and encourages exploration and connections to the world that the child is studiously building bridges to discover. The esteemed child will have many opportunities for individual interchanges with the kindergarten teacher, who will communicate the value of the particular discoveries and contributions that the child is making in school.

The child who enters kindergarten with a strong sense of self-worth but then encounters an unsupportive environment may initially experience shock and disorientation; he or she may also become somewhat depressed while functioning within that environment, employing defenses and developing self-protective strategies. The child may insist on bringing lunch from home, even though lunch is served at school, to retain an intimate connection to the food even when it is served in a hostile environment. He or she may use the art or entry period to pursue self-expression that provides internal gratification. He or she may take all work home to appreciative parents who can compensate for the teacher's lack of enthusiasm or personal attention.

The child who has not experienced esteem at home and enters an unsupportive kindergarten environment, however, is at great risk. He or she will not have the internal or experiential resources that act as an alternative source of information about self-worth; thus, the risk is great that the child will consolidate the negative self-image that he or she formulated in toddlerhood. Feelings of worthlessness, isolation, and peer alienation are three of the risk factors associated with violent outcomes in middle-school and high-school children (National Institute of Mental Health, 2000).

Too Much, Not Enough, Just Right: The Meaning of Daily Routines

All early-childhood programs depend on stable routines to function efficiently. As all-day kindergartens become prevalent in the United States, and extended day options or ancillary day-care programs are used by increasing numbers of families, kindergarten children are spending many hours each day structured by the routines that their schools have in place. It is therefore important to examine these routines closely in terms of their meaning to the kindergarten children who experience them.

Examining the meaning of routines for kindergarten children may initially seem superfluous, even to early-childhood professionals. We are conscious of the need for caution when imposing routines on infants and toddlers. High-quality day care for those age groups seeks to develop routines that are in sync with babies' natural rhythms and individual needs. Preschool children are still developing their ability to function independently within daily routines, such as eating and toileting, and therefore require a supportive environment and a respectful pace to allow the children's explorations to proceed as they develop competence. Most kindergarten children are able to function more or less independently within daily routines, raising a question about the need for caution.

Five-year-olds need meaningful routines because such routines are the beams that support the psychological bridges that they are working so frantically to build. Supportive routines ensure that a 5-year-old's basic needs are met during the school day, thus freeing her energy for social forays and adventurous learning. A 5-year-old who is overwhelmed at lunchtime by a crowded cafeteria staffed by a few school aides who shout at the children to maintain a fragile sense of order is unlikely to be able to focus on eating, to enjoy her food, or to muster the energy for social interaction. She is likely to shut down or become overstimulated by the fray. She is likely to return to the classroom feeling less competent, more exhausted, and less receptive to learning. Her functioning as a learner may be depressed by this unsatisfactory routine experience. By contrast, a 5-year-old who has lunch in the classroom, in the presence of her teacher or class paraprofessional, is much more likely to eat, experience the food on as sensory level, attune herself to peer behavior and food preferences, engage in social interchange, and seek supportive contact from the teacher or paraprofessional when she needs something. After lunch, she is likely to present as somewhat restored, with new energy from the food, and open to what the afternoon curriculum brings. If that curriculum includes something new, interesting, or inviting, she is likely to have the physical and emotional energy to engage in the adventure of exploring and responding to the challenges.

A 5-year-old who is exhausted after lunch and is not offered an opportunity to rest cannot function at his or her best. Although the teacher may understand this—and perhaps expect it—the 5-year-old may be less tolerant of shifts in his or her functioning level. Considering how vulnerable 4- and 5-year-olds are to feelings of inadequacy, if their competence level is diminished by fatigue, they may experience hopelessness and an inability to compete. A 5-year-old who is offered a nap by a supportive teacher has many options. If tired, he or she can sleep and awaken with renewed capacity to take in experiences and demonstrate competence. If tired but not sleepy, he or she can rest mind and body, read alone, engage in internal fantasy, or use a stuffed animal to play quietly about what is on his or her mind. The child will generally arise in a more receptive and able state. If the 5-year-old is physically mature and neither body nor mind needs rest, he or she may feel frustrated by the lack of activity but should, in the meantime, be able to engage in quiet activity that keeps the mind engaged. Although this child may experience some frustration, his or her sense of self-confidence and competence will remain intact.

If the kindergartner has had a traumatic history, rest time may be difficult. The lack of activity may leave the child vulnerable to unwanted feelings or memories, and a teacher's presence and support may be required for the child to feel rested. Therefore, kindergarten teachers and supervisors should not consider rest time a period in which the teacher is expendable. Indeed, adult comfort, support, and watchfulness is what allows the children to learn to relax.

Any teacher who has taught kindergarten will recommend having a bathroom in the classroom. That is certainly ideal for an age group that is almost always toilet trained yet easily distracted by external stimulation from their bodies' signals. "Don't wait until the last minute," parents constantly advise their 5-year-olds; a bathroom in the classroom helps children compensate for that tendency. Of course, many school buildings are antiquated, and ideal classroom space is not available to accommodate all of the young children that the school serves. When there is no bathroom in the classroom, and when there is a lack of paraprofessional staff, teachers are often forced to take the whole group at once at intervals during the day. This practice may run counter to the biological rhythms of some of the children in the classroom. Even more detrimental is the tendency among some teachers to deal with the logistics and organization of toileting a whole group of children mechanically and somewhat militaristically. This is contraindicated for kindergarten children, who can master toileting but are often still dependent on intimate contact to feel secure and comfortable in toileting situations. This need for intimacy is demonstrated each time the kindergarten child announces to the teacher his or her intention to visit the bathroom, even when the classroom has a bathroom and the child is free to use it as needed. The child feels better when the teacher is informed and when he or she makes individual contact with the teacher before going.

Five-year-olds are engaged in mastering self-regulation on a higher level than was available to them in preschool. Although preschool children explore their ability to regulate, they frequently are more invested in forays that allow them to experience too much of a good thing. For example, 3- and 4-year-olds at the water table giggle when they overfill a cup, and they do it intentionally over and over. Many children love the feeling of immersing themselves in what they are doing. Thus, painting their bodies after painting on the paper on the easel—and painting the easel itself—-are common and comfortable occurrences in preschool, but they would be unwelcome and much less common in kindergarten. Five-year-olds are more invested in mastering the concepts of not enough, too much, and just right, and they want to discover their competence within their real experiences as well as in play.

Designing routines that give kindergarten children input into self-regulation supports their developmental agenda. A good working formula for the kindergarten teacher may involve the teacher's taking responsibility for external order and rhythm while giving the children the freedom to work within the structure toward creating experiences that suit them individually. For example, the teacher might determine that it is rest time and that everyone must be on a mat. The children would decide what to hold on their mats, whether they will sleep or rest, or whether they want to use a blanket. Or the teacher and school schedule announce that it is time for lunch, and the child decides what he or she will eat, how much he or she wants, and how he or she will eat it. The teacher in a classroom without a bathroom may have to determine time for group toileting. Each child must decide how much privacy he or she requires, how much paper to use, how long he or she needs to be in the bathroom, and who he or she wants to help fix clothes if he or she cannot do this alone. The children who are waiting decide which book to take from the classroom so they can read while awaiting for their turn in the hallway. The kindergarten teacher's affects are the key ingredient in determining whether these routines will be comfortable and emotionally supportive. If the teacher's attitude while engaging in these routines is nurturing, she will communicate that the children and their individual needs are worthy.

To do this, the teacher must also understand her own worth in her capacity of caregiver and teacher. It is appropriate to encourage independence in kindergarten, but this must occur in an atmosphere that acknowledges individual dependency needs as valid. If the teacher is annoyed by the expression of individual dependency needs, she will communicate her wish for these needs to disappear, and the children will probably try to deny the needs. But in so doing, they will diminish their own joy in accomplishing routines independently, as the independence will occur by necessity instead of through personal evolution and triumph.

Relationship: A Core Capacity for Kindergarten Teachers

In Chapter 4, I will explore the connection between teacher–child relationships and the development of young learners' symbolic capacities. This is a relevant concept for all early-grade teachers, but it is particularly salient for preschool and kindergarten teachers, who give children their foundation for learning. This foundation is much more complex than school administrators imply; it does not consist solely of the actual curricular material that a child is exposed to at the pre-kindergarten or kindergarten level. Indeed, this foundation is what makes children ready to receive curricular material. It allows the children ultimately to make sense of, explore, internalize, and apply that to which they have been exposed so that they can be receptive to learning on the next level.

To give children a foundation for the development and evolution of their symbolic capacities, kindergarten teachers must connect to each child in the classroom. The teacher must get to know the children as individuals in a deep way, and the children must get to know the teacher. The classroom must become a holding environment for the individuals in the group, as well as for the collective experience that the group shares. The teacher can then help the children to develop the symbolic tools they need to process these individual and collective experiences and symbolize them through language, play, drawing, and, eventually, writing.

The teacher herself must have the capacity for relationship and connection to each child, because if she does not, she will have no way to know what the collective experiences she provides mean to individual children. Without relationships, the kindergarten teacher cannot help individual children use symbols as vehicles for true expression, because she will not know enough about the content of what the children want to express. In contexts that are devoid of personal relationships, early-level schoolwork is likely to be produced rotely and mechanically, running the risk of making the schoolwork meaningless instead of an empowering means of self-expression. A child who does not know the teacher and is not known by the teacher is on his or her own in the school setting. The structure of the school routine may provide the 5-year-old with some sense of containment, and the lessons or activities may provide stimulation, but the child's ability to make meaning and communicate the meaning to others may be compromised, potentially compromising his or her search for meaning while moving through the grades.

Kindergarten teachers must know how to relate to children, and they must know how to help children relate well to one another. Highly structured kindergarten minimizes peer contact in favor of teacher-focused activities. Thus, the children's peer relationships tend to develop on the playground, in the lunch room, and on the school bus, where there is no adult supervision. As noted earlier, 4- and 5-year-olds are still learning about friendship, tolerating difference, living through rejection, being kind, and being inclusive. Thus, when there is little teacher input concerning the real and often adverse dynamics that develop, children may miss critical opportunities for pro-social learning. Teachers may not know that certain unpopular children are excluded by the peer group and feel isolated and undesirable.

How does a kindergarten teacher come to know her students, and what might constitute the collective experience that the kindergarten environment provides? The effective kindergarten teacher must spend time observing the children as they play and interact with one another. Her day must include time for children to engage in open-ended activity so she can use play and interaction as a primary source of information. The effective kindergarten teacher is attuned not only to the affects but also to the performance levels of her students. She knows what makes the children in her class excited, comfortable, sad, angry, afraid, worried, and triumphant. She regards behavior and play as primary avenues of communication about the motivations, concerns, anxieties, and interests of her children, and she informs her practice through observation and interaction. This information is useful in designing and orchestrating collective experiences for the group. For emotionally responsive kindergartens, the curriculum is always at least partially emergent because it is designed to support the developmental and experiential agendas of the children in the particular group. An effective curriculum for 5-year-olds is experientially based (Katz, 1995) and requires interactive explorations as well as personal discovery, experimentation, and documentation (Calkins, 2000).

Teacher–child relationships are critical to 5-year-olds' emotional well-being and receptivity to learning. Thus, the teacher herself must believe in the value of her relationships with the children, and she must feel that she is an important attachment figure in each young child's life. Her presence counts in part because it is organizing for her students; conversely, her absence is upsetting and disorganizing. She must acknowledge the meaning of her emerging, then real, connections with students to the children and to herself and inform her practice with her commitment to those relationships. This means she will tell the children ahead of time if she knows she will not be present, and she will give them information about where she will be to help them create imagery when they do not see her. She will gradually get to know the children's families so the children will not feel cut off from their families while at school and will not have to segregate home experiences from their learning. She will create curricula in concert with the children's interests and developmental issues and will present options for children to explore the curriculum on various levels through various modalities.

Above all, kindergarten teachers must have the capacity to form relationships with young children. They must like young children and be comfortable with their dependency needs. Being a successful kindergarten teacher today requires enormous intelligence, empathy, and creativity and excellent organizational skills. Administrators must realize the critical import of placing well-educated early-childhood teachers with good relationship capacity in kindergarten classes. Administrators must give kindergarten teachers permission to invest in emotionally responsive practices and refrain from bombarding the teachers with requirements that focus all their energy on assessing children's performance levels before she knows the children she is assessing.

The practice of staffing kindergarten classes with upper-grade teachers who could not maintain order in the classroom or convey academic subjects to older children must stop. Putting incompetent teachers in kindergarten classes, imagining that will ensure high-level performance of upper-grade children, is an incredibly short-sighted intervention. Kindergarten-age children grow up to become upper-grade children. If they do not acquire a strong foundation for the use of academic symbols as vehicles of true expression, and if they do not experience emotional well-being at school in the early grades, they are less likely to perform well in the upper grades. At the same time, they are more likely to be isolated with and overwhelmed by emotional distress and to act out this distress in the upper grades.

Kindergarten teachers can protect children when they are in the classroom, but they cannot protect kindergarten itself. Protecting kindergarten is the job of administrators, elected officials, and parents. The introduction of public pre-kindergarten does not diminish the need for excellence in kindergarten. Five-year-olds need a kindergarten experience that nourishes the emotional well-being that underlies their developing concept of themselves as capable, creative learners and desirable friends. Saving emotionally responsive kindergarten from the trend toward performance-oriented kindergarten is a matter of national urgency. Saving kindergarten may result in saving hundreds of thousands of children from becoming overwhelmed by the feelings of inadequacy and peer rejection that can haunt them throughout their school careers and produce frightening consequences in adolescence.

PART II

The Emotionally Safe School Environment

SAFETY HAS ALWAYS *been a priority in public schools. However, it is only recently that we have gone beyond physical safety to recognize the critical need for emotional safety in our schools. In schools that heal, all staff members take responsibility for children's emotional well-being. Each professional in the school building has an important role to play in maintaining the emotional safety of the whole school environment. Part II discusses the role of teachers, principals, and school-based clinicians who want to support the emotional health of children in their buildings. This part of the book emphasizes the need for emotional health to become a priority for all staff members, including the cafeteria worker as well as the social worker. No in-school mental-health component can compensate for the negative effects of an unwelcoming, controlling, or demeaning school environment. In the early grades, children depend on an emotionally safe environment to become attentive, productive learners. Therefore, the children's potential to be successful rests in part on the school's ability to organize around supporting the emotional health of children throughout the school day.*

CHAPTER 4

Teacher, Teacher!

The Teacher's Role in the Emotionally Responsive Classroom

Teacher, Teacher!

THE DEMANDS of teaching are unrelenting and varied and impossible to imagine for people who have not spent their days in an early-grade classroom. Pressure to quantify the results of teachers' labor in terms of test scores has become pervasive, but the far more powerful results of teachers' labors are largely unseen by politicians; they are also impossible to quantify instantly and persist for years after a child leaves the classroom for the next grade. These unquantifiable but potent results include disposition for learning (Katz, 1993), social competence and confidence, access to creativity, feelings of personal worth, opportunity for attachment and positive identification, and ability to use symbols in a meaningful way (Koplow, 1996).

Although children constantly demand the teacher's attention, their demands are often diffuse and frequently often made in an irritating way. Needy children may know that they need something, but they do not always know what it is that they need and therefore they do not make it easy for the teacher to respond helpfully. Because the teacher cannot always read the child's behavior in a way that facilitates a positive response, the power of her relationship to all of the children may not be felt sufficiently in an average classroom. The children who are well behaved and perhaps at less risk are likely to get the most positive responses, leaving out the children who are at the most risk and who are dependent on the school environment to develop a sense of emotional well-being.

Meeting all of the social, emotional, and learning needs of a diverse and needy group of children is an overwhelming prospect and unlikely to occur in even the best of circumstances. Yet the task becomes less overwhelming when teachers understand the power of organizing the classroom environment to promote emotional health. Teachers who see this possibility both design and implement curricula that support emotional health and engage in responsive interactions with the children at a moment of crisis or unmet need. To develop her repertoire for emotionally responsive practice, the teacher needs to think about what goes on in the classroom. The experience of teaching requires the teacher to be totally present in the moment of interaction with the child or group. The role of an emotionally responsive teacher also requires reflection and consideration of classroom life for herself and for the children. Many teachers take pride in keeping their personal lives out of the classroom. Others take pride in their ability to bring the person they are into the classroom and share that person with a group of children. The number of years a teacher has been in the field, the issues in her adult development, and the unresolved issues of her childhood interact with the developmental issues of the children she teaches and creates a complex personal and professional story. A teacher who learns to read this story to herself and allows her students to connect to its meaning contributes to her own emotional well-being and to the well-being of her students.

Inviting and Containing: A Guiding Principle

Teachers with emotionally responsive classrooms have achieved a balance between creating an open atmosphere where expression is welcome and creating a safe atmosphere where clear boundaries contain self-expression and behavior. Selma Fraiberg, a psychologist who has specialized in working with children and parents, has written about the therapist's need to invite expression while helping people feel contained by the therapeutic relationship so that the expression will not be overwhelming and frightening for everyone (Fraiberg, 1980). Inviting and containing is a valuable organizing concept for the classroom teacher who must find developmentally and academically appropriate ways to invite children's expression but retain enough authority and structure to contain the expression that she is inviting. Every teacher has had the experience of going into a colleague's classroom where chaos reigns. This colleague may be able to invite or enable children's emotional expression but does not have enough structure or personal authority to contain the children's emotional energy. More frequently, one enters classrooms in which the teacher contains the group in an authoritative way and uses a highly structured, rigid approach to teaching and classroom management. She minimizes the children's opportunity to interact with one another and silences their emotional expression. This teacher's classroom is orderly but does not provide any invitation for expression of self.

Although it is unlikely that children will be able to grow emotionally in a classroom of chaos, it is equally unlikely that they will be able to grow emotionally in the overly rigid classroom. Inviting without containing leads to chaos, and containing without inviting leads to emotional and social isolation. Children deprived of avenues of expression will become isolated with their issues and at risk for depression, or they will become explosive when they are on the playground or school bus, where the rigid structures are absent. Children who are denied the opportunity to interact with one another under the watchful eye of the teacher may develop dysfunctional patterns of relating to peers, resulting in the destructive dynamics of bullying or social withdrawal. Dynamics that are not allowed to express themselves in the classroom will have ample time to express themselves on the playground, on the school bus, and in the cafeteria, and they will go unaltered because there is no professional involvement at times that peer interaction is permissible.

Achieving a balance between inviting and containing is often a developmental process for teachers. New teachers may strive to be responsive to the children but have difficulty exerting their authority and may struggle to maintain control of the group. New teachers may lack role models for achieving a healthy balance of inviting and containing, and after a hellish first year they may return to the school sounding like their colleagues down the hall who yell all day and seem unempathic to the children's needs. One urban teacher looked back at her history as a first-grade teacher as she began her fifth year of teaching: "The first year, I cried every night. Now I never cry, but I'm not as responsive as I was. It's like half the time I don't even hear them." Feeling ill-equipped to meet the emotional needs of her children, this teacher learned to manage the group better over time and to tune out what felt overwhelming.

A teacher who is not yet able to embrace her authority in the classroom is at risk for feeling constantly assaulted, first by the children's never-ending demands and difficult behavior, and then by administrative and peer pressure to get her class in hand. Although she may believe that the classroom should be a supportive place and that she is helping the children by being permissive, the more she feels the stress of the assaults, the more her receptivity and responsiveness may diminish and her feelings of resentment toward the children and co-workers may increase. Although owning authority may seem antithetical to the wish to create classrooms that extend invitations for children to express themselves, it is that owning of authority that ultimately makes productive expression possible for many children. A teacher who owns authority in her relationship with the group and with individual children provides the security of knowing that the adult is in charge. It is comforting to know that someone is steering the ship and that you will not be allowed to drift out to sea, be thrown overboard by rowdy shipmates, or be left helpless in a sudden storm. The crucial balance lies in the teacher's ability to take charge of the classroom's external order and of implementing routines and activities but allow children to be in charge of and to find avenues of expression for their inner lives during the school day, *while they are with her* in the classroom. The school that tries to meet children's need for expression only through extracurricular activity misses the opportunity to use the potential healing power of the teacher–child relationship as an organizing force for emotional health and social relationships.

Teacher as Midwife: The Birth of Symbol

Children cannot succeed in school without a strong hold on symbolic expression. Drawing, reading, writing, math, and language development are all representational processes that require an increasingly sophisticated ability to recognize, use, and create metaphors with symbols. However, many early-grade teachers of highly stressed urban children report that the children seem compromised in their ability to recognize and generate symbols. These teachers feel frustrated as pressure mounts to ensure that the children are competent readers and writers as early as kindergarten when the children are not able to listen to stories and grasp the main idea, use language to express complex thoughts or feelings, or play elaborate sequences in the dramatic-play area. There is a feeling that the cart is being put before the horse, and that both teacher and child are being run over in the process.

There are good reasons that highly stressed children come to school with what looks like impoverished symbolic development, but there are no good reasons for overlooking the importance of this fundamental developmental process before creating expectations for academic performance. Highly stressed children often come to school without having experienced the foundations for symbolic development typical to their age (Koplow, 1996). These experiential foundations include stable, undisrupted attachment relationships; the opportunity to separate gradually and to discover, explore, and act on objects in the intimate environment; and the opportunity to reconnect with the attachment figure to share the discoveries verbally and affectively (Mahler et al., 2000; Stern, 1985). If children from stressed families are to succeed in school, they must be provided with opportunities in the early grades to acquire these experiential foundations for symbol development. This means that the opportunity for a strong attachment relationship with the teacher and other school adults is an essential component of the young child's experience in schools that heal. Therefore, children and their teachers in preschool, kindergarten, and first, second, and third grades must connect deeply with one another, share interesting experiences, separate to make discoveries, and reunite frequently to share their discoveries verbally and affectively. They must then generate representations of their collective or individual experiences that are meaningful to themselves and to their teachers and, frequently, to their peers as well, because there is a common ground of collective experience. Symbols generated from strong teacher–child relationships and developmentally appropriate collective experience will be elastic, strong, effective, and truly creative because they are personal, meaningful, and learned from intimate contact with people and things, not rote. Children who can play about what they do in school, draw about what they do in school, dictate stories about their discoveries, and write about them will not be at a loss when symbol recognition is demanded and reading becomes the academic focus.

Children who have facility with symbols are able to use language, drawing, play, and writing as avenues of emotional expression; they are therefore less likely to become isolated and depressed or to develop disruptive behavior patterns. (Sheridan, Radlinski, & Foley, 1995). Children who have the opportunity to become attached to their early-grade teachers and to share experience with them have more potential to become symbol users on par with children who have had the good fortune to experience strong and undisrupted attachments in early childhood. Promoting attachment between at-risk children and their teachers has been recognized as a protective factor in preventive mental-health practice in schools (Koralek, 1999). The practice of looping—keeping groups of children together with their teacher for more than one year—supports child–teacher attachment and therefore may be one of the ways in which teachers and administrators can collaborate to support the emotional health and learning potential of lower-grade children. The teacher as attachment figure and "midwife" for the birth of symbols in early-grade children is the facilitator of both learning potential and emotional well-being for her students.

Whose Classroom? The Art of Collaboration

No one knows what it is like to be a teacher unless he or she is a teacher. Spending many hours a day often as the only adult in a room full of children demands a level of energy, vigilance, connection, intelligence, and mediation that few other professions demand. Many teachers work in a windowless world, and no one sees how things really are for them. The only eyes that peer between the blinds are administrative or supervisory, and these seem to observe for short periods that may or may not capture the tone of the classroom or provide understanding and support for that teacher's need.

Therefore, it seems almost paradoxical that many teachers seem uncomfortable when other adults want to be with them in the classroom. It is difficult to have an emotionally responsive early-grade classroom without building in the presence of parents, school-based clinicians, and other adults in the school community. It is easy for teachers to feel territorial about their space, which is their home base for many hours each day. It is difficult to integrate others, such as potentially intrusive parents and clinicians who want to ask distracting questions about a child in the middle of morning meeting. The payoff of collaboration can be worth the trials, but the art of collaboration develops gradually, slowly expanding the universe of the teacher and her students.

Successful collaboration that involves other adults in the classroom may depend on another application of the inviting-and-containing principle (Fraiberg, 1980). That is, teachers can comfortably invite other adults into the classroom if they define the parameters of contact. For instance, an early-grade teacher may invite parents to stay for the first half-hour of the morning but may request that they refrain from actively using materials. They may invite parents to do an art project parallel to their children's but explain that they may not add to or take away from what their child designs on his or her own project. A teacher may invite a social worker in to observe but make clear ahead of time that there can be no discussion of the children until lunch or prep, when the children are out of earshot and the conversation will not be disruptive to classroom process.

The teacher who invites participation from others will probably feel more a part of the school community and less isolated in the "windowless world" of the classroom. Parents and clinicians may become more realistic about what the teacher can do in the group setting if they experience the daily demands in person. Parents may become more trusting and invested in the child's learning process if they can see the teacher's work and concern firsthand. Watching a competent and supportive teacher at work may replace negative images that the parent may have of teachers from her own experience as a child or as the parent of an older child. If the teacher can invite parents to participate when appropriate, she will help children build important bridges between home and school. If she invites the social worker in and asks her to work collaboratively in return, the teacher can use school-based clinicians to stay abreast of psychosocial history to inform her practice, thus addressing both the developmental and experiential realities of her students and improving their potential to learn unencumbered by worries and confusion about their lives.

The Classroom Community: Beyond the Job Chart

Although all early-grade teachers knows that peer dynamics are an important part of classroom life, teacher training rarely addresses this subject or offers a blueprint for the creation of classroom community.

When the classroom functions as a community of learners, the teacher's authority will be augmented by community rituals and values. If the classroom does not constitute a community with common concerns and values, the teacher will find herself trying to control unruly children without support.

How does a classroom of children and their teacher become a functioning community within the larger community of the school? Surely, the whole school's ability to function as a community supported by a strong administrator will be somewhat influential. Yet there are always classrooms that manage to do this despite their school's lack of integrity, and there are always classrooms that do not function as communities although the feeling of whole-school community is palpable.

It is the principal's responsibility to articulate her school's mission to become a functioning community, but it is the teacher's responsibility to articulate her classroom's mission to become a functioning and supportive learning community for all of its members. Leaving the evolution of community to chance is too risky, because the developmentally appropriate tendency of children to exclude one another is too strong. Early-childhood teachers have long struggled with the dilemma of respecting children's peer preferences while making all children feel valued and included, a topic that is well illustrated in Vivian Paley's *You can't say you can't play* (1993). Recent current events have dramatized the need for the entire profession to make the building of inclusive communities a priority. This means that teachers will have to have many discussions with their children about community building so that common goals for safety, well-being, and learning can be articulated, written down, and upheld by the community. Groups of children who have had no prior experience as community members, or whose experience as family members has been tenuous and does not serve them well, may need to see the teacher demonstrate her devotion to the community's values again and again before their "membership" truly takes hold.

All early-grade teachers are familiar with the benefits of a job-chart routine, which gives each child responsibility for some function of classroom life, helping to facilitate connections to the classroom and a feeling of being essential to it. In addition, almost all early-grade teachers post a list of classroom rules, which are often dictated by the children themselves. They usually include such rules as "No hitting" and "Raise your hand before speaking." Teachers often comment on the disparity between children's ability to suggest and talk about the importance of these rules and to actually follow them. Children who verbalize the importance of rules such as these but constantly behave in a ways that are contrary to them may be attempting to feel identified with the authority figure, but they may also not have a sense of cause and effect that allows them to anticipate their negative outbursts or inhibit them to avoid the rejection that results from the impact of the behavior on peers. If classroom groups are to constitute intentional communities, the teacher's intervention must go beyond the initial posting of rules and assigning of jobs. Her repertoire must include facilitating group dialogue about community life and group process addressing difficulties within community life.

To facilitate group dialogue that can help consolidate classroom communities, teachers have to avoid relying on phrases such as "We're all friends in school" and "In our class, everyone can kick the ball far." Although those phrases may communicate the teacher's values, they do not acknowledge the dynamic that is taking place among the children; thus, the children are left to their own devices except in the particular moment that the teacher is intervening. It is more powerful for teachers to say, "It looks like kids are only wanting to work with their best friends and are leaving other kids feeling left out." It is more effective to say, "Every time we have to play a game that involves teams, the same kids get picked right away because they are known as the 'kick-ball experts,' while other kids never get a chance to play the key positions, so they never get the practice they need to become kick-ball experts," then pretend that the whole second grade has equivalent kick-ball skills. If the teacher brings up a dynamic that is happening within the classroom community and addresses it simply and honestly, she invites the children to do the same.

The invitation may provoke anxiety in some teachers, who worry about what they will say if children say something that is too direct or embarrassing to someone else. For example, in such a discussion, a child might say, "I don't want to be Suzanne's partner. Her clothes smell funny," or "I don't want to pick Michael for my team. He kicks like a girl." The classroom teacher may have to preface her discussion with a conversation about the community problem-solving process. She might need to say something like, "I'm going to bring up a problem we're having in our classroom to see if you have ideas about it why it is happening and how we can change it. If you have an idea that you think might hurt someone's feelings, you need to keep it to yourself and talk to me about it later in private."

The evolution of community in classrooms is enhanced by a strong schoolwide community and by a teacher who is kind and respectful to children. The teacher must embrace her authority, be able to articulate her devotion to community, and enact a curriculum that provides collective experience as well as group exploration of emotionally salient topics.

A common definition of a subculture includes having collective experience and a common language to code and communicate about those experiences. For the classroom to become its own community or subculture within the school, children must learn through shared experience and be able to discuss their learning process with one another. Emotionally responsive curriculum, called "Therapeutic Curriculum" in the book *Unsmiling faces* (Koplow, 1996), allows teachers to read the common-ground emotional and social issues in her group and use symbols for these to create curriculum. Emotionally responsive curriculum is a natural companion to a core social-studies curriculum that provides collective exploration of the external environment, because emotionally responsive curriculum extends a parallel invitation for children to explore inner-life issues within the school community. Emotionally responsive curriculum can also be a key facilitator of literacy skills, because it requires children to integrate their experiences in academic learning rather than leave life experience behind in favor of the teacher's agenda.

Emotionally Responsive Curriculum

Emotionally responsive curriculum (ERC) allows children to focus on issues that preoccupy them or hinder their functioning at school; it also gives teachers tools that facilitate emotional well-being and the evolution of community and cognitive growth. Emotionally responsive curriculum gives children the opportunity to address unresolved developmental issues that might compromise their foundation for more mature learning. To implement Emotionally responsive curriculum in the early grades, teachers must familiarize themselves not only with the developmental issues that are salient to the age groups that they teach, but also with the experiential realities that constitute common ground for their population of children. In addition, because Emotionally responsive curriculum allows children a chance to focus on unresolved developmental issues, teachers of early grades must reacquaint themselves with the essential social and emotional milestones of infancy, toddlerhood, and early childhood that they learned in graduate school. The developmental chart (Table 4.1) may be helpful for teachers who feel the need for a refresher course.

Those who have read *Unsmiling faces* may already have a sense of designing and implementing Emotionally responsive curriculum in early childhood programs, but they may feel at a loss to do it in the early grades of elementary school. *Unsmiling faces* gives early-childhood teachers a blueprint for designing these curricula by observing the themes in children's spontaneous play and drawing, noting their behavior, observing interactions with peers and teachers, and listening to their spontaneous conversation. For example, children who cry when they enter and leave school, have difficulty with transitions throughout the day, and seem too preoccupied to play with one another might do well with a curriculum that focuses on separation (see Koplow, 1996, p. 149). Children who have had a lot of experiences with hospital emergency rooms, injuries, doctor visits, and other threats to their physical well-being would probably be well served by a curriculum focusing on body integrity (see Koplow, 1996, p. 156).

Certainly, pre-kindergarten and kindergarten children in public school would be well served by curricula such as those described here, while first-, second-, and third-grade children may want to study these themes on a more sophisticated level. Kindergartners who have trouble tolerating the darkness of rest time and cannot function with a substitute teacher when their group teacher is out sick may respond well to a curriculum that uses transitional objects, as does "My Special Animal" in *Unsmiling faces* (see Koplow, 1996, p. 163). However, because kindergartners are more competent physically and cognitively than preschool children, their use of this curriculum will be more elaborate and appropriate to the capacities and preoccupations of 5-year-olds. For instance, 4-year-olds may distinguish their stuffed animal by choosing a ribbon for the teacher to tie around its neck; 5-year-olds can choose and tie their own ribbons. While 4-year-olds simply give them animals names, 5-year-olds name their animals in the context of studying the meaning and origin of their own names by interviewing their parents. While 4-year-olds talk, play, and draw about what their animals like and do

TABLE 1   Developmental Milestones for Emotional/Social Well-Being

Age: 0–1	1–2	2–3	3–4	4–5
reciprocity, nurture, attunement	locomotion	autonomy	mastery	peer group
↓	↓	↓	↓	↓
attachment	psychological home base	"no" and "mine"	"why?"	"are you my friend?"
↓	↓	↓	↓	↓
regulation of state	transitional object	toileting	cause and effect relationship	identity issues
↓	↓	↓	↓	↓
symbiosis	language bridge	body integrity issues	parallel play	gender
↓	↓	↓	↓	↓
differentiation	early level symbolic play	integration of positive and negative affects	cooperative play, dramatic	power vs. powerlessness
↓	↓	↓	↓	↓
object permanence	separation issues in behavior and play ambivalence	object constancy	same and different	body integrity
↓		↓	↓	↓
pointing, labeling		symbolic play sequences elaborate	monsters, dreams	birth, death, injury
				↓
				fantasy vs. reality

not like, 5-year-olds do so within the context of a study about what makes them the same as other people and what makes them different.

A group of 6-year-olds who are displaying symptoms of fearfulness and peer antagonism also may be well served by this curriculum. They might be asked to distinguish each animal by designing and making clothes and the focus might be on creating a safe environment for the animals to live in, necessitating a study about what makes their own classroom environment feel safe or dangerous. Literature chosen for reading aloud would reflect the theme of emotional safety, and the teacher would invite group discussion and individual elaboration through projects and story writing, allowing each child to use the curriculum both to build community and as an avenue of personal expression.

TABLE 1 *Continued*

Age: 5–6	6–7	7–8	8–9
need to compete and win, feels powerless easily	same sex friendships dominate	conceptual intelligence is evident	needs to perceive meaning in academic material in order to thrive in class
↓	↓	↓	↓
identity issues dominate	peer group pull increases	fantasy and reality lines are more clearly drawn	internalizes feelings of inadequacy or acts them out
↓	↓	↓	↓
gender is a more salient identity maker	concern about self presentation increases	"best friend" or group membership is important	can argue position coherently
↓	↓	↓	↓
authority issues are evident	roles of inventor, builder, and detective are satisfying	group projects are motivating and satisfying	can look at past, present, and future on new level
↓	↓	↓	↓
licence with truth is common	fantasy and reality factors are both used to explain perceptions and inform play	inadequacy stimulated by peer rejection or not achieving in school	image of self includes dreams and fears of future
↓	↓		
royalty and dinosaurs are play themes	interests and talents emerge		
↓	↓		
new level of eloquence competence is increasing markedly	new level of individuation from parents is evident		

The use of transitional objects in early-grade curriculum can be useful for children of all ages in times of community crisis. In response to the recent attack on the World Trade Center, schoolchildren in New York City were given bears for comfort. Curriculums were developed that kept children's developmental issues in mind as well as their shared experience as children living in a city that experienced terrorism (see chapter 12). The same curriculum could have been adapted to help children process group loss, bearing witness to violence or any other shared experience that was difficult for them to integrate.

The teacher who has never used ERC but wants to integrate it into her classroom begins by observing children and identifying common-ground issues that are salient to them. To identify the salient issues, she observes how the children interact with one another and with her; makes note of the themes in their spontaneous play, language, drawing, and writing; recalls their responses to learning activities; and looks at their behavior during the day's routines. If a school social worker or guidance counselor is involved with some of her children, she may want to consult with that person concerning the themes that emerge in the therapeutic context and to stay current about psychosocial factors that may be affecting the child's social and emotional status.

Once the teacher has identified an issue that seems relevant, and sometimes pressing, she can begin to consider ways to invite group exploration and individual expression on a symbolic level. These usually include children's literature that introduces the issue, songs that raise the issue, and projects that allow children to explore the issue and express their personal relationship to it. For example, Ms. H's second-grade class does not do well with the special teachers while she is on her prep and completely disintegrates, becoming disorganized and aggressive, when a substitute teacher is called in. Ms. H knows that several children in her class are in foster care and that a few children are now with their parents but spent years of their early lives separated from them. Ms. H decides to create a curriculum about teacher presence and absence. She introduces the curriculum by reading *Miss Nelson is missing* (Allard, 1977) or *Jamaica and the substitute teacher* (Havill, 1999). She invites the children to talk about what happens when she is not in the classroom. How do they act? Why? How do they feel? She invites conversation about where the kids imagine she is when they come to school and find that they have a substitute. The children are engaged by this topic and make lively contributions.

Ms. H listens to the dialogue in a deep way, because ERC is a form of emergent curriculum. The teacher knows the issue is relevant because of how the children are behaving. She uses curriculum to invite an elaboration of the issues, which she then can respond to through curricular means. Ms. H is surprised to discover that many children cannot imagine her at all when she is out of sight, and others imagine that terrible things are preventing Ms. H from coming to school. Therefore, the first part of the study is organized around helping the children's developing imagery for Ms. H when she is not with them. She brings in photographs of herself at home, in her neighborhood, and on vacations. She invites the children to make books about what they do when there is no school and Ms. H does not see them. The class takes field trips to one another's homes and to Ms. H's home so they have images to help them think about one another when apart.

The study then becomes more focused on helping the children anticipate their reactions to the teacher's absence and understand their behavior. Discussions focus on the differences in being with one's own teacher and being with a substitute. Some of the children's remarks are particularly informative: "The substitutes don't like us. They keep telling us to go sit down"; "The substitutes don't respect you. We say, 'Our teacher does it this way,' and they say, 'I don't care what your teacher does. She's not here now. I'm here now.'" Ms. H uses this information in many ways. First, the children and she make a chart of everything they and she would like a substitute teacher to know. The chart includes information about the children and about the how the classroom runs. For instance, one child says, "Let her know that we don't like anyone to turn the light off. It scares us." Ms. H writes down everything the children say and promises to leave directions for substitutes to look at the chart before they start to teach. Ms. H and the children also talk about the difference in ability that exists among experienced classroom teachers and inexperienced or less capable substitutes. Ms. H invites the children to let her know about what has happened during her absences by writing them down or telling her when she comes back. She is pleased when the school principal remarks on the children's improved conduct the next time that she is out.

Presence and Absence

The topic explored in Ms. H's curriculum illustrates the importance of teachers' presence to children's functioning. Clearly, if child–teacher attachment is a cornerstone of prevention for students at risk, frequent absence by teachers is detrimental to children. Of course, absence will at times be unavoidable, such as during illnesses and family emergencies. At times such as these, curricula such as Ms. H's can be enormously helpful and, at the same time, give school personnel, such as paraprofessionals and administrators checking in on groups, information about the teacher's whereabouts and a time line for her return.

When teachers can anticipate their absence, it is enormously helpful to let the children know ahead of time and, if appropriate, to give them imagery for thinking about the teacher in her absence. For young children, these images may need to be concrete: An assistant teacher, for example, draw a picture of the teacher who is home in bed with the flu for a group of anxious kindergarten children. Having this image may improve the children's ability to focus on their activity for the entire day.

Presence and absence can be defined concretely or relatively. A teacher who is physically present but mentally absent cannot be helpful to a child who is dependent on the connection. This tends to become a pervasive problem for teachers at the end of the year. Many teachers feel stressed by the demands of the end of the year and burned out by events that have taken place throughout the year. Therefore, during the final weeks of school, many teachers tend to take time off, and some of the teachers who are physically present are mentally absent, imagining that they are where they would like to be during summer vacation. This is problematic for children who have not always had an opportunity to separate from important people and important places and who desperately need the teacher to be present for the goodbye. An emotionally responsive curriculum that includes a collective retrospective about the experiences that the class and their teacher have shared, as well as a study of the next grade, can be tremendously helpful, but it must be offered within the context of the teacher's full presence in order to take hold.

Teachers who manage to "stay in" until the end of the school year may actually experience less post-season exhaustion and depression than teachers who have not, because they have let themselves participate in the separation process in a real way. Saying goodbye to a group has meaning for both the children and their teacher when real attachments have been formed. Even the children who are the most difficult and stressful for the teacher to deal with evoke complex responses for the teacher as the year ends. On the one hand, a teacher may feel enormously relieved that she is no longer responsible for the difficult student; on the other, she may realize that the the person on whom she has expended huge amounts of energy all year long is suddenly out of her life. The loss demands a kind of psychic reorganization that may be delayed if the teacher avoids a real goodbye.

Creating a Context for Responsive Teaching

Early-grade teachers who are committed to emotionally responsive practice often find themselves swimming against the tide when the school environment is dominated by pressure to raise students' performance without offering students the kinds of support that are likely to bring about such improvements in the long run. If a teacher is not working with a supportive administration, school-based clinician, or in-school peer group, she must find outside sources of support and professional development. She might find a peer support group, study group, or counseling group for people in stressful professions. She might enroll in continuing-education classes to become more knowledgeable about the kind of work she wants to add to her repertoire. She might look at other primary schools in her area to see the range of possibilities for an early-grade professional seeking a supportive environment for engaging in emotionally responsive practice and apply for a transfer. Certainly, it is unreasonable to expect early-grade teachers to devote their energy and talent to fostering their schoolchildren's well-being if the school administration is unconcerned about the well-being of its teachers. Responsive teaching in isolation may be initially exhilarating, but over time it may cause teachers to become disillusioned, exhausted, and burned out. In order to stay the course, responsive teachers require connection and support for their efforts.

CHAPTER 5

Creating a
Healing Environment

The Role of the Principal

IT IS IMPOSSIBLE for schools to support emotional well-being in students without a wholehearted commitment by the administration. The school principal must set the interactive tone throughout the building, communicate the importance of emotional well-being as a precursor to learning to all staff with the building, and create school-wide policies and practices that support the needs of the children and staff. If the principal lends only nominal support to making emotional well-being a priority, it will not be a priority. Teachers and other members of the school staff are generally well attuned to the building administrator and often seek status and approval by mirroring the administrator's vision of school success. Indeed, when teachers in the early grades are interviewed about implementing practices that support well-being in children, they often explain apologetically that they cannot devote energy to emotional well-being because the building principal is concerned only with academics. The building principal may be well spoken about the advantages of attending to social and emotional health in the early grades but may feel extreme pressure from the district to disregard all concerns except those directly related to test scores. Most school districts have yet to recognize the connection between students' emotional well-being and their performance (Schonkoff & Phillips, 2000).

There are many studies that principals and school-district personnel can read to become acquainted with the connection between emotional health in children and school functioning and performance (e.g., Arnold, Ortiz, Curry Stowe, Goldstein, Fisher, Yershova, & Zeljoja, 1999; Bronson, 2001; Ladd, Birch, & Buhs, 1999; Schonkoff & Phillips,

2000). These studies indicate that investing in the emotional health of children is not only a compassionate, responsible approach to designing educational programs for children in the early grades, but also that it actually affects children's learning in remarkable ways. A recent study of the New Beginnings Project in Newark, New Jersey, surprised officials by documenting higher scores in reading and math for children who had spent two years or more in child-centered classrooms with a developmental interaction approach to learning and an active commitment to the emotional health and social competency of the students (Kopacsi & Onsongo, 2001). Children in this program also had significantly higher rates of school attendance than did a control group.

Although there are relatively few elementary schools that make emotional well-being a conscious priority, the most recent surgeon general's report on the unmet mental-health needs of U.S. children strongly states that school-based mental-health programs are essential in order to provide for children's well-being and prevent issues from becoming serious and debilitating later (U.S. Public Health Service, 2000). Although principals of schools that serve children age 4–10 may feel that risks of incidents of psychiatric instability that result in school violence are relatively low with this age group, profiles of middle-school- and high-school-age school shooters have revealed patterns of peer isolation and alienation or unhappiness that have sometimes been present since kindergarten. All elementary-school principals strongly consider their students' academic futures when they plan for each grade. It has become critical for elementary-school principals also to strongly consider their children's future as adolescents and adults who must be able to maintain a stable sense of positive self-worth and remain socially motivated beyond their elementary-school years. These considerations need to inform both policy and practice in elementary schools throughout the nation.

The idea of school-based mental-health programs has been interpreted in many ways. Sometimes schools collaborate with existing providers, such as community mental-health clinics, to offer evaluation and treatment services on-site at school. These collaborations can be extremely valuable and can give access to children whose parents would not be able to get them to the clinic to receive the services. However, to be effective, the collaboration has to go beyond including the services within the school's walls. No school-based mental-health program can succeed in improving the emotional well-being of children if school practices themselves undermine emotional well-being. For instance, if a child is identified for school-based treatment for issues of poor self-worth and acting out in the classroom and leaves the treatment session to return to the classroom by way of a security guard's desk, where the security guard makes berating about the child's having been taken out of the classroom, the positive experience that the child has just had is likely to be negated.

Although collaborations between schools and mental-health providers are an important resource for many children, they cannot and do not replace an in-house commitment to making the school environment support emotional well-being and prevent the deterioration of students' mental health.

Setting the Tone

The building principal sets the emotional tone in the school by the way in which he or she interacts with teachers, children, and parents and by the way in which he or she responds to students' and the staff's expressions of need. If the principal is harsh, authoritarian, and uncommunicative, many teachers will model this tone in the classroom, and children may take a harsh tone with one another when outside of teacher earshot. If the principal's tone is kind, firm and concerned, teachers are more likely to relate to children in this manner as well. Although the principal becomes a model for practice by virtue of having the leadership position, modeling is never enough to address fundamental aspects of school practice. The school principal who is committed to having a school that is a healing environment for children will have to articulate her position about the tone of relating to children and parents in her building, and will probably have to evaluate this aspect of staff performance at intervals and enforce it the way she enforces other school policies.

In addition to the principal's articulating her vision and modeling an emotionally supportive tone, introducing the commitment to providing an emotionally supportive environment will require staff development. This will probably need be carried out over a number of months, because many people speak to children the way they themselves were spoken to as children, regardless of whether this is optimal for the children they are addressing. Staff development will have to be offered for all levels of building staff who are present during the school day, so that the entire community is involved in the transformation. Administrators should expect to hear frequent regressions to the kind of language that was used before the staff-development process began and should respond with reminders when this occurs. "Remember, we're not using that kind of language or tone here anymore; let's think of another way to communicate that thought" may become a frequent comment made by principals in schools that are in transition.

The tone that adults use to address children and the language that they use to communicate with children must be genuine, clear, and respectful and convey appreciation for the child's point of view. Take, for example, the second-grader in an urban school who is accidentally stepped on by the child in front of him in line. He in turn shoves the child, who falls and hits her head. Comments made by staff people might range from, "Tyrone! If you don't stop hurting everyone you'll end up in jail when you grow up" to "Tyrone, you've done it again. You've lost your recess time." The school principal can model a different response. "Tyrone, I know Kyra stepped on you, and you probably didn't mean to hurt her when you shoved her, but you know that there is absolutely no shoving allowed here. That did hurt Kyra and could have been dangerous. You'll have to spend recess indoors thinking about what you can do next time someone steps on you by accident." Without administrative intervention, the comment about one day going to jail is at least as dangerous to Tyrone as Tyrone's push is to Kyra.

A mother who is upset because her daughter repeatedly loses clothing at school bursts into the school office, demanding to see the principal and loudly cursing at the teacher, whom she feels has not done enough to keep track of the kindergartner's clothes. The principal emerges from her office, having heard the mother state the issue. "I'd be happy to talk to you about your concerns about Anna's clothes," the principal says, "but in our school, there is no cursing or yelling, so if you're feeling calm enough to work on the problem now, come in; otherwise I'll give you an appointment to come back." The mother is taken aback but agrees to calm down and talk about her concerns. When the meeting is over and the parent leaves, the principal hears the office staff talking about her in derogatory terms. "She's worth nothing to that child. She probably doesn't know where her clothes are at home, either," one of the secretaries says, who is exasperated at having had to deal with the mother when she first walked in. The principal responds, "I know she's hard to deal with, but she's Anna's mother, so we're going to have to figure out a way to deal with her. Let's figure out a strategy for the next time it happens."

Policy, Routines, and Quality of Life at School

The principal has the power to determine quality-of-life issues for his or her school building. The way in which policies are implemented, and the way in which routines are carried out, will have enormous impact on the way in which children feel about being in school and teachers feel about working in the school building. Although they certainly affect the attendance of both students and teachers, and these factors clearly affect students' performance, quality-of-life issues are not generally acknowledged except when students and employees complain among themselves. Yet quality-of-life issues are crucial to the creation of emotionally responsive school environments. How students and teachers feel about being in the building can be a litmus test for the emotional health of the school. The creation of child-friendly and employee-friendly policies will go a long way toward fostering emotional health in the building.

All schools must deal with personal emergencies among the staff that come up during the school day. A staff member may become ill while in the building or may get a call to come to pick up a hurt or sick child from school. If the school's policy demands that the staff member remain in the building until officially excused by the principal, difficulties may arise if the principal is called away from the building or is attending a high-level meeting and cannot be disturbed. Teachers who are called about an emergency and are waiting to be excused are likely to be distracted and ineffective. When formal policy feels too constraining, informal policies or networks are likely to take over. Therefore, one teacher may try to cover for another who has already left for the day, leaving the principal in the dark about coverage in her own building. If the policy accounted for the lack of availability of the principal and gave teachers another way to proceed, teachers would be more likely to find the policy bearable and would therefore be more likely to abide by it

Every school has a teachers' lounge, where teachers spend some of their down time during the day. Every school has a lunch period for teachers in which they are free of the responsibility of caring for their group. A teachers' lounge can be stark and barren or it can be warm and inviting. The administrator's commitment to making routines comfortable for the people who work in the school may be the determining factor. District policy may define the lunch period as 30 minutes, barely enough time for the teacher to deliver her children to the cafeteria or special activity, eat, and return for them. The principal can try to schedule prep periods so that each teacher has a prep adjacent to a lunch period for at least one day each week. Although teachers may still feel stressed and may rarely express gratitude, the actions of the attentive principal will go a long way toward creating an the emotionally responsive environment; it will be felt by staff and be seen in fewer sick days and more willingness to participate in additional projects. It will also ultimately be felt by children, who will have a more rested and less stressed teacher with a greater capacity for emotional attunement when she rejoins her class.

All schools share certain basic routines that make up what is considered the "non-instructional" school day. Routines such as daily entry, snack, rest time, toileting time, lunch time, after-lunch recreation time, and dismissal make up the "non-instructional" school day for children, teachers, and paraprofessionals. Although these routines are not considered "instructional," they do teach important life lessons to the children who engage in them day after day. The quality and experience of those routines repeatedly provide participants with either positive or negative messages about their self-worth, their relationships, and their dependency needs. If the messages are positive, the repetitive nature of the routines ensures that the positive messages will be internalized. If the messages are negative, those messages are likely to be internalized and become problematic, perhaps even dangerous, for fragile children. Thus, to the professional concerned about children's mental health, routines are an important part of school life.

Paradoxically, many educators consider routines to be incidental and therefore not worthy of professional time. Thus, significant staff members are often absent during those routines in which children require the most intimate contact in order to gain positive messages about themselves. Young children's lunch and rest routines are often supervised by paraprofessional staff instead of by the teacher, for example, who has the strongest relationship to the individual children involved. This usually results in the children's feeling needy and over-whelmed, acting out, and becoming difficult to manage. Paraprofessional staff, who may not have the resources to contain difficult children, may then resort to techniques to gain control that are demeaning to them and disturbing to the children who are behaving well. When parents are asked to volunteer to help in the cafeteria or on the playground, they often do so without receiving adequate orientation or training. Their only model is the staff member who is having trouble managing the children.

The developmental meaning of routines is important to consider for the age group of children engaged in the particular routine. For example, lunch time is an important time for all age groups. For children in kindergarten and first grade, food responds to and evokes their need for nurture. Although they enjoy socializing as they eat, they generally eat better in small surroundings, with a low level of external stimulation and a lot of opportunity to have contact with important adults. Some schools recognize that the experience of eating in a crowded and noisy cafeteria supervised by cafeteria aides is too much for 5-year-olds and arrange for children to eat in their classrooms with their teacher or a classroom aide. Other schools are not able to arrange this because of union regulations about teachers' lunch hours and other logistical problems and face the challenge of making the existing routine more intimate and more grounding for the youngest children. Under the principal's direction, children can make individual place mats in their classrooms and take them into the lunchroom to make the experience more personal. The cafeteria staff can be instructed to save a certain table every day for kindergarten children, so that they have a place to eat that becomes their own. The staff can be instructed to serve the kindergartners' food on a rolling cart instead of having them wait in a long line that cuts down on the time available for eating. The principal may choose to create additional lunch hours, dividing the children into smaller groups that are likely to cause less commotion and be more conducive to comfort for the children eating their lunch there.

For fifth- and sixth-graders, lunch time is almost strictly a social time, and complex peer interactions dominate the cafeteria. Although the older children can be independent about getting and eating their food and clearing their places, the principal may be aware of the need for another level of supervision that the lunch aides cannot be expected to provide. Without professional supervision of some kind, the principal fears, damaging peer dynamics may be occurring that leave some vulnerable preadolescents feeling excluded and rejected over and over again. The attuned principal may elect to spend her valuable time in the cafeteria when the older children are present to observe the children's interactions and intervene when they are damaging, and to inform teachers and school social workers about children who are on the fringe of the group and may require additional support. Administrative and clinical attention or the services of a recreational expert are certainly warranted during the outdoor time that follows lunch in many public schools. In cases in which the children are largely unoccupied with sports and games, playground equipment, or organized activity of some kind, unsupervised peer dynamics again threaten the well-being of fragile children who are ostracized or humiliated by the group.

In recent years, many school administrators have instructed kindergarten teachers to stop having rest time in order to give instructional time more opportunity to take hold. This has worked for some physically mature children, but it is often unproductive for less mature children, who are exhausted at the end of the day unless they rest or nap. Although we recognize the importance of school lunch programs for families in poverty, who may not have the resources to provide nourishing food, we sometimes neglect to recognize the importance of rest time for children from stressed or disorganized families who may not get enough rest at night. Energy for learning is affected not only by nutrition, but also by rest. Rest time may provide refueling for many young children.

In schools where rest time is part of the daily routine for the youngest learners, administrators may consider the teacher's presence to be unnecessary and call meetings or expect her to attend to paperwork at that point in the school day. However, the rest-time routine demands the early childhood teacher's professional attention in order to be helpful to the children. Many 5-year-olds can settle down only when an attachment figure is present. Many children fear darkness or begin to feel separation anxiety at rest time. Children with traumatic histories are frequently disruptive at rest time, because being on their own in a quiet place allows them to be overwhelmed by memories of trauma. Without teacher contact and intervention, those children are likely to become disruptive to the children who are resting.

When considering the best way to make the rest-time routine productive, staff must again look for ways to make the routine more personal for fragile children. Inventive kindergarten teachers have purchased night lights for their rooms for use at rest time, have used transitional objects as part of rest-time comfort, play soft music, and, above all, stay in the room while the children are resting. In interviews, teachers of young children made many interesting comments about the value of rest time. Kindergarten teachers who had reinstituted rest time after suspending it under pressure to pursue academics found children to be more attentive and productive later in the day (Koplow, 2001).

The developmental needs of early-grade children are best met when classrooms are equipped with bathrooms that children may use when the need arises. When antiquated buildings make this impossible, policies and routines govern children's bathroom experience at school. Principals should become involved with the ways in which these policies are carried out and with the nature of the routines that are being enacted in their buildings. For example, one kindergarten teacher had a policy that children could not leave the room to use the bathroom during an activity; they had to wait until the activity was over. Her expectation was not developmentally appropriate for 5-year-olds, who have a tendency to become absorbed in their activity to the extent that they wait until the last minute to ask to go. Indeed, over time several children had accidents and ended up in the school office in tears, waiting to see the nurse, who, according to school policy, could help them change their clothes. The nurse was often busy with an ill child, which caused the children who were wet to stay in wet clothes and feel embarrassed when children were brought to the office for other reasons. The principal made a policy that all early-grade children be given permission to use the bathroom as soon as they made a request. She also instructed the teacher to ask each parent for an extra set of clothes to be kept in school. The number of accidents decreased dramatically, and for the few that did occur, children were often able to change themselves into their dry clothes, avoiding additional embarrassment and unnecessary loss of instructional time.

Many young children are still struggling with issues about control, privacy, and achieving comfort while engaging in intimate routines without their parents present. When groups of children are taken to the bathroom together, teachers often use military-style group management to accomplish toileting in an orderly fashion. The experience may provoke anxiety in some children, who may feel tense or hurried in a way that is uncomfortable and counterproductive for them. Principals may remind teachers that the toileting time needs to be low-key and relaxed, while organized. Children might take books with them to read while waiting for a turn. If they are engaged, they will be less likely to act out and require a disciplinary response.

Administrative collaboration with teachers in the design of daily routines communicates the administrator's acknowledgement of the importance of routines in the school lives of young students. It lets teachers know that the principal values all of the time that she spends with the children, and that, although daily routines are not considered instructional in the traditional sense, they are full of lessons about personal worth and respect. The lessons that the children learn are essential if they are to thrive emotionally.

Embracing Authority:
The Value of Being at the Top

The school principal has a unique role. No one else in the school building has as much decision-making power. No one else has as much power to set the emotional tone. Although administrators themselves feel the weight of being responsible for children, teachers, and parents, as well as the weight of pressure from the district, those pressures are invisible to children and at times ignored by parents and teachers.

Children see their own parents as all-powerful, although in the greater scheme of things they are not. Children, parents, and teachers may experience the school principal as all-powerful, although in the greater scheme of things he or she is not. However, in the eyes of the children, parents, and teachers in the building, and within the confines of the school hierarchy, the principal has ultimate authority within the building. This means, among other things, that people will behave differently in her presence, as they will probably see the principal as a maternal or paternal figure, eliciting complex emotional reactions. Principals sometimes complain that teachers must think they are magicians, capable of miraculous feats, even in the face of evidence to the contrary, such as a low budget or lack of supplies. Indeed, authority figures are often endowed with "magical" powers by those who see them as powerful (Fraiberg, 1984). This can be facilitative or it can be detrimental, depending on the how the administrator chooses to use the "magical" powers given to him or her.

Many children, teachers, and parents have had complicated experiences with people who have more authority than they do and meet authority figures with mixed emotions that may include respect, fear, mistrust, wish for approval, and hopefulness. The principal may experience a variety of complex emotional reactions from children, staff, and parents that can make administrative life more difficult than it already is. Those who mistrust authority present a special challenge for the principal, who may need to respond constantly to oppositional behavior that seems designed to provoke an authoritative response. Principals react to this constant demand for limit setting in various ways. Some principals use memos to state and restate school policies to staff and parents; other principals divide administrative labor and have assistant principals interact with children and staff members on most issues while they deal with parent issues directly. The principal who responds to these challenges in person by becoming a partner in development to the child, parent, or staff member who is driven to test her may accomplish a great deal. If he or she is able to set limits clearly and articulate the purpose of the limit in person, yet invite an ongoing relationship with the person seeking limits, the principal will ultimately be exercising the "magical powers" of her authoritative position. These powers include the ability to give people experience with authority that is embraced but not abused—authority that is necessary to uphold the priorities of the school, including the emotional well-being of children.

Principals are often called on to enforce policies that come from the school district. Some of these might be consistent with her own beliefs and goals; some of them might not. When administrators are called on to enforce policies that are not in the best interest of the population she is serving, she may feel frustrated with the limits of her power. She may also struggle with presenting the new regulation to staff members. It is important that principals acknowledge when there are conflicts that affect the school's mission and create identity issues for her and potentially for the staff. For instance, a school committed to an experiential curriculum in the early-childhood classroom is suddenly mandated to engage in standardized testing in the early grades. The principal calls a meeting to explain the mandate from the district, addressing the staff in the following way: "Given our beliefs about how young children learn and our approach to teaching them, I have concerns about how this will affect us. It seems like there will be implications for children, parents, and for you. I'd like to hear what your concerns are. We're going to have to figure out a way to implement this that is the least intrusive to our overall functioning. What do you think?" By acknowledging that the policy is dissonant with the priorities of the school, yet also acknowledging the necessity to comply, she both embraces her authority as she restates her own vision and priorities, and clarifies the limits of her authority by inviting a realistic dialogue about implementation. In contrast, the principal who simply restates the mandate of the district and gives instructions for implementation paradoxically undermines her own authority, because she appears to be only a vehicle for the directives handed down from above.

The administrator who runs an emotionally responsive school often articulates her school's vision concerning learning and emotional well-being and uses her authority to make sure that the actual experiences that children have at school are commensurate with that vision. Because there is no one else with the authority to protect that vision, the extent to which the school functions as an emotionally safe environment depends almost totally on the administrator's willingness to embrace her authority and enforce standards for how adults at school relate to children and relate to one another.

Saying "No," Saying "Yes"

Principals who embrace their authority have a unique opportunity to give children, parents, and staff a positive experience with limit setting. Many children have had experiences with limits being set in overly harsh and absolute ways, in ways that deny them permission to have their own feelings about the limit, or in ways that leave them with no positive choices. Many children have confusing experiences with adults at home that may allow them to have too much power in certain situations and not enough power in others. For example, a little boy may be punished if he does not eat all of the food on his plate, regardless of whether he likes it, but is free to watch anything wants on television, even if it is not suitable for children. Another boy may have any toy he wants, as long as he does not cry or complain that his parents work too many hours and he rarely sees them. A little girl is allowed to make the rules at home and commands her parents to get things for her but is not allowed to connect to adults or children outside the home, even though she is 6 years old and in need of friends. Another girl gets a spanking for wetting her pants but is not allowed to get up to go to the bathroom in the middle of church services. All of these children come to school with authority issues that play themselves out in the school setting. When these children grow up, some of them will become teachers and administrators with authority issues that are likely to play themselves out in the school setting, as well. A wise administrator will understand her own authority issues and recognize the power of her position to evoke authority issues in the children, parents, and teachers in her school.

Principals and teachers do well to realize their authority in external matters and to realize the importance of leaving internal matters to the individual or group in question. This "external order, internal freedom" formula is useful in limit-setting interactions with children as well as with staff and parents. Say, for example, that a crossing guard comes to speak at an assembly about safety on the street near the school. The speech is long and boring at times, and several third grade boys are making rude noises that distract other children. The principal speaks to them sternly. "You might not find this interesting, but you are not allowed to be rude to the speaker and disruptive to everyone else. If you think it 's boring or you have other opinions about it, you can write about that in your journal this afternoon." This principal uses her authority to support her agenda but acknowledges that the boys might have another agenda, which they have the right to express at an appropriate time and place.

A group of girls complains about going outside after lunch and give the lunch aides a hard time by running into the building every chance they get. The principal sees this in action one afternoon and asks the girls what is going on. "We're cold and bored out here," they say. "It's not fair that we have to go outside; it's only good for the kids who play sports." The principal responds, "Everyone has to go outside after lunch because we have no indoor space large enough for all the kids, and we need the cafeteria for the next lunch period. If I see you run into the building again, you'll be sitting in my office. Meanwhile, why don't you have a meeting out here and think of some ways to make the outdoor time work better for kids who don't like sports?"

A first-grade child who is crying loudly is brought to the office by her teacher. The teacher explains that the little girl brought a talking stuffed animal to school, but the toy is disruptive to the group, and the teacher has taken it away to keep until the end of the day. The girl has been crying so loudly and for so long that the children could not concentrate during the morning meeting. The principal gives the girl a tissue: "I know you love your stuffed animal, but no one can bring talking toys to school because the talking disturbs the class. Your teacher will give it back before you go home, and we'll send a note to mommy so she knows not to send it again. Sit down here until you're finished crying and you feel ready to go to your class."

Parents of kindergarten children storm into the principal's office demanding to see her. They are upset to learn that the kindergarten children are excluded from a field trip to a haunted mansion for Halloween. The principal comes out of her office to greet them and listens to their grievance. "Kindergarten children will visit the pumpkin farm for their Halloween trip," she says. "Its part of their curriculum about harvest. The mansion is too scary for 5-year-olds who don't know that what they are seeing is make believe." One parent replies, "But our kids aren't scared. They see every horror movie around with their older brothers and sisters. They want to go." The principal hears this familiar argument. "Well, I know they want to see those movies, but there are a lot of scared kids around here when the lights go out for rest time, so we're not going to give them anything else to be afraid about. But I know you have PTA money for special events, so why don't you plan something just for the kindergarten kids after school hours— something that captures the excitement of Halloween that and isn't too frightening for young children. Let me know what you come up with." These parents decide to put on a Halloween carnival for the kindergarten children and are delighted by the enthusiastic response of the youngest members of the school community.

A school in a large urban community has a problem with teachers' arriving late and trying to cover for one another when administration becomes aware. The principal addresses the problem in a staff meeting, restating her expectation that teaching staff will arrive by 8:00 each morning. One teacher protests, "I prepare in the afternoon after the kids leave. I never leave before 4:30 or 5:00. I'm much better with the kids in the morning if I take more time to relax and drink another cup of coffee. I'm always here before the bell, and I'm always organized and prepared." The principal restates her expectation. "I want everyone here at 8:00 A.M. If something comes up, I want to have access to you before the kids are here. If you use afternoon time to prepare, come in and sit in your room and relax with your coffee. Just be here."

In each of these scenarios, the administrator deals with the kind of issues that call for her attention several times during the school day. In each case, she must exert her authority concerning what people must do and when but is able to leave how they do it and how they feel about what they need to do up to the individual. Children, parents, and staff then have the opportunity to experience someone who embraces her authority to maintain order and philosophical integrity but does not use the authority to over-control, attack self-worth, or deny others the right to their feelings. By embracing the power allowed by her position, she serves as a role model for the people with whom she interacts, whom she then invites to be powerful within the confines of their respective positions.

What Teachers Carry

Whether teachers are talented or struggling, experienced or brand new, they carry the enormous responsibility of teaching large numbers of children with diverse learning needs and often with intense social and emotional issues that make themselves felt in the classroom. Principals who were classroom teachers earlier in their careers can remember both the joys and the burdens of their teaching experience. The complexity of the teacher's task has probably increased at the beginning of the 21st century, as the lives of children in the United States have become more complex regardless of where they are on the socioeconomic continuum and the political pressures for frequent assessment and prescriptive teaching have become enormous. In one large urban district, kindergarten through third-grade teachers are required to give each of their children six different assessments annually, which constantly disrupts the creation and implementation of curriculum projects that help to establish the classroom as a community of learners. Teachers express frustration about this. Principals who choose to acknowledge the teachers' many serious challenges openly within the school community help to alleviate some of the stress that teachers feel by affirming their experience. Principals who know what teachers carry, talk about the enormity of the teachers' task, and articulate the value of what teachers give to the children each day empower teachers on many levels. Principals who can be expressive in this way become a model for teachers who need to be able to give the same respect, empathy, and affirmation to their students.

Most teachers live a double life of sorts. The experience of teaching can be exciting, but it is certainly draining. It can be joyful to be with young children, but it is also intense and painful to be with young children whose lives are complex and who have desperate needs. People who do not teach, however, tend to have an idealized view of teaching. They tend to focus on long vacations and short work days, art projects and field trips, but they do not consider the day-to-day stresses and challenges of classroom life. Their vision does not include being with the confused and lonely child who has two incarcerated parents, mediating among children who are driven to express their anger and desperation physically, or coping with the child who throws up all over the class science project. Often teachers are alone with the stressful part of teaching, with only their fellow teachers as potential sources of support and understanding; their spouses and friends may be in the dark about what their actual day to day lives are all about. Principals who use their authority to acknowledge these stresses help teachers integrate the positive and negative experiences that are part of teaching and give teachers more access to their own energy because they do not have to exhaust themselves by traveling between the actual world of the classroom and the idealized image maintained by the world outside.

For example, a school district directs all first-grade teachers to use a new assessment tool that demands that the teacher sit with each child for 20 minutes. The district may imagine that the rest of the class will sit quietly and do their work during this time or use learning centers without the need for teacher intervention. Ms. E's class is needy and incapable of working on their own unless they can connect with her. Therefore, countless children come to interrupt her assessment time, although she has strictly forbidden it. Yet she knows that the arrangement is flawed because it assumes that her children are more mature than they actually are. She feels pressure to bring them to a higher level instantly, which is unlikely to work. If Ms. E does not expect support from her principal, she is unlikely to bring this to anyone's attention and will try to cope alone. As a result, she will become stressed, short-tempered, and less empathic toward the children and herself. If she expects validation, she will be more likely to approach her principal, Ms. R, with the problem. Ms. R acknowledges her dilemma simply and clearly: "I know that group is not going to function on its own all day long while you attend to only one child." Ms. E can then sigh with relief, and together they can try to come up with a plan for using special teachers and other methods while the assessments are in progress.

Every principal has some teachers who seem unable or unwilling to participate in schoolwide efforts to promote children's emotional well-being. There are teachers who seem to need to exert their power over children in a controlling or demeaning way that is counterproductive to both learning and emotional well-being or who feel that learning is not influenced by well-being and therefore that emotions are not within their arena. Although principals have channels for reporting and dealing with behavior that is outright abusive, there are many instances in which teacher–child interactions and teacher–principal interactions lack respect. Administrators have the enormous task of giving feedback to the people in question, providing them with opportunities for emotional growth through staff development or helping them transfer to classes in higher grades or other schools when union regulations allow this.

Principals with years of experience may be able to recognize teachers who can grow when given the opportunity and teachers who are entrenched in negative styles of relating to children. When teachers who embrace a hopeful attitude outnumber those with a negative style, administrators may notice small, positive changes in the staff members of concern over time, as the power of the teacher peer group may provide a strong yet subtle motivation for change. The administrator may decide that her energy is well spent in developing the skill and commitment in the receptive staff members before addressing the resistant staff members about emotional well-being.

Being in Good Company

No principal can create a healing environment in isolation. In the absence of peer support, the stresses of administration become oppressive and force even the most committed and talented administrators to shut down, making them less emotionally available to staff and to themselves. Administering without empathy for other staff creates a rigid and emotionally unresponsive environment. Administering without the empathy for oneself creates a stressed, angry, and depressed administrator. Acting as principal of a large urban school is essentially an impossible task, and it is helpful for the principal to acknowledge this to herself and gain access to peers who can help her regain perspective when she has lost her own. Because there is no built-in peer support for principals, the principal must make peer support a conscious priority if she or he is to survive emotionally. Teachers can spend some part of the day in the company of other teachers and gain support from one another; principals have no such luxury. Without a plan in place, principals are thrown back on family support systems, which vary widely depending on the particular situation of the individual administrator. Therefore, schools that heal must collaborate with other schools in their area that are committed to the emotional well-being of children and organize regular peer-support meetings for principals.

Isolation has been named frequently throughout this book as a primary risk factor for children and families. Without social connections to hold difficult experiences, children or families can become trapped in private hells that may erupt when children become adolescents and are unable to contain their impulses and fantasies. Administrators are not immune to the dangers of holding distressing experience and chronic stress in isolation. The nature of their job is continually to multitask, address crisis, and be responsible for vulnerable children and staff while answering to a school district that may or may not acknowledge the weight of their day-to-day load. The administrator who feels isolated may find herself experiencing physical symptoms of chronic stress, such as asthma, anxiety, or chronic sleeplessness (Clarke, 1985). He or she may also find herself fantasizing about taking revenge on the district or on difficult staff members. Yet ultimately, most administrators have a high regard for law and order, and they rarely act out their fantasies against others. They may, however, be at risk for engaging in self-destructive behavior, such as smoking and overeating (Clarke, 1985). They may be vulnerable to feelings of extreme guilt or inadequacy if unable to perform at the level that they consider optimal. To compensate for these feelings, struggling administrators may need to appear more powerful than they feel, increasing their sense of internal isolation and widening the gap between their behavior and their underlying feeling. A peer support group or professionally facilitated group for principals may go a long way toward ameliorating the potential for the psychological dangers that threaten school principals.

Conclusion

There can be no real possibility of creating a healing school environment without the commitment, energy, and compassion of the school principal. The principal alone has the authority and perspective needed to make the vision of emotional well-being a reality inside the school building. Embracing authority in a way that supports the vision of emotional well-being, enforcing policies that are friendly to children and staff, and creating child-friendly routines are important components of the emotionally responsive school experience. Just as important is the principal's ability to empathize with teachers and herself as professionals who are trying to provide for the well-being and learning potential of children in a political climate that is often hostile to efforts that cannot be immediately quantified. Although the principal can certainly invite evaluation of emotionally supportive practice over the long run, her understanding and empathy for the teachers' burdens, and for her own burdens, in the present can empower her to make a difference in the emotional climate of the school that can be felt by children, parents, and staff.

CHAPTER 6

The Role of the School-based Clinician in Schools That Heal

Evaluating Our Resources

MANY PUBLIC SCHOOLS have school-based clinicians as part of the team of professionals who work to help children and families. Most often the school employs a guidance counselor, social worker, or school psychologist, or a team of these mental-health professionals is assigned to a primary school or cluster of primary schools. Although these mental-health professionals ideally are present to help children in all grades, teachers, administrators, and clinicians themselves often say that the majority of the clinician's time and energy is taken up by the crises and transitional needs of upper-grade children. There is much less focus on children in pre-kindergarten to second grade unless their mental-health needs constitute an emergency. Indeed, some early-childhood pediatric social workers in urban schools complain about being assigned administrative detail because of a perception among school administrators that young children do not need their services and that they are therefore available for clerical duties. Other systems use mental-health professionals in elementary schools to evaluate and identify learning or severe emotional problems in children but rarely to treat these problems once they have been identified.

It seems paradoxical that many public-school systems employ school-based clinicians but do not seem to know how best to use them to foster the emotional growth of children in the early grades. Many public schools already have the resources necessary to implement primary prevention in the early grades, but few systems are devoting clinical hours to this purpose.

When clinicians work in schools that go from pre-kindergarten to fifth or eighth grade, competition will exist for the clinician's time and resources. Because upper-grade children's crises sometimes manifest themselves in dramatic and even dangerous behavior, clinicians may find their time occupied in outside-of-school family advocacy in situations that urgently demand attention. However, if we do not ensure that clinical time for primary prevention in the early grades is built into the school-based clinician's schedule, the number of urgent needs among upper-grade children will increase, because these children's early-grade indicators of stress went unattended. When sufficient resources exist, two different clinicians should be assigned to the lower and upper grades; when resources do not support two clinicians, school districts need to rethink allocations to make this feasible.

Why are school-based clinicians an essential resource for early-grade children? How can we use school-based clinicians in a way that is optimal to promoting the emotional well-being of all young children in school settings? How can school-based clinicians help to bridge the great divide that exists between themselves and the educators who work alongside them? Every school district must search for answers to these questions if young children are to benefit from a valuable school-based resource. School districts must find answers to these questions if they intend to respond to the mandate for preventive mental-health practice in the early grades.

What We Say Versus What We Do

Most districts commit themselves to enhancing the emotional well-being of their students in their standards and policy manuals. Most schools refer to teaching the whole child and to addressing social and emotional development as an essential learning avenue. But most public schools do not actively address these goals or enforce standards regarding these goals in the way that they address literacy goals and goals for test-taking behavior. When interventions designed to promote academic performance are counterindicated for the social and emotional health of children, the devotion to emotional well-being may continue only in name. Often, the school-based clinicians are the only people in the building who have studied the connections between emotional well-being and learning and who actively embrace the mandate to address emotional well-being to improve learning outcomes. If they voice this knowledge passionately, they are perceived as being self-serving, and are generally ignored by building administrators and district personnel. School-based clinicians often work in a system that claims to value their services but acts to devalue their work, disempowering them and creating a work climate that encourages them to huddle together to find strength and solace and the resolve to keep going. The need to huddle for safety may contribute to the strengthening of walls between educationally and psychologically oriented professionals in public-school settings, as educators may perceive the huddling not as a survival need but as a "holier-than-thou" attitude.

Professional development is a major need and a major problem for the majority of school-based clinicians. More resources and more understanding of the need to offer professional development are available to educators than to clinicians. Yet systems that hire school-based clinicians often ignore the individual's background and area of expertise when placing a clinician in a job. Take, for example, the social worker who has had eight years of experience working in an in-patient unit for adolescents who is placed as a pre-kindergarten social worker but given no initial orientation or specialized training or supervision concerning the developmental issues of 4-year-olds. She must either learn from experience or rely on more senior coworkers to enhance her professional development. Or the school psychologist who has worked for the board of education for years doing only psychological testing and is suddenly reassigned to work in a struggling district with a project designed to address the needs of high-risk toddlers who eventually will be entering the school system. Although a completely different set of skills is necessary for this job, no training or supervision is built into the assignment.

To continue these examples, an experienced, knowledgeable teacher observes the first social worker working with her pre-kindergarten children. She correctly identifies the social worker's lack of skill and concludes from it that school-based clinicians have nothing to offer her. A parent in the program for high-risk toddlers complains about the psychologist to the building principal, who then feels that clinical projects are useless and deserve less support. Instead of increasing support to clinicians to offer them the supervision and professional development that they need to do their jobs well, or placing them carefully so that their job demands are in concert with their skills, clinicians are marginalized within the system that neglects them. If school-based clinicians are to become major players in primary prevention in the school setting, their position in the school community will have to change, and there will need to be sufficient resources for their supervisory needs and professional development needs to be met.

The Great Divide

When conversing with a group of teachers about school-based clinicians, it is easy to observe a great distance between the way that teachers see themselves and the ways that they see clinicians. When conversing with clinicians about teachers, it is just as easy to observe a great divide between the ways that clinicians see their own performance and the performance of teachers. A process of mutual judging and devaluing goes on between teachers and clinicians and between clinicians and teachers.

Typically, teachers feel that clinicians do not understand the demands of taking care of large groups of children and the impossibility of attending fully to individual needs. Clinicians may fail to appreciate the pressure that teachers face from administrators to focus solely on academic gains. Teachers tend to perceive clinicians as idle or as having a relatively luxurious position that gives them freedom to work outside the classroom and one-on-one with the children. Many teachers feel that if they had those privileges, they, too, would have the energy to meet the children's emotional needs.

Clinicians, for their part, often feel that teachers are too harsh, are not sufficiently attuned to individual needs, and are not careful enough about the messages that they give to children. Teachers who are overly harsh and not receptive to children's needs also tend to be the least likely to collaborate with school social workers. Clinicians often feel unwelcome when they enter these teachers' classrooms, as if they are intruders or sent to judge the teacher's performance. Clinicians often feel that teachers blame them for children's difficult behavior and wonder whether teachers attribute a kind of magical power to clinical intervention, because at times the teachers seem to expect any clinical involvement to result in an immediate improvement in children's conduct.

It is easy to see the individual factors that have opened the great divide between teachers and school-based clinicians over the years. In many school settings, administrators have made early-grade teachers feel that their sole responsibility is to insure that young children are able to behave and attend. Teachers have been discouraged from seeking clinical consultations about young children's needs and have often internalized their inability to meet all of the emotional needs of their students as somehow indicative of personal failure. It is difficult but essential to close the great divide so that true collaboration between educators and mental-health professionals can become a reality in school settings. To diminish the power of the divide, teachers have to become more knowledgeable about clinical intervention and clinical processes and about the conditions under which school-based clinicians work, and social workers need to become more knowledgeable about the demands of group care and about the pressures under which teachers work. Teachers and school-based clinicians need joint staff development in order to demystify their professions to each other and to create an experiential opportunity to walk in the other's shoes. Both groups need to become more knowledgeable about the developmental needs of the age groups that they serve and about the ways in which difficult experiences affect developmental processes and learning. Teachers and social workers in collaboration need to become a collective voice of support for promoting the emotional well-being of schoolchildren—a voice that administrators and policy makers can hear loudly and clearly. If teachers and school-based clinicians had a collective voice, it would demand school policies that humanize school routines and give early-grade children opportunities to become effective learners within an emotionally safe environment.

Being a Partner

School-based clinician who are effective in their practice enter into many partnerships. They become partners in development to children who are struggling because they have been unable to resolve early developmental issues and are therefore at a loss to meet age-appropriate demands. Effective school-based clinicians enter into partnerships with parents who need help to access services or to understand their children's difficulties, and they enter into partnerships with teachers who want to support children's emotional well-being and benefit from clinical input. These partnerships give school-based clinicians a unique perspective, because if the clinician is truly engaged in a productive process, she will hear from all of the important people in a child's circle. What she hears is privileged information, and the privilege goes beyond the confidential nature of the material: It is the school-based clinician's privilege to gain access to the various contributing factors in a child's world and her responsibility to use privileged information to support the partnerships that are crucial to the child's emotional well-being.

School-based clinicians often struggle with issues of confidentiality when treating children in a school setting. Traditional definitions of confidence forbid the clinician from sharing the content of a child's or parent's session with the teacher; it therefore becomes difficult to know how to include the teacher in a way that will allow her to benefit from the information that the clinician has. Some school programs have addressed this by redefining confidentiality as information that may be shared only among the team of professionals that is helping the child and including the teacher in this team. Programs that regard confidentiality this way explain it to parents from the beginning by saying something such as, "In our program teachers and social workers communicate when we're working together on behalf of a child or family. What you tell me cannot be shared outside of that partnership."

Parents may indicate that certain sensitive information is for the ears of the school-based clinician only. The clinician must then use his or her judgment about whether simply to respect the request or to work with the parent about letting the teacher in on it if it seems crucial to the teacher's ability to be effective.

For instance, a first-grader named Joey was acting out frequently and angering other children by boasting about his prowess and the prowess of his father. He teased other children in the class whose fathers were not around. The clinician met with the boy's mother and learned that Joey's father was actually in jail, but his mother did not want other children in the neighborhood to know, so she had made up stories about his being away in the army. The mother told the story to her son, yet she knew that Joey's paternal grandmother spoke openly about visiting her son in jail. The school social worker suggested that the boy and his mother have some sessions together so they could explore what Joey actually knew about his father and clarify the situation for him. Simultaneously, she asked for permission to share the information with the child's teacher, with the understanding that she would not refer to the situation in front of other children but would use the knowledge to inform her practice when she had to respond to his teasing behavior. The social worker suggested that knowing the story might make the teacher more empathic when dealing with Joey's constant teasing. The mother was able to agree, and the social worker and the teacher worked together to change the dynamic in the classroom. The teacher was then able to use the information to inform her curriculum, using "power and powerlessness" as a theme for the children to explore, which invited Joey to express the emotions evoked by his confusion about his father's incarceration. The teasing behavior became less prevalent, and the teacher was able to enjoy Joey more, as were his peers.

True educational–clinical partnerships on behalf of early-grade children are rare but can be an extremely effective form of prevention. Without the intervention of his teacher–social worker team, Joey's constant teasing of other children might have resulted in the peer group's ostracizing him. That undoubtedly would have exacerbated his feelings of abandonment and worthlessness and increased his feelings of alienation and subsequent depression, leaving Joey at high risk for developing violent behavior as an upper-grade student (Hazler, 1994).

The Weight of Stories

School social workers have the privilege of hearing children's personal stories. Almost all school systems will ask that a psychosocial history be taken as part of a formal evaluation process, and less formal parent meetings will include a request for psychosocial information, as well. In some instances, psychosocial information may be available to the school social worker from the beginning of a child's school career, particularly if the child is in foster care or is receiving some kind of preventive or psychiatric services outside the school. The school social worker feels the weight of those crucial stories. Sometimes she alone knows the terrible realities that a child has faced before attending public school. She hears about the little girl in kindergarten who lives with her aunt because she was sexually abused repeatedly by her mother's live-in boyfriend. She hears about the first-grade boy who has been moved back and forth among relatives who are overwhelmed by his needs because his father is in prison for killing his mother and he observed the tragedy. She is told tearfully about the financial stresses that a single mother faces, forcing her to work many hours and leave her 7-year-old daughter in the care of a neighbor whose 17-year-old son taunts and demeans her child. She hears the chilling denial of a mother who works in the television industry and travels four days a week, leaving her children with a nanny who seems oblivious to their needs. She watches an 8-year-old boy come to school with his custodial grandmother because his parents have died of AIDS. The grandmother herself looks weaker each day, and the social worker wonders how much longer the arrangement will last.

These stories can be enabling or debilitating for the school-based clinician who is hearing them, and they can be extremely helpful or detrimental to the children themselves. The clinician who hears the stories, then puts their recorded version in the file drawer, without ongoing individual contact with the students, has no outlet for using the stories that she has heard. If a story is intense, compelling, and upsetting, it is likely to haunt the clinician who carries it. It is unlikely to be helpful to the student in question, because its value is sealed in the record. No professional can use this story to inform their practice with the child. The school-based clinician who hears many such stories and is unable to interact with any of them in a meaningful way may become overwhelmed and despondent under their weight. The occupational hazard of burnout may even be higher for clinicians who constantly hear about tragedies that children live with but are not allowed to be active to help the children heal.

However, if the story is held in confidence within the team of professionals helping the child, its value is enhanced considerably. The development of 7-year-old Darrell, for example, was delayed in several areas. His language was unclear and not specific for a child his age; his activity level was high, and his attention span was short; and he was not yet reading. All of Darrell's areas of functioning were evaluated, including his psychosocial history, which revealed that Darrell had been in the custody of a maternal aunt since age 2, when his mother was shot in a drive-by shooting at which he was present. While Darrell's functional level indicated a need for language therapy and individual help with reading, his psychosocial story indicated a need for counseling with the school social worker. Because Darrell's school had made a serious commitment to the emotional well-being of children, it did not consider his story to be incidental but assumed that life experience had interfered with Darrell's developmental process and therefore required the same level of professional attention that other areas of need required.

Darrell's social worker worked in partnership with Darrell's teacher to help her understand the ways that life experience might be affecting the boy's classroom functioning. Together they realized that part of Darrell's difficulties came from his hypervigilance to sounds outside of the classroom—loud trucks, banging from old pipes in the hallway, and shouting from the street were troublesome for Darrell. The social worker pointed out that unspecified loud sounds might cause Darrell anxiety, and perhaps terror, because he might associate them with the gunshot that had killed his mother. The teacher integrated that information into her curriculum, having her whole class take a walk through the building and around the neighborhood looking for the source of the sounds that they hear during the day. They took photographs of the things they discovered and made a classroom book about the sounds and their sources. The teacher gave Darrell the book when he began to be distracted during the day, and it was helpful for him. His ability to stay focused improved.

Without the clinical–educational partnership attending to his story, Darrell might continue to suffer in several ways. First, his functioning would be less likely to improve significantly, even with the addition of other services, because a core problem still would have been neglected. Darrell would probably stay isolated with his painful history because he would have no invitation to share his experience of it. Indeed, members of Darrell's family who were also affected by this traumatic loss were trying to "forget" about what had happened. At the same time, many people who live in the school community were around when Darrell's mother was killed; thus, the likelihood existed that neighborhood children would refer to bits of his story in unkind or hurtful ways, especially while on the playground, in the cafeteria, or during another part of the public-school day when there was no teacher supervision. This would subject Darrell to being assaulted with his story and made to feel somehow responsible for it. That is, all the wrong people would have access to Darrell's history, while all of the people who might helpful would be protected from it.

The Right Place, the Right Time

School-based clinicians are at the right place at the right time if they are in the position to attend to the mental-health needs of early-grade children. Almost all children of school age attend school. Therefore, if we as a society are committed to preventive mental health, our greatest access to young children comes through their school communities. A number of intervention techniques are available to school-based clinicians beyond the usual "school-based counseling" model. Often, school-based counseling consists of a clinicians' checking in on a student in a regular way and organizing around behavior management of the student during periods of the day that the student finds difficult. This kind of counseling can be helpful for various reasons. The most powerful feature of this kind of school-based counseling is the potential connection that can develop between the clinician and the child if there is regular contact. Many troubled children are helped by the opportunity to attach to an adult and organize themselves around the attachment relationship itself. The secondary feature of the focus on the student's behavior may be helpful because it may help the student feel contained, and if he is able to improve, he may take pride in his own progress. He will then be more likely to get positive feedback from teachers and perhaps feel more valued in the group. The increased acceptance may prevent him from becoming marginalized as he moves toward adolescents.

Another prevalent model for school-based practice might be described as the "identify and refer" model, in which school-based clinicians are called on to observe, evaluate, and investigate situations with children about whom teachers are worried. Often, after meeting with a child's parent, the school-based clinician will refer the family for therapy or will research resources in the community that might be helpful for the family.

As useful as these typical models may be for certain early-grade children, they are not the only models of practice, or even the preferred models for all early-grade-school populations. This model of school-based counseling tends to neglect the student's psychosocial story, which may have too powerful a hold on the student to resolve without attention. Often, children in need of school-based counseling are more enabled when the attachment that unfolds from ongoing contact with the clinician is used to hold their psychosocial story. In play-therapy sessions, children may want to play or draw as a way to integrate their difficult experiences, and the school-based clinician is then freed from depending solely on the children's language output as a source of information about their mental status. When school-based clinicians use play and drawing with early-grade children as therapeutic technique, they are actively allowing children to symbolize their stories and integrate the difficult pieces.

Limitations of clinical time may motivate clinicians to make referrals instead of offering on-site treatment. Yet clinicians are painfully aware that the families in the most need of therapeutic services are often the least able to gain access to and attend these services. Frequently, family members are unavailable to transport children to therapy after school or they lack health insurance that covers outpatient mental-health care. Clinicians need to be a voice of reality within the system, as administrators and policymakers assume that the clinician's referral function is effective and thus meeting the needs of many more children than can be treated by a single school-based clinician. School-based clinicians should try to keep track of the outcomes of their referral work and record resulting statistics. The recorded results may help to make a case for staffing elementary schools with sufficient mental-health resources.

Experienced clinicians know that, when referrals are indicated, simply meeting a child's parent and giving him or her the information is unlikely to result in follow-through. Parents rarely take a referral from someone with whom they have no connection unless they made the initial request for the referral. The need for referral requires the school-based clinician to make a connection with the family of concern. Usually, this means that the clinician must have some relationship with the child or observe the child enough to understand him or her in a deep way. In addition, parents may have to make several visits to the school, spend time in or observing the classroom, and participate in school celebrations or traditions before they feel comfortable enough to share issues and be receptive to school personnel. The parent and clinician or parent and teacher have to have some relationship before the parent will be able to listen to concerns. The parents will have to feel that what is being proposed has value because the the teacher or clinician "really knows my child and knows my family."

Because most schools are diverse in their population of children, many clinicians know that, when dealing with fragile families or families who lack resources, the most successful referrals are those that have the school-based clinician in attendance for the initial contact. Again, these field trips consume an enormous amount of clinical time, and clinicians tend to feel pressured to account for time spent in this way. Administrators may not understand why the presence of the clinician is required unless school-based clinicians record the results of referrals made with and without their presence and make administrators aware of the needs of multi-issue families. If school-based clinicians are treating a certain number of children on-site at school and are using time to visit early-grade classrooms in an ongoing way to do preventive practice, the need to leave the building frequently to accompany parents to service providers is disruptive and difficult. Clinicians who are assigned to one school only and who can organize their own time may find it helpful to keep two half-days free of ongoing appointments in order to devote time to referrals and the need for phoning or off-site follow-through.

Preventive Practice in Early Elementary School

Clinical practice that meets the needs of schoolchildren cannot be limited to the availability of a single clinician to do individual sessions with children in an entire school building. Neither can effective practice be limited to the making of referrals. Rather, clinical time in early-grade schools needs to be devoted to preventive practice with children in classroom groups or smaller groups and to facilitating preventive practice by teachers throughout the day.

What does preventive practice mean to the school-based clinician? How can an emphasis on prevention translate into addressing issues with children from pre-kindergarten through third (or fifth) grade? Certainly, preventive practice implies ongoing interaction with teachers and children in classrooms. In many settings, school social workers, guidance counselors, or psychologists go to the classroom to talk with children after a crisis, such as a death in the school community. The clinician may ask the children what they knows about what has happened, how they are feeling, and so on. She might read a book about a similar situation and allow the children to respond to the content. She may organize a project following their reading and discussion that invites further expression on the topic. These are the very methods that school-based clinicians can employ when doing preventive practice, using them to address developmental issues and everyday difficulties that may not be considered crisis, as well crisis when it occurs. For example, a clinician practicing prevention may address separation, peer dynamics, difficulty with classroom routines (such as rest time for pre-kindergarten and kindergarten), issues of safety and danger, fears, reality testing, and so on.

Frequency of contact for preventive practice will certainly vary depending on how the number of classrooms and clinicians in the building. Because mental-health resources are usually scarce, clinicians will do well to identify teacher–partners who can and will take on the use of techniques that help children express themselves and help the classroom contain their expressions comfortably. Clinicians will probably find themselves identifying classrooms in which they can collaborate with the teacher; those in which they can rely on teachers to implement preventive practices in consultation; and those in which the teacher is not welcoming and makes it impossible to intervene. In such classrooms, techniques addressing the teacher's issues may be the precursor to other forms of child-centered preventive practice. The school-based clinician engaged in preventive practice will rotate through designated classrooms at scheduled intervals so that the practice is woven into the school week or month and children and teachers can depend on her presence.

School-based clinicians should be familiar with Selma Fraiberg's work and her use of the terms "inviting" and "containing" (Fraiberg, 1980). Although these concepts were not initially applied to school settings, they are extremely relevant and useful for school-based practice. In essence, the clinician engaged in preventive mental-health practice in the early years is finding ways to invite expression in children that is compatible with sound early-childhood educational practices; she is also engaged in developing strategies that help children feel safe and contained in the school environment. The clinician must be deeply involved with both processes, because if her invitations for emotional expression are not held by containing strategies, children and teachers will feel overwhelmed, and the atmosphere will be chaotic. If the clinician devotes energy only to managing the children's behavior, the children will be likely to lack avenues to express their core issues.

Although behavior may be less problematic in situations of high-level structure, trouble will re-emerge when high-level structures are not present because core issues will not have been addressed.

For example, a second-grade teacher expresses frustration with her group because the children constantly tease one another, leaving at least one child in tears. Sometimes the teasing escalates into physical violence on the playground and in the lunchroom. The social worker and the teacher collaborate to engage the children in a group discussion about teasing. All the children dutifully repeat their teacher's prohibition and voice the value of mutual caring and concern. Yet during the session, while sitting on the rug, children frequently confront one another about being bumped or intruded on and insult one another when defending their territory. The social worker points out to the children that they are saying one thing but doing another. Why is this? The children seemed bewildered; a few of them voice theories about it. The social worker the children how many of them have older brothers and sisters, and how many have older brothers and sisters who tease them. More than half of the children raise their hands. They all have stories about being teased at home, which they tell eagerly and in detail. The conversation fills the time that the teacher and social worker have allowed. The social worker asks the children to follow up their discussion by writing a story about being teased and how teasing feels. "We really have to understand teasing if we're going to help you make your classroom a safer place without people saying mean things to one another," she says. "Write a story about being teased at home or somewhere outside school, and when I come back next week we'll all talk about it."

The teacher and social worker recognize that peer teasing can be destructive for all children, and particularly for fragile children. By talking about it out of the moment, they can capture the children's attention and enable them to think about their behavior and the teasing dynamic without feeling threatened. By inviting them to write, the social worker asks for expression within a containing form—the written word—to be read by her and the group during their next interaction. She conveys her belief that the relationship will be strong enough to hold the material that surfaces.

At the next meeting, the written stories are shared, and the children easily empathize with their peers who have been victims of taunting by older siblings. The clinician then distributes teddy bears to the children and announces that the bears will be living with them in the class-room for the rest of the school year. The group will be in charge of making the classroom environment welcoming and supportive for the bears so they will feel safe and happy in their new home. The children have many ideas about how to do this. The clinician reminds them that they also had many ideas about the value of not teasing one another but had not been able to stop. "The bears will help us stop," one boy says, "because they need us. We have to take good care of them." The teacher agrees but adds that she has tried her best to take good care of the children when they are with her, but they also needed to take good care of one another.

As the year goes on, the teacher and social worker use the bears to address peer issues when they arise, but the teacher reports that the teasing has become less prevalent, and acts of kindness more common, in her group.

Beginning with Teachers

No school-based clinician can be effective without teacher sanction. Because classroom teachers are likely to have strong relationships with the children in their classes, these relationships—whether positive or negative—will affect the clinician's ability to do her work. When teacher–clinician alliances are strong, the clinicians know they will have access to the children; will be able to interact with them as is clinically indicated; and will have a partner in the classroom who may be able to support a child's therapeutic process.

Situations in which teachers are not receptive to a partnership with the clinician in the school setting tend to be extremely frustrating to the clinician, who may feel that the teacher is not allowing her to do her job. Indeed, if an elementary school is responding to the mandate for preventive mental health in the early grades but many early-grade teachers do not embrace this value, the school's efforts will not succeed. Administrators must take responsibility for enforcing the mandate and provide ongoing development to help staff understand the connections between emotional well-being and learning, but they should not overlook the potential of school-based clinicians to affect classroom practice. Clinicians do not have the authority to enforce the mandate, and they will not succeed if they put energy into trying to persuade teachers to practice differently. However, if school-based clinicians regard unreceptive teachers as one portion of their clientele, they can "start where the client is" and start the slow process of connecting with the teachers to give them the kind of attuned attention that they want the teachers to be able to give to their students. The clinical task is often to begin where the teacher is. If clinicians embrace this as part of their jobs, they may feel less frustrated and more empowered, because they will certainly be using their clinical skills. Although beginning with the teacher may initially translate into checking in with her whenever possible, eating lunch together, offering to listen to her frustration with the children or with her position, the clinical focus on teachers' well-being may later translate into organized programs to support teachers' mental health. With administrative support, clinicians may be able to offer groups for teachers who feel overwhelmed by the dual demands of needy children and pressuring school districts. Or they may be able to give workshops for teachers that focus on stress. Or they may decide to make office hours available for teachers who feel as though they are in crisis. The practice of teacher-focused mental health is an innovative and exciting way to work toward creating healing early-grade environments in public schools. Because teachers provide hours of care each day, as well as the foundations for children's symbolic development and complex learning, attending to teachers' well-being is a sound investment. School-based clinicians who develop the art of school-based practice should regard the avenue of teacher-focused mental health as an important part of their preventive mental-health repertoire.

PART III

Possibilities for Emotionally Responsive Practice

COUNTLESS OPPORTUNITIES *exist for professionals who are com-mitted to supporting children's emotional well-being to integrate emo-tionally responsive practice into the school day. Part III offers models for making emotionally responsive practice a schoolwide priority and to help staff members imagine themselves as engaged in roles that initially may feel unfamiliar.*

All schools have staff development for their employees. Most schools include a training session on social and emotional issues as part of their focus. Part III points out that, as helpful as single-session training can be, it is unlikely to foster deep changes in professional practice. Instead, training in emotionally responsive practice must be ongoing, continue over a long period of time, and address issues on several levels simultaneously.

Possibilities for emotionally responsive practice include models and techniques that focus on the child and the family and techniques that focus on the teacher. This part of the book is designed to help readers envision how they might implement the techniques of emotion-ally responsive practice in their own settings and within their existing structures and resource parameters.

CHAPTER 7

A Staff-Development Approach to Responsive Practice

MANY SCHOOL DISTRICTS wisely include staff-development days in their calendars—that is, three to ten days in the year that are devoted to keeping staff current on effective techniques for early-childhood practice. Children do not attend school on staff-development days so that staff can concentrate on their own learning and are not distracted by simultaneously meeting the needs of children. Emotionally responsive practice can be taught within a staff-development model as long as the sessions are multiple and occur over time. Once a school or district has decided to devote staff-development time to emotionally responsive practice, however, confusion often exists about how to design an effective curriculum. The staff-development curriculum that follows can be used as a model for schools seeking guidance in this area. Suggestions for implementation follow the outline.

The Ten-Session Model for Emotionally Responsive Practice

All are half-day sessions.

Session 1

Topic: Understanding Development, Understanding Experience

Part 1

The facilitator uses an overhead projector to focus the presentation on early developmental processes and precursors for social and emotional health (see Table 4.1). Each participant should also have a handout of this chart. The presenter points out that each milestone on the chart is in essence a partner activity, meaning that each requires a relationship between a child and an adult to be accomplished.

After offering vivid descriptions of each milestone, the presenter should revisit the column that describes how life experiences can affect developmental processes. For example, a well-attached child uses attachment as a cornerstone of development. The attachment relationship becomes an organizer of other experiences. If a child is removed from his or her biological parents and put in three different foster homes in the first year of life, how would he or she be able to achieve attachment and the partner-dependent milestones that follow? There should be a special focus on the achievement of object permanence, its uses as a developmental springboard, and the ways in which establishing object permanence depends on experience.

For example, a well-supported baby plays games by dropping toys and having adults retrieve them to help support the concept of object permanence. Once object permanence is in place, this baby is likely to start pointing at and labeling objects. A baby who is not in a supportive environment may drop coveted objects that no one retrieves. His experiences negates the concept that things last even when out of sensory contact. What is likely to happen with this child's concept of object permanence? The presenter would do well to use chapter 1, "The Development of Personhood," to inform the presentation during part 1 of session 1. The first part should be approximately an hour and a half long.

Break (15 minutes)

Part 2

The presenter should pose two questions to participants, verbally and in large, poster-type writing: How do children's unresolved developmental issues express themselves in pre-kindergarten, kindergarten, and first-, second-, and third-grade classrooms? What are the implications for our practice in the early grades of public school? Participants should be free to offer as many relevant comments and suggestions as they want, and these should be recorded by a facilitator or scribe. The facilitator should then pose one last question: What do the participants see as barriers to emotionally responsive practice? The responses to this question also should be recorded. The facilitator and program administrators should then articulate the school's (or district's) commitment to emotionally responsive practice and announce the intention to devote the staff-development sessions to the process of achieving emotionally responsive practice so that the participants' concerns can be addressed and they can feel empowered to create responsive and effective classroom environments. The session should conclude with questions and comments. Part 2 of session 1 should be an hour and 15 minutes long.

Session 2

Topic: Inviting and Containing in the Classroom

Part 1

The facilitator introduces the concepts of "inviting" and "containing," crediting their initial use to Selma Fraiberg (Fraiberg, 1980) and using handouts and overhead transparencies (see Handout 1) to develop the meaning of the terms for classroom teachers. The facilitator should describe classrooms in which there is too much inviting but no containing, which results in chaos; she should then describe classrooms in which all of the teacher's energy goes into containing, which creates environments that may be orderly but that are also rigid and lacking in built-in avenues of expression for children to resolve issues. Children who have been constricted in the classroom are likely to behave in explosive ways in the lunchroom or play yard. A classroom environment that balances inviting and containing is ideal for emotional well-being. In such an environment, children are invited to express their feelings and voice their experience in ways that are commensurate with sound early-childhood practice. The routines, structures, and relationships in the classroom are strong enough to contain the material that is expressed.

The participants should then be asked to explore their understanding of the concepts of inviting and containing by completing the group exercise "Inviting or Containing: Which Is Which?" (Handout 2). The participants are divided into small groups to chart the interventions, routines, and learning opportunities that they use in their classrooms as "inviting," "containing," or both. After the activity, a spokesperson from each group shares the information with the whole group, elaborating when an item qualifies as both inviting and containing.

Break (15 minutes)

Part 2

The facilitator introduces a menu of inviting and containing techniques sorted into categories that include techniques for teacher–child interaction; techniques for designing classroom environments and routines; and techniques for curriculum development (see Handout 3). These categories will serve as focal points for the next three staff-development sessions. Teachers should be given enough time and space to develop each of these categories of intervention fully so they will become truly useful in the classroom. For the remainder of part 2, small groups are designated providers of either anecdotes or interventions, and each group is paired with a group with the opposite designation. The anecdote groups collect and record stories from their practice in which a child or group of children's emotional needs were difficult to meet. The intervention groups listen and consider the menu of inviting and containing interventions. They then offer a scenario based on the anecdote group's input, altering the story to include a selected intervention. The anecdote groups are asked to comment on whether they view this technique as useful or not useful in such a circumstance. If they do not see the technique as useful, they should be asked whether another technique could be substituted. The large group can then be reconvened, and each group should be asked to share one of its anecdotes and elaborate on one of its inviting and containing responses.

Session 3

Topic: The Meaning of Routines and Environmental Design

Part 1

A list of common classroom routines should be available on overhead or large white board. Participants should have their developmental milestone handout (see Table 4.1) available for reference. The facilitator's presentation should focus on the fact that routines are not an incidental part of a child's school experience. Young children count on routines for a sense of stability. Routines by definition are containing for children; the job for school professionals is to create routines that are inviting as well as containing; that are developmentally appropriate; and that acknowledge the meaning that routines have for the age groups we serve. If we understand the meaning of routine and the messages communicated by classroom design, we have a powerful avenue for enhancing the emotional well-being of children.

Participants should be asked to focus on the routines listed on the overhead and instructed to consider routines involving food, toileting, resting, arrival, and dismissal. In small groups, each person is asked to describe her classroom's or school's routines in these areas. A recorder should write the descriptions down on one side of a piece of large paper that has been divided down the center. Participants are then asked to consider the routines on the overhead in light of both the developmental milestones on their chart and handouts on inviting and containing. They should be asked to consider several questions, such as:

1. How can adjustments be made in existing routines that invite children to experience the routine in a meaningful way? For example, how can goodbye time be handled to acknowledge the separation experience and provide reassurance about reuniting the following day?
2. How can routines be made more intimate and thus heighten the meaning as well as the feeling of being held for participating children? For example, if kindergartners must eat in a school cafeteria with children from other grades, how can that routine be handled to ameliorate the inappropriate features of large-group meals for 5-year-olds?
3. How can staffing patterns enhance important routines in the early grades? For example, if the teacher must attend meetings during rest time, leaving rest time to be supervised by a floating staff member who does not have a solid relationship with the children, what is likely to occur? If the cafeteria has only aides managing large groups of children, what is likely to be the experience of eating there for early-grade children?

Play with the reorganization of staffing patterns or primary-teacher interventions that enhance routines but that teachers can live with without being deprived of essential down time. Record the ideas on the other side of the easel paper.

Break (15 minutes)

Part 2

The reporters present their adjustments to the large group, with comments by the facilitator about the meaning of the particular routine under discussion and from other teachers about the proposed modifications. The facilitator should also help the teachers consider proposed routines in terms of inviting and containing features.

Each participant should then be given a large diagram of a classroom, with essential furnishings such as a coat-hook area, chalkboard, and shelves drawn in. Each participant will be asked to draw in the other features of the classroom environment that can serve important functions in how they invite children to explore what is important for well-being at that age level and how they contain children's expressions and potentially difficult behavior. Teachers should be given as as much time as they need to work on this. Then the small groups will reconvene to discuss the features that the teachers have included and the role that these features play in the classroom. Recorders should note each item and function on a large sheet of paper, and when they are finished, each group's classroom drawing should be mounted on the wall, with the function descriptions alongside them. The participants are then invited to move around the room and view the work of their peers.

Session 4

*Topic: Story-Gathering Technique as a
Precursor to Responsive Curriculum*

Part 1

The facilitator introduces the topic of psychosocial histories. For years, teachers were discouraged from learning about their students' life experiences, even when the children's histories played a significant part in their development and receptivity to learning. Teachers were kept in the dark for fear that the information would be prejudicial. Emotionally responsive practice depends in part on teachers' having access to information that is important in the lives of their students so the classroom agenda can incorporate this information in positive ways. For example, if several children in a class have medical issues that have resulted in trips to the hospital, the group may be interested in a study of the emergency room. Children in this group are likely to have unresolved body-integrity issues and might benefit from a curriculum that invites them to explore these issues further. If the teacher has no access to this important information, she can do nothing to address the likely outcomes in the classroom. If a child is preoccupied because her building had a fire over the summer in which her family lost everything, including their home, the teacher who knows the information can be empathic, invite expression related to the child's experience, provide curriculum that may be interesting to her and to several other children in the room, and increase her attention and participation in class. If the teacher is kept in the dark, she may conclude that the child has an attentional disorder or does not understand the material being presented.

During part 1, the participants are invited to read the handout titled, "Why Gather Stories?" (Handout 4) and to make comments or ask questions about its content. Each participant is then asked to focus on "Story-Gathering Day" (Handout 5). The handout is a form of teacher story-gathering used in early-grade programs that are committed to enhancing emotional well-being.

For story-gathering days to be successful, administrators must support the process by arranging for classroom coverage while the teacher speaks to each parent in her class for 30 minutes. The teacher will not talk about how the child functions in the classroom; instead, she will explain that she did not know the child before he or she came into the classroom and that she wants to ensure that each child is known and that each child's stories and experiences are valued. The teacher has a form with questions on it to ask parents and with space to record the stories so that she does not confuse one child's story with another's. Parents are invited to respond but can, of course, choose not to address a questions that are uncomfortable.

The facilitator should invite discussion of the questions, the parent interview process, and the issues of confidentiality that story gathering raises. Handout 6, a statement of confidentiality to be signed by participating teachers, should be included in the story-gathering packet. The statement should be read aloud in part 1 of session 4 and the definition of confidentiality discussed. Each school that participates in the story-gathering process must come to a common understanding about defining confidentiality in its setting. For example, some schools will tell parents that everything they say will be held in confidence unless there is a threat to the child's well-being. Others will say that the teacher, the school social worker, and the school nurse function as a team, and that no information will be shared outside this unit.

The school administrator or administrators need to be attend session 4 so that an administrative voice is present when definitions of confidentiality are created.

Break (15 minutes)

Part 2

The facilitator talks about the skills necessary to conduct time-limited interviews. She can use the resource *Microcounseling* (Ivey, 1974) to introduce such skills to teachers as attentive listening, use of open-ended and closed questions, reflective techniques, and refraining from providing solutions. Participants can be given handouts with this information (with the required author's permission), or the microcounseling techniques can be outlined in an overhead.

The teachers should then be paired up, with one teacher acting the role of parent and the other acting as interviewer. The interviewing will also record the responses on the form. When they are finished, they will switch roles. The group should then reconvene, and the partners should be asked to share their experiences as interviewers and interviewees. How did they feel about asking, and how did they feel about being asked, the questions? Did they find getting elaborate responses difficult? Was it difficult to get people to move to the next question? Did the interviewees feel that certain questions invaded their privacy? Did it feel reassuring to know that the teacher was interested in certain information, and if so, which information? How do people envision parental responses? How do teachers think this kind of interview will affect the teacher–parent relationship?

The principal is instructed to bring in his or her school's plan for story-gathering days when the group meets the following month. The teachers are instructed to read the curriculum section of *Unsmiling faces* (Koplow, 1996) and chapters 9 and 10 of this book before the next meeting.

Session 5

Topic: Emotionally Responsive Curriculum

Part 1

The facilitator shows overheads of the developmental chart, inviting and containing workshops, and the groups' work on creating emotionally responsive routines and classroom environments. She also has copies of the handout "Why Gather Stories." Teachers who have done story gathering since the last session are invited to share their experiences with the larger group. If none have done so, the participants are asked to have their filled-out story-gathering forms from previous session handy.

The facilitator then introduces the concept of emotionally responsive curriculum (ERC), a curriculum designed by teachers to reflect the agendas of the children in her classroom. ERC allows children to study or explore topics that are compelling to them because of their developmental significance or experiential relevance. To include ERC in their repertoire of preventive mental-health techniques, teachers must both understand the developmental issues that affect their children and know as much as they can about the children's life experiences. If the teachers have done story gathering, they can use the common ground in the children's psychosocial histories to inform their curriculum. For example, pre-kindergarten and kindergarten teachers know that friendships are of paramount concern to children in these age groups. Peer dynamics demand a lot of teacher attention and intervention throughout the year. A curriculum that addresses the complexities of friendship is guaranteed to compel the interest of classrooms of 4- and 5-year-olds. If a child in a kindergarten classroom becomes seriously ill during the year and dies, the kindergarten children in his or her school will be profoundly affected. Their understanding of friendship, object constancy, and body integrity will be shaken, and they will benefit from a curriculum about those issues and that addresses their experience of loss.

When the facilitator finishes her introduction, many teachers are likely to have questions. Most will ask the same question: "How can we do this and do all of the other things that the district expects from us?" The answer is twofold. On the one hand, many of the skills developed in ERC are the same skills that the districts are promoting, but they are emerging from different topics. For instance, a group of children who hear a book about loss and then write their own stories about their experiences of loss are still listening, writing, and reading. On the other hand, it is impossible to have multiple priorities when the priorities contradict one another. Teachers will need time to create the material necessary for ERC, and it is not reasonable to expect them to use only their own time. Schools and districts that are committed to emotional health and prevention will have to articulate and show their commitment by removing something from the teacher's plate when they add emotionally responsive practice. After the question-and-answer period, the facilitator should ask the teachers to break out into the same groups they formed during the previous session to review their story-gathering forms and list topics that the group has in common that can be elaborated as curriculum. For example, if several children were affected by a scary experience in early childhood, "Scary and Safe" might be an emotionally responsive curriculum to explore. Spokespeople from each group share the lists and submit them in written form to the facilitator.

Break (15 Minutes)

Part 2

After reviewing the lists, the facilitator will assign each group one topic to develop as curriculum at various grade levels—for example, at the kindergarten level for one group, and at the first-grade level for another. The facilitator should have many books on hand that support a curriculum on topics related to the previous week's story-gathering information. She should advise teachers to think of songs, stories, writing activities, art projects, and possibly field trips that would support exploration of their topics. She should advise them to consider the ways in which the curriculum can invite expression and ways in which that expression can be contained in the classroom. She can also distribute sample curricula from *Unsmiling faces* (Koplow, 1996) and from chapters 9 and 10 of this book.

The groups will work together for the remainder of session 5, using a variety of art supplies, books, and classroom materials to support their work. Each group should shares its curriculum with the whole group before dismissal.

Session 6

Topic: Making and Using Emotionally Responsive Books

Part 1

The facilitator brings several children's books that relate to topics elaborated for ERC during session 5. She reads them to the group and invites discussion about how to use the books for curriculum and for discussion.

Issues of group process are discussed. How do participants imagine that the children in their current classrooms would respond to the books that have been read? What would they say? What questions would be asked? In which directions might the conversation go? What happens when children reveal "family business," such as having an incarcerated parent? What happens when children say something that is frightening to other children? What happens when children say something that is frightening to the teacher? What if children ask for more information about a topic of interest or concern? The facilitator records useful responses from experienced teachers and provides guidelines of her own (see Handout 7).

The facilitator then produces several teacher-made books reflecting children's issues. She models several types of books, including those with children's input and illustrations and those made entirely by the teacher. Participants discuss the various uses of this kind of literature. What is its power? How does it differ from existing literature? The facilitator then calls the participants' attention to an overhead projection of Handout 7, which is designed to help the teachers organize the form and content of their own book projects. The participants also focus on guidelines for illustrations in emotionally responsive literature made by teachers.

Break (15 minutes)

Part 2

Participants are given several sheets of 8.5-by-11-inch oak tag, markers and crayons, hole punches, notebook rings, pencils, and pads of paper. They use the remainder of the time to organize, write, and illustrate a story in book form. The story will have to support one of the issues raised during the discussion of ERC. the facilitator acts as a consultant to participants during the book-creating process.

Before session 6 ends, participants should be asked to share their productions and offer comments. They are encouraged to cover their books with clear contact paper or laminate them for use in the classroom and to report back to the group on the book's reception in the classroom, the group process that followed its use, and the experience of using it with the group.

Session 7

Topic: Valuing Stories

Part 1

The facilitator reads from the book *The need for story: Cultural diversity in classroom and community* (Dyson & Genishi, 1994). The participants then talk about the many ways in which healing environments express the value of story in the classroom. The list includes story gathering, reading stories from the existing literature that support young children's agendas, writing stories and making books for children that reflect their emotional and experiential agendas, and allowing children to tell experiential stories to the teacher and to the group if they wish to. It also includes making collective classroom stories, with contributions from everyone concerning a certain topic or experience, and individual books that give children a voice for feeling or experience. Teachers may bring up family history projects for second and third grades, having children interview parents and grandparents, family tree projects, etc. They may bring up the use of tape recorders for inviting personal or collective storytelling. Some teachers may have invited parent to come to school to share stories about their own childhoods, about their children as infants or toddlers, or about their cultural celebrations or rituals. The facilitator asks these questions of the whole group and facilitates the discussion that ensues. What is the value of children knowing the real stories of their own and their family's experiences? What is the value of children being able to articulate their own stories? What is the value of a historical perspective for children? What do stories of actual events in their own history, their family's history, or their community's history offer to 4-year-olds? To 5-year-olds? To 60-year-olds? To 7-year-olds? And to 8-year-olds?

Break (15 minutes)

Part 2

The facilitator invites the participants to consider how their personal stories, their family stories, and their cultural histories affect them as teachers—how they define or affect their teaching styles and otherwise express themselves in the classroom. Teachers are asked to consider this silently for 10 minutes and to take notes on their thoughts. They then break out into small groups. Each teacher is asked to tell one personal, family, or cultural story to the group that has had a meaningful impact on his or her style of teaching. Each group is given a copy of the book *Cherry pies and lullabies* (Reiser, 1998), and one participant is selected to read out loud to the small group. When everyone has heard the story, the facilitator puts a large pot in the middle of each group's circle. A basket is also put under the table. The facilitator explains the next activity this way:

> Think about effective and responsive teaching as a stew of essential, just-right ingredients that blend together to make something that is nurturing and builds strong foundations in children. Think about the ingredients from your own childhood that you want to include and pass along to another generation. Write these down one by one and put them into the stew pot. Also think about the ingredients of your own childhood and experience as a student that were not good for you and that you don't want to hand down to another generation. Write these down one by one and put them in the basket under the table. When you're done, have one person serve portions of the stew to everyone and examine the ingredients in your bowl. Comment. Invite the group to come together as a whole group and talk about the process of considering the past in this way.

Thus, the participants are invited to share the stories that came into their minds during the activity if they want to.

Session 8

Topic: Teacher–Child Interaction: A Complex Constellation

Part 1

The facilitator notes that teacher–child interactions are determined by multiple and complex factors, including aspects of the teacher's own history. How can teachers insure that their interactions with children are facilitative and the way that they want them to be? Can "ingredients" be identified for facilitative teacher–child interactions? A discussion ensues, and the facilitator notes significant contributions. The facilitator then documents and organizes group responses on an overhead transparency entitled "Teacher–Child Interaction." Sub-headings are teacher–child language use, teachers' expressions of affect during interaction, teachers' relationship to and expression of authority, and teachers' actions in response to children's behavior. The participants are asked to comment on each of these interactions in terms of their inviting and containing function and in terms of their potential efficacy. The participants are then asked to respond to the following questions: Would children have a different experience if the teacher following these guidelines for facilitative interactions were genuinely attached to them? How would the experience differ? From the teacher's perspective, does strong attachment to students enable or hinder the teaching process? What are the complexities of strong teacher–child attachments from the teacher's point of view? Participants are asked to discuss these questions in small groups and take notes on the responses on easel-mounted pads. A spokesperson then shares the array of responses with the whole group, and the facilitator notes key points from the collective on her easel.

Break (15 minutes)

Part 2

Each teacher is given book-creating material identical to those given during part 2 of session 6 on making emotionally responsive literature. The teachers' assignment this time is to create a book about their experience in having become attached to a child or a group of children in their classroom. THIS BOOK IS NOT FOR A CHILD AUDIENCE! It is only for the individual author and the teachers participating in the group process. Teachers are encouraged to be as honest as they can be. Teachers who find the assignment difficult can create a book about being attached to a teacher as a child or about wishing that a teacher would notice or respond to them in a special way. Participants who want to read their books to the group are encouraged to do so. Discussion about the collective themes follows the reading of the books.

Session 9

Topic: End-of-the-Year Issues

Part 1

The facilitator asks teachers to hold up a hand if they have noticed regression in their students in late spring. She asks them to hold up a hand if the regression includes deteriorating behavior, a greater number of children crying, and a resurgence of separation anxiety at the end of the day. Many teachers will raise their hands. Questions for discussion can include: Why do children behave this way at the end of the year? What comes up for children at the end of the school year? What comes up for teachers at the end of the school year? Are teachers more anxious, and if so, why? The facilitator notes responses on easel paper or an overhead transparency, and the responses are discussed in the context of the material distributed by the facilitator and by other participants in earlier sessions—for example, teacher–child attachment, separation histories of the children, separation histories of the teacher, end-of-the-year pressure from school district, and so on.

The participants are asked, Which strategies can be implemented that address end-of-the-year issues in the early grades? How can we apply what we have learned so far in this training series to attend to end-of-the-year issues? A list should be made of suggested interventions, such as specific responsive curricula, end-of-the-year books and scrapbooks, and so on. What are the barriers to addressing end-of-the-year issues in public school? What are the last months, weeks, and days of school actually like for children? For teachers? How can these conditions be ameliorated?

Break (15 minutes)

Part 2

Participants are broken out into small groups according to grade levels and given the assignment to invent strategies, activities, and interventions that address end-of-the-year issues for the children in their grades. Many materials should be made available for their use, such as blocks, puppets, book-creating materials, scrapbooks, and instant cameras. Participants can also use the end-of-the-year curricula from *Unsmiling faces* (Koplow, 1996) as a reference point.

Each group must share its work with the whole group at the end of the session.

Session 10

Topic: Working Toward Emotional Well-Being: The Joys and the Torments

The last session encompasses the following segments: Questions and answers about end-of-the-year classroom practices; open-ended discussion about what it has been like to participate in the training series and to implement strategies and techniques to support emotional well-being in the classroom; and projects that invite participants to express their feelings through various modalities. After the question-and-answer segment and the initial discussion about the series and the real experience of implementation, participants will be invited to use paint, clay, haiku, or narrative writing formats to express the joys and torments of the task before them. The break should come after the discussion and before the artistic expression. When most participants are finished, the expressions should be mounted and displayed and the artists invited to comment on their own work. Then the participants can be invited to view one another's works before lunch is served. The facilitator will invite further comment, questions, or discussion before dismissal.

Conclusion

Staff development is one avenue for informing teachers about emotionally responsive practice in the early grades. For staff development concerning emotionally responsive practice to be effective, the program must include frequent sessions that are offered over time—perhaps longer than a single school year. The sessions must be both didactic and experiential to be integrated on a deep level, and they must address teachers' well-being as well as children's well-being if they are to bring about change.

Each staff-development session described in this chapter can stand on its own and can be used when the issue addressed is particularly relevant to a particular school. The other modalities described in this book, however, will need to accompany the training if the outcome is to go beyond the immediate aftermath of the session. The staff-development program must exist within a school community that is well supported by an administration whose vision for an emotionally safe environment is maintained as a priority months and years after the training is finished.

CHAPTER 8

The Power of
Teacher-focused Mental Health
in Public Schools

A ROOM FULL of urban teachers filled a graduate-level seminar in the use of bibliotherapy techniques in the early-childhood classroom. After three days of making books for children that address essential developmental and experiential issues, teachers held up their hands to ask questions and comment about the course. One said, "This is an amazing tool. I wish I had known about it sooner. What I want to know is, who is going to make a book for us? Who is going to give us permission to discuss *our* emotional responses to these kids so that we survive the profession, and our spouses survive our marriages? My husband is getting pretty tired of hearing the grim stories that I have to tell him when he gets home every day."

Several people chimed in to support their classmate, who had voiced an unmet need for most people in the room. Unless they went into their own therapy, most teachers felt overwhelmed by the stress of their job and felt inadequate support to help them maintain their emotional balance. Use of peers for support was the most frequently reported way to manage, but teachers felt that this was of limited value because such informal peer support networks often deteriorated into gripe sessions.

"What happens when you feel completely overwhelmed and there is no one to talk to?" the instructor asks. "Mental health days!" people chime in in unison. Various teachers explained that they used sick days in order to feel restored and regain their balance. The more stressful the time of year, the more sick days they used. Several teachers described their schools during the last few weeks of the school year as schools without teachers. Substitutes generally supervised the majority of classrooms while teachers took their sick days to escape the stresses of the end of the school year. "Is this effective?" the instructor inquired. Many people responded, expressing the sentiment that it was effective for individual teachers to a degree, but debilitating for the school on the whole. One insightful teacher commented, "The more days I missed, the more impossible my children became to deal with. It became a cycle. I couldn't face being with them. I was afraid I was going to snap when they acted up like that, so I took the easy way out."

Clearly, if the only way that teachers can recover from the stresses of teaching and restore their emotional balance is to be absent from school, teachers' well-being and students' well-being are being endangered. For schools to function as healing environments for at-risk children, teachers have to be present physically and emotionally. We need to build in avenues for helping teachers to retain emotional well-being and balance *at school*. If schools themselves find ways to attend to teachers' mental health, teachers will be more likely to be present both in body and in mind. If the emotional reality of teaching is acknowledged and given credence, teachers will be able to acknowledge the emotional realities that their students bring into the classroom and will be better able to find ways to give their students constructive voices for their emotional lives.

There are many possibilities that schools can explore that would allow them to provide some form of teacher-focused mental health for their staff members. Schools may want to use their own mental-health professionals to attend to this task, or they might want to collaborate with outpatient mental-health programs, private practitioners, or other institutions to provide the services. Initially, it might be necessary to use discretionary moneys or foundation grants to get such a program off the ground, with the hope that the results will help to make a case for systemwide funding. Teacher-focused mental health can include a variety of supports or one or two projects, programs, or services. This chapter does not elaborate an infinite number of techniques; rather, it seeks to help administrators and district personnel imagine the possibilities and consider the value of making this commitment

The Retreat: An Intensive Intervention

Many educators are familiar with the concept of retreat, and some school systems have retreats built into the school calendar for various staff members. Retreats are sometimes used to bring about new learning or to focus people on specific problem-solving tasks. Leaving the school environment and spending many hours together in a less formal atmosphere, minus the stresses of the school day and the demands of the children, can be a powerful experience for teachers and other school staff members. Retreats designed to be part of teacher-focused mental health are organized with the goal of promoting the teacher's emotional well-being by giving her a voice for the emotional experiences that are evoked by teaching. Retreats can be organized during non-instructional days, because they are considered a form of staff development, or on weekends. Although weekend activity might initially be unappealing to staff members because it can conflict with family responsibilities and thus generate more stress, those people who do attend and experience relief from the retreat will probably inspire greater participation from their peer group for the next retreat.

Retreats can be a powerful part of a teacher-focused mental health plan for a school or district. The retreat can be used to initiate the teacher-focused mental health process or to provide an intensive experience for consolidating input from other forms of intervention. The fact that the school or district organizes and funds a retreat that focuses on teachers' mental health strongly communicates the school's priority for children's and teachers' well-being. The message to teachers is: If you are extremely stressed, and no one is attending to how stress is affecting you, you will not be an effective teacher. It is then easy to conclude the same about children. If young children are extremely stressed, and no one is attending to the ways in which the stress is affecting them, they will not be receptive learners. Thus, focusing on teachers' mental health becomes an avenue for acknowledging the connection between teachers' well-being and children's well-being and acknowledging the connection between emotional well-being in people in general and functioning level. It allows participants to understand the need to attend to emotional well-being in schools for everyone who spends many hours a day there.

Schools and districts that are interested in using retreats as an initial form of teacher-focused mental health may feel the need for direction when planning the event. There are several possibilities, the most effective probably being a topic that focuses on an aspect of the teachers' experience that is acknowledged in informal networks but typically denied at the systemwide level. For instance, a project in a stressed urban neighborhood emphasizing developmentally appropriate practice in the early grades held a retreat titled, "The Joys and Torments of Our Practice." The title itself acknowledged the fact that, although the project was deeply committed to developmentally appropriate education in the early grades, it was not always a rosy experience for the teachers who were trying to implement it. Indeed, teachers who had been teaching using a traditional model, in which children sat at desks doing structured, teacher-led lessons, were suddenly experiencing children working freely in centers, using them as resources, and often telling them personal stories. Although some teachers instantly embraced the changes, most were suspect and overwhelmed and felt a huge loss of control in their professional lives. Many teachers spoke of the torment they went through when they heard about their students' traumatic experiences and realized how difficult their lives were.

Teachers who attended that retreat were invited to express their joys and torments through a variety of avenues. The facilitator began by reading them several compelling passages from the book *A teacher's voice* (Raphael, 1985), written by a teacher of urban children. She encouraged participants to use the retreat to find their voices for their own professional experiences. No one but teachers know what it is like to be a teacher with young, needy children. That becomes a problem not only for teachers who are isolated with the painful realities of teaching, but also for society, which creates plans, standards, and policies that adversely affect the lives of children and teachers without having any insight into the teachers' reality. The retreat used an inviting-and-containing model to give teachers means of expression that were safe and could be held by the collective. Teachers were invited to paint, write descriptive stories in pairs, and write haiku about the joys and torments of their professional lives. At the end of the afternoon all of the work was mounted. The gallery of material astounded and impressed the participants themselves, many of whom denied having a voice or the talent to express their joys or pain artistically.

Another retreat was organized by the clinical staff of an urban school who perceived that many teachers were behaving the way that their own parents and teachers had behaved with them when they were children. They decided to organize a retreat that invited teachers to explore both the strengths and the dangers of intergenerational patterns in child care and teaching. The retreat was entitled "Teachers Past and Present." The facilitators started by reading two children's books to the group: *Sophie* (Fox, 1994), the story of a young African American girl's relationship with her grandfather over time, and *Cherry pies and lullabies* (Reiser, 1998), a story about mothers handing down traditions to their daughters over generations and changing those traditions as they are passed along. The facilitators invited teachers to consider their own experiences as schoolchildren and the parenting and teaching practices that were typical at the time in their communities, and many teachers shared their experiences. Small- and whole-group exercises were made available to help participants consider that the positive experiences they have been able to hand down to their own children and the children in their classrooms and the destructive practices they were conscious of getting rid of and preventing from affecting the next generation. Dialogue then unfolded about things that various teachers swore they would never do to their own children or to the children in their classes that somehow have emerged. The dialogue was rich and compelling for listeners as well as for more active members; it also resulted in a consciousness about the topic that allowed for a different level of conversation about practice once back in the school environment.

If schools have a precedent for offering retreats to staff to introduce new types of curriculum or to acquaint them with higher standards, then the modality of retreats certainly can be made available to those same schools or school districts as an avenue for teacher-focused mental health.

The Ongoing Group: A Work in Progress

Ongoing groups focused on teachers' mental health are a very accessible form of teacher-focused mental-health practice. If they are held monthly or bimonthly, these groups can take place during the school day, if the principal can arrange for participating teachers to take adjoining lunch and prep while children are being covered by special teachers, lunch teachers, and so on. Other schools may want to use substitutes in order to ensure high attendance that results from holding groups during the school day. After-school options will be sought out by motivated teachers but not by teachers who are less familiar with the benefits of this kind of support. Therefore, the school as a whole may not gain as much if the group or groups are attended inconsistently or by only a few staff members.

School 8, a public school in the Boston area, was part of a collaboration with a neighboring college of education. The principal of School 8 worked with a mental-health consultant at the college to make her school an emotionally safe place for children, teachers, and parents. In the first three years of this involvement, School 8 held one-day-long retreats addressing children's and teachers' mental-health issues; during the fourth year, however, an ongoing group was started for teachers that met monthly during the school day. The group was organized around the understanding of the developmental framework taught by Erik Erikson, a framework that the teachers at School 8 had studied the year before as part of a school-reform project. The mental-health consultant who facilitated the ongoing group reviewed the Eriksonian framework. She then invited participants to think about the ways in which their students' developmental issues interacted with their own and made their work lives complex. She invited the group to think and talk about the connections between their personal and professional lives and to use the group to express their own emotional reactions to the issues and trauma that the children brought to school with them each day.

The teachers at School 8 were astounded at this invitation. Although they had all been involved in the mental-health consultation projects that the college had been initiating for the past few years, they expressed disbelief about their school's and their district's willingness to invest in their well-being in this way. "I just can't believe they're letting us meet like this to talk about us," said one teacher. "Wow!" a new teacher exclaimed. "Ms. B [the principal] must be really progressive. At the M school, no one cared about us one way or the other. They just told you to shut your door if you were having trouble. No one would think of how it was affecting you in a million years—unless you freaked out or had a heart attack or something."

"I thought I was going to have a heart attack last year," recalled a first-grade teacher. "That group was just so difficult, and then they kept adding kid after kid, all with these tremendous problems, and it was too much for me—too much for anyone. I just resigned myself to it by the end of the year. I just thought, 'Let me get through these last few months and they'll be gone.'"

"Good thing they didn't make you loop," a coworker commented. Everyone laughed.

"I used to stay up nights worrying about them when I first started teaching at my old school. I actually used to cry thinking about their lives, and then I used to cry because they made me feel so angry and helpless. But then I decided, 'Wait a minute!' I got to keep some distance and not get so involved. Otherwise I won't be able to teach much longer."

"How can you do that? I could never do that," asserted a coworker. "How can you keep a distance all the time?" Turning to the consultant, she asked, "That isn't good for them either, is it?"

"Well, maybe not, but it is better for me, I know that." commented the teacher who had been talking.

"Well, in your old school, it doesn't sound like you had a lot of choice. Either you let yourself get isolated with all of their issues and difficulties or you tried to keep a distance from it. There was no one to talk to about it or share it with," said the leader.

"I just can't believe what these kids coming up now go through and what they talk about and what they get into. I remember being in the second grade, and, you know, I just did my work and played at recess and that was it. If I cut up like they do now, I would have gotten a whipping for sure. But you can't blame them, because they're just doing what they see their young parents do, and it's a shame."

"Who else remembers being the age that the children in your class are now? Who remembers what school was like for you and what your teachers were like?"

Many voices responded to this invitation to remember. The teachers recalled strict teachers, punitive teachers, and attuned teachers. They recalled successes and failures, winning awards, getting spankings. They recalled years when school was their oasis during family instability, and years when school was torture.

The hour and a half came to a close. The teachers left slowly and reluctantly. They had more to say and were only partially reassured by the statement that they would reassemble in a month. They had had things that felt right come and go before. They remained incredulous about the possibility that the group might actually go on for as long as they needed it.

When the teachers returned to their classrooms to resume their day, what had they accomplished? How would the children reap the benefits of the time the group had spent together? Certainly, the answer is "over time." Some of the teachers who participated in the first group session might have felt some relief in being able to tell their stories. Some might have felt affirmed and less guilty about their own ambivalence toward difficult children as they listened to their colleagues. Some might have felt refreshed from the midday break from classroom life and the opportunity to talk with other adults. But what the group became for each participant was impossible to know from the onset. The benefits were varied, personal, and incremental. The topics touched on in the first group set the stage for a deeper dialogue about many fundamental issues for professionals who spend many hours each day in the company of young children. The group talked about the difference between the way children behaved when they were young and the way they behave now. They talked about the parallels and disyncronies in their own teaching styles and they ways in which they were taught. They talked about what school meant for them as children and a little bit about what it means to them as teachers. They talked about the dilemma that they all face concerning closeness and distance with needy families and needy children. They talked about topics that, if left unconscious and unexplored, would be likely to play themselves out in the company of children in positive and negative ways.

The group facilitator made some notes at the close of the group so she could remind participants what their prior agendas had been if they had trouble getting started the next time. However, she did not structure the topics ahead of time. She allowed the teachers to determine relevant topics for themselves. She followed the topics each time and sometimes reminded them of emerging themes or contradictions. She occasionally offered interpretations or a framework for understanding confusing content. The group did not need more guidance than that, and, at the end of the school year, the evaluations were uniformly positive. "I thought I'd have to leave the profession soon," said one teacher. "Now, I think, if I can keep talking about it, maybe I can stay."

Behind Closed Doors, Letting Doors Open

Another option for integrating teacher-focused mental health into public schools is to set aside some clinical time that teachers can use, as needed, before school and during their lunch and prep periods. Including the option of office hours acknowledges the reality that teachers may be overwhelmed by feelings or experiences that they would like to talk out with someone in a private and confidential setting. Some teachers, of course, seek their own therapy, but there are many factors that affect teachers' access to private therapy, including health insurance, time, availability of services, and personal finances. On-site office hours for teachers is unlikely to substitute for ongoing therapy for teachers who want treatment, but it may be extremely useful as a resource for teachers who need to talk something through, who are in crisis, or who are having a complicated reaction to something that a child has brought up. The advantage of speaking with someone who is intimately acquainted with the stresses that teachers face may be one of the strongest arguments for on-site office hours for teachers. Employee-assistance programs tend to lack this expertise; they tend to be more familiar with treating the poor outcomes of teacher stress, such as alcoholism and other kinds of substance abuse.

In addition to setting aside clinical time for teachers' use, schools that heal recommend making clinical time available to administrators. Whereas teachers may have be able to some rely on some peer support in the building at difficult times, administrators typically have no such resource. Apart from those principals who are lucky enough to work with an assistant or vice principal whom they trust and can befriend, principals are most often going it alone when it comes to mastering their emotional reactions to their jobs. Arranging for clinical consultation that is built into their schedules may be a form of prevention that benefits not only the individual principal but also the entire school.

Policymakers may find it difficult to understand how focusing on teachers' mental health can possibly justify allotting sparse clinical services to teachers' needs when there are so many children who need clinical services but do not get the therapy that they need. Yet, that being the case, children bring their distress to school; teachers inherit that distress. A teacher's ability to be emotionally responsive to those children may depend on her having someone be emotional responsive to her. Assuming that all teachers have someone who fills this role in their personal lives leaves too much to chance. It stands to reason that a certain number of teachers do not have this resource in their personal lives as adults and may not have had it in their childhoods. Thus, it becomes essential to consider how to build this resource into the system.

Imagine a scenario such as this one: A first-grade teacher, Ms. A, has been teaching for eight years. She is asthmatic and gets bronchitis easily in the winter; thus, she is out sick frequently during the winter months. Her class comprises 27 6-year-olds, many of whom have disruptions in attachment in their histories. During Ms. A's absences, the group is reportedly rowdy and disruptive with the substitute. When she returns, she manages to restore order, with the exception of two children, Eric and Randy, whose behavior remains difficult. Randy begins to do dangerous things, such as climbing up on pipes in the bathroom, and sliding down the school's banister. Each time Randy does something dangerous, Ms. A finds herself getting extremely anxious. When her anxiety level rises, her breathing difficulties increase. She stays home to prevent the return of bronchitis and to control the asthma symptoms. Each time she returns to school, the class is less and less manageable, and the two children who have become disruptive are completely out of control, with Eric acting out aggressively with other children and Randy becoming almost suicidal in his behavior. One afternoon, Ms. A finds Randy caught in twisted pipes in the boys' room when the boys return from the bathroom without him. She takes him to the nurse to be sure that he is alright and goes into the teachers' room, crying hysterically. A coworker volunteers to use her prep to cover Ms. A's group and takes Ms. A to the school-based teacher-focused mental-health clinician.

Ms. A begins by apologizing: "I'm sorry. It really wasn't such a big deal. The nurse said he was fine." She resumes sobbing.

The clinician assures Ms. A that there is no need to apologize. Obviously, Randy needs help. His reactions to Ms. A's absences are becoming dangerous. Maybe something about the kids in the classroom is adding to Ms. A's stress and increasing her vulnerability to asthma and her need to stay home.

Ms. A responds by telling the story of her health difficulties. "I've never had a group like this one in my eight years of teaching. They were O.K. in the fall before all of this started, but it's like they fell apart when I was out, and now. . . ." She sobs again. "It's like I've lost them and can't get them back."

The clinician has a lot of thoughts. "I wonder what the kids are being told when you're out. I wonder what you've been telling them when you return. I think they need a lot of information to help them stay connected to the here and now and not become overwhelmed by feelings of abandonment that belong to the past. We need to develop a plan for your class that helps them see what's happening and helps them find their way back to trusting you. I also wonder about your own history—whether you've had losses that were unrecoverable."

Ms. A responds to the first part of the clinician's response. It is true that the children have been told very little about their teacher's absences and that the substitutes have not helped them to stay connected to her through her absences. Then she pauses and is silent.

"Is there more?" the clinician inquires.

Ms. A begins to cry wordless tears. She finally reveals that her younger brother killed himself when he was 10 and she was 8 years old. He jumped into an open elevator shaft. No one was sure whether the death was intentional, because he had always been reckless and not very expressive.

"I can't believe I didn't put that together—that Randy reminded me of Calvin—and Randy's behavior is so obviously a reaction to something I did. . . ."

"It's common for kids who lose someone to assume that they are the cause of the tragedy," the clinician adds.

"We have to find a way to help Randy with this," Ms. A says emphatically. She and the clinician make a plan to meet with the principal to develop plans for her class when she is out. They also plan a meeting to design a curriculum for the children around their teacher's presence and absence issues. The clinician invites Ms. A to come in again during a lunch or prep period within the week to check in and talk about how she is feeling about everything.

Ms. A returns to see the clinician twice in the next three weeks. She does not need to miss school for health reasons for the rest of the winter season.

Safety Net

The conventional wisdom is that everyone in the education field needs to have a life outside the classroom, and that this life has to include many outlets for emotional expression and sources of emotional support. When we assume that such outlets and supports are built into all teachers' lives outside the classroom, we are operating as if our young children are spending many hours each day with adults who can maintain their emotional balance in the face of constant stress and regression. When we assume that teachers have adequate support in their outside life, we close our eyes to the fact that the thousands of teachers who lack these supports are left alone to try to survive the emotional turmoil that classroom life engenders. Teachers who are struggling alone this way are unlikely to be able to function as emotionally responsive adults in the lives of their young, often desperately needy, students. Indeed, teachers who are struggling and losing the battle to maintain their own emotional well-being may be behaving in ways that exacerbate the problems that children bring to school. At-risk children can ill afford to have primary adults in their lives who cannot be consistently physically and emotionally present. When teachers act out their frustration in the classroom, at-risk children will be profoundly affected.

Children look to their teachers for confirmation of their potential and self-worth. Teachers who have lost sight of their own potential and sense of worth cannot be a source of well-being for children. We as a society will suffer the results.

CHAPTER 9

The Tools of Emotionally Responsive Classrooms

Basic Tools, Ongoing Results

EMOTIONALLY RESPONSIVE classroom practice is within reach for good early-grade teachers. The basic tools for emotionally responsive classroom practice are low-tech, readily available, and highly implementable. The tools that are recommended here are essentially conceptual, as opposed to highly prescriptive. It is necessary to use them every day, during each activity of the day, as opposed to enacting them periodically as adjunctive to the general educational practices of the classroom. It is unlikely that the use of these tools will result in immediate results, but it is very likely that ongoing use of these tools will enhance the emotional tone of the classroom and that children will integrate gains over time that do not disappear.

The basic tools of an emotionally responsive classroom include attachment, symbols and metaphor, respect for experience, respect for development, emergent curriculum, routine, and environmental design. These tools have been described in prior chapters but not listed as discrete organizing concepts. This chapter will include an elaboration of the value of each basic tool and the ways in which it can be used to inform practice in early-grade classrooms. After discussing these basic tools, I will explore the use of more clinical approaches that can be adapted for classroom use.

Attachment

Emotionally responsive early-grade classrooms need to invite children to become attached to teachers and teachers to become attached to children. Teachers need to recognize their importance in the lives of young children. The teacher is a pivotal figure for a young child who spends hours of the day with her. During those hours, the child must feel that he has a partner in development who cares about him and can take care of him and keep him safe physically and emotionally. Teachers who do this naturally engage in a powerful avenue of preventive mental health without even knowing it. Research has shown that attachment is a critical protective factor for at-risk children (Koralek, 1999). Children who have not had opportunities to attach to a consistent, nurturing adult cannot develop well and are often difficult, inattentive, and disruptive in the classroom. If children do not have this opportunity at home and have not had it historically before coming to school, their need for attachment, rejection of relationships, or disorientation in the face of attachment deprivation will thwart all of the teacher's attempts to intervene unless attachment becomes part of the goal for intervention.

There are several ways to heighten the opportunity for child–teacher attachment in early-grade classrooms. The teacher who wants to invite attachment relationships addresses children in a personal way. She always calls children by their first names, not "Mr. Newman," "Ms. March," an so on. She makes contact with each child as he or she enters the room, recalling and referring to experiences that she knows they have had and things they have brought to school with them. She makes reflective comments so that children know that she is able to see them. For instance, if a child did not sleep the night before and looks very tired, the teacher might say, "You seem so tired this morning, Annie," instead of asking questions in an information-seeking mode.

An attached teacher lets children know that she remembers the collective experiences that she and the class have shared, and that she thinks about the children even when they were out of sight. If a child has been out for more than a few days, the teacher may want to call his or her home to check on the child's well-being and to touch base with the child herself. Teachers who reach out to children across time and physical distance and refer to important experiences that she has shared with them make a big impact on the young child, who then has help "holding" the different parts of her life experience. An attached teacher helps children to think about her when she is out of sight by helping children create imagery for her across time and physical distance: "Next week is the week that I will be out to attend a conference in Texas. Has anyone here been to Texas? Can you tell the class what it looks like?" This teacher may also use transitional objects to help children stay connected during vacation breaks that are uncomfortably long for them. These may be given in the form of small stuffed animals given as a holiday gift before the winter break, or they may take the form of a journal that each child keeps during the break to convey the nature of his or her vacation experience to the teacher when classes reconvene.

Young children learn about reading affects in others and about expressing their own emotions effectively from their attachment figures. Babies and toddlers watch their parents express emotion and learn which affects convey which meanings. Children whose parents are unable to display genuine affects, are depressed, are not in control of their affects due to substance abuse or mental illness, or express emotion in a dangerous or overwhelming ways cannot serve as partners in the developmental task of affective communication. Teachers who want to help children read and express emotions constructively have to have strong attachment relationships with their students, and they have to express a range of genuine emotions themselves without being scary or overwhelming. An attached teacher who expresses happiness, sadness, anger, fear, and concern appropriately has the potential to be a model for her students in the development of this important human skill.

Many schools discourage teachers from making physical contact with children because they are concerned about vulnerability to accusations of abuse. This is problematic for young children for a number of reasons. The literature tells us that, for early-grade children, the most powerful communicator of warmth and caring is touch (Currie, 1988). In addition, research supports a correlation between academic achievement and perceived warmth (Rohner, 1986; Starky, 1980). Teachers who are comfortable holding a crying child, giving a reassuring hug, or sitting in a rocking chair with children on their lap are likely to enjoy strong attachment relationships with their young students; they are also likely to promote a sense of well-being and a decrease in anxiety in their environment. Indeed, an elementary-school program that instituted a positive touch policy, giving the school principal the key role of receiving children as they entered in the morning and hugging those who looked upset, found that the incidents of child-to-child aggression in the building decreased by 46% and that test scores increased dramatically (Currie, 1988). The caregiving aspects of teaching young children, such as handing out snacks, helping children with coats, and attending to children who are sick, are powerful attachment behaviors that ultimately enable children to succeed in school.

Symbols and Metaphor

Symbols are among a teacher's most powerful tools in emotionally responsive practice. In chapter 4, the teacher is referred to as a "midwife for the birth of symbols" in young children. Teachers who have strong attachment relationships with children have the power to help children endow symbols with meaning. There is a crucial difference between the ability to produce and use symbols in a rote manner and the ability to produce and create symbols with evolving meaning. When teachers read books aloud that are intrinsically interesting to the children; invite them to use clay, to draw, and to play about experiences that they have had; and model the use of writing as an expressive outlet, symbols become tools that children can use for self-expression rather than products that are produced merely to satisfy adults. The child who learns to make symbols meaningful gains ways to resolve issues, express feelings, and communicate with others that protect him or her from emotional isolation and enhance his or her potential for academic success.

Most early-grade teachers have had experience with music and movement, which are compelling and organizing for children. Often, music and movement are taught by special teachers who visit the group once a week while the classroom teacher is having a prep period. However, there are wonderful opportunities for classroom teachers to integrate music and movement in the curriculum during the time that she is with the group. Not only are these activities good for supporting a feeling of unity in the classroom, but they are also potentially great conveyers of symbol and metaphor. Children can be invited to write lyrics for familiar tunes, focusing on specific aspects of their learning, using words that carry meaning for them and symbolize their collective experiences. Movement and drama can be used to help children invent metaphors that portray feelings and perceptions in complex ways. The creative early-grade teacher will use language arts in an integrated way, choosing literature that is relevant and that can be linked to emerging concepts and self-discovery; can be expanded on during music, movement, and drama; and can build on themes that emerge from spontaneous language and play.

Chapter 4 talks about the importance of teacher–child attachment as a precursor to effective symbol use. It is easy to understand why symbols are critical to school achievement in such core curriculum areas as reading and math; it may be more difficult to understand their essential value to children's mental health. Collective experiences that are treasured and captured in symbol and metaphor communicate the value of children's participation in school events and encourage them to make connections between one level of experience and another in ways that can be mutually appreciated.

Children who create metaphors based on collective experience enhance not only the connections among group members, but also their cognitive abilities to generate ways of conveying complex experience. For example, a teacher asks a small group of interracial third-graders to have lunch with her to talk about her perception that they sometimes feel excluded by the other children. Some of the kids are able articulate how they feel when African American kids tease them about having a white parent or do not include them socially. Some children talked about feeling different and being different. One girl whose best friend is white talks about feeling torn about where she belongs in the classroom community. The teacher asks whether any of the children would be interested in developing a skit about how they feel to communicate their experience to the other children. She asks them to use metaphor, which the children have studied in language arts, to convey their complicated feelings. They respond enthusiastically to the invitation. One of the boys who has not been vocal in the meeting says that he does not want to be on stage, but he is willing participate as a writer. The group agrees and meet to practice each day during recess.

"This is our play with no words," the actors announce to the class. One child walks onto the "stage" wearing a huge white-cloud costume. Another comes from the other side wearing a huge black-cloud costume. They hold hands. Then three small gray clouds come from behind them and run around the stage. The two large clouds disappear, and the children who played them re-emerge. One holds a sign showing many white clouds; the other holds a sign showing many black clouds. The gray clouds try to join the white clouds, but the white clouds stay distant. The gray clouds try to join the black clouds, but the black clouds move away. Then the wind blows all the clouds together. They crash into each other and make thunder sounds. Finally, when the thunder and wind stop, all of the clouds are intermingled, and a rainbow flag waves over them.

The kids applaud. "What was the play about?" asks the teacher. Many children respond. One says, "First I thought it was about weather, but then I knew it was about being biracial." Another says, "I thought it was science, and then I thought it was a book they read, and then I thought it was social studies." The teacher responds to the comments. What made the children's thoughts change? What did the skit make the children think about that they might not have thought about before? What metaphors were used to convey the children's experiences? How did the kids know what the message was? What questions would they like to ask the actors and writers? The kids have a lot to say:

"Well, I knew it was that way sometimes, but I didn't think it was all the time."

"I think the biracial kids must feel bad, like they don't belong."

"Why did it end happy?"

"Why did they make a storm happen?"

The class talks about these issues and is able to use the metaphor and more direct references to racial dynamics more comfortably during the balance of the year. The biracial children are visibly relieved to have had a voice and to be less isolated with their painful experiences.

The social and emotional health of the group as a whole is enhanced.

Routines

Teachers whose classrooms function according to stable routines practice preventive mental health only if these routines are carefully designed to offer a balance of inviting and containing throughout the day. For instance, morning meeting should happen at the same time each morning and should include some rituals that do not vary. Within the meeting, however, there must be an invitation for the children's voices to be heard. Writing time may be built into the daily schedule, but within that structure there must be some opportunity for writing to be used as an expressive art. Snack time may not vary, but within that routine children must have the right to accept or refuse food, to talk quietly to a friend sitting next to them, or to voice suggestions about the menu or the amount of food given. The teacher has the right—indeed, the obligation—to set limits about these things, but she needs to welcome the dialogue. Routines must be designed by teachers who decide when things will happen and what will be offered, but that allow children to decide how they are going to engage in the activities and how they feel about the activities. Routines that offer this kind of external structure complemented by internal freedom enhance the mental health of children. Routines that provide external structure but deny internal freedom thwart emotional well-being, because they force negative feelings to go underground or to become confrontational.

If children must go out to the play yard after lunch because that is how the school operates and coverage is arranged, those who have trouble with this will withdraw or act out unless their difficulties are addressed. A teacher who says, "I know going out is hard for you. Let's talk about what makes it hard and see if we can make it work better," provides more potential for positive resolution than the teacher who says, "You're going out, and that's that. I don't want to hear any more about it."

Teachers need to appreciate the value of caregiving routines for these routines to support children's mental health. Caregiving routines such as snack, lunch, toileting, rest, and response to illness or injury may be considered incidental to a teacher's mission, but they are in fact primary in the life experience of young children. Teachers who want to support emotional well-being in their group can think about ways to make caregiving routines more intimate and more integrated as part of the classroom experience. Caregiving routines that are enacted mechanically without the participation of the teacher/attachment figure often do not support emotional well-being, and caregiving routines that are pressured or demeaning of children's needs undermine children's well-being. The first-grade teacher who cannot eat with her students because of school protocol may want them to brainstorm about making their cafeteria table more comfortable, arrange things in the classroom to make the table a more homelike experience, and check in with the children about how lunch went each day when they return to the classroom. If the children report that a lunch aide screamed because a child did not eat anything, or that children spilled their food as they walked from the line to the table, the teacher can empathize with the children involved, then bring the matter up at a grade-level meeting at which an administrator is present as a topic worthy of ongoing discussion and potential reform.

Classroom Environment

Teachers can extend invitations for expression to children and provide a containing feeling to hold those expressions in part through their design of the environment. A classroom that consists of rows of desks, a globe, a flag, and some bookshelves communicates that the priority is order and teacher-directed learning. A classroom that has a variety of materials, such as crayons and paper, a block corner, and wood-working and dramatic-play areas, communicates that symbolic activity, self-expression, and social endeavors are valued. A classroom that is loaded with materials that flow from one space to another, and in which every inch of wall space is covered with posters or children's work, is likely to be an over-stimulating environment. A classroom with few materials and barren walls is likely to be an under-stimulating environment. A classroom with clearly defined centers where children can explore various kinds of learning and move between personal and social endeavors may be the most conducive to emotionally responsive practice when it coexists with a well-thought-out and well-balanced routine, an attached teacher, and an emphasis on the use of symbol and metaphor.

Environments conducive to emotionally responsive practice need to have defined areas that contain invitations for expression. The classroom also needs to maintain a balance between whole-group areas, such as a meeting corner, and spaces for small groups and individuals to work. Early-grade classrooms should have carpeted spaces as well as space where the floors can be easily washed. Children's work should be displayed at eye level. The room should be warm and inviting, with plants, fish, and other signs of life and projects that come to life in the classroom. Some teachers in early grades find it helpful to designate an area of the classroom for children who need comfort or a quiet space to work something out with another child. This space can be made semi-private by placing classroom furniture to carve out some kind of enclosure. Teachers may put material in this corner that children find comforting, such as pillows or a quilt made as a group project or books that reflect emotional issues. Having a place in the classroom where children can go when they need to take a break, seek comfort, or resolve conflict communicates the teacher's understanding that these things come up in the classroom and can be accommodated in a hopeful way.

Environmental design must also support the teacher's particular teaching style. For example, if a very traditional teacher is forced to work in a room that invites openness, she may spend considerable time and energy trying to prevent children from responding to the invitations that surround them. If a teacher trained in a progressive education model has nothing in her room but desks, chairs, and textbooks, she is likely to become frustrated and feel constrained in what she can offer the children. The classroom environment must support the philosophy of the school and of the teacher in order to become an adjunct of emotionally responsive practice.

Truth

Schools that heal are truthful with children and families. This means that administrators have a vision and a mission that they state and by which they live, and that teachers have a connection to that mission and bring it to life in the classroom. When this ideal construct does not exist, the school and classroom will acknowledge the disparity in a way that affirms the experience of those living with it. Take, for example, the parent who reports that her son does not want to return to school for his first-grade year. Everyone in the building knows that the kindergarten teacher who taught the child was demeaning to her students. The principal has been trying to get her out of the building for years. The boy's new teacher says, "I know Ms. E yelled a lot and sometimes hurt the kids' feelings, but in my classroom, I respect children's feelings. I think it will be pretty different. But if something happens to hurt your feelings, tell me." In this way the teacher legitimizes the boy's feelings and expresses her commitment to communicating truthfully. She engages in preventive mental-health practice not by reassuring the boy that his former teacher really loved him, but by supporting the facts.

Denial robs children of the foundations of emotional security by undermining their process of reality testing. Being truthful with children is thus critical to emotionally responsive practice. Not only must the content of the teacher's communication with children need to be truthful; her affects and tone of voice must also be genuine in order to be helpful to children. Many children desperately need adult role models who express a genuine range of affects without being overwhelming or out of control. For young children who do not have role models for this kind of emotional learning at home, the early-grade teacher can be among the few adults who has enough contact to provide a corrective experience.

Being truthful with children is sometimes difficult because it may feel as though truthfulness makes offering children the reassurance they need to feel secure impossible. A child who is crying because his guardian has forgotten to pick him up for the sixth time in two weeks may be reassured by a well-intentioned teacher who says that the guardian "really loves him and probably just got delayed." Although these are meant as words of comfort, they can cause immense confusion for a child who feels neglected because he is actually being neglected. In the long run, it is more comforting to make a truthful comment that supports the child's experience, such as, "This has happened so many times lately. Does it make you feel sad and mad and worried?" This kind of comment is reassuring because it communicates the fact that, although the guardian is missing, the teacher is present and can share the moment with the child in need.

Clinical Tools in Classroom Practice

Teachers often must go beyond the basic tools of good practice in order to facilitate emotional well-being in the classroom. Many clinical approaches are classroom-friendly and can be incorporated comfortably into the educational milieu. One such tool is the use of reflective technique. Reflective technique simply is a way of helping people to feel heard. Reflective technique may consist of the speaker repeating or restating the essence of what the other person has communicated. A teacher has countless opportunities for the use of reflective technique. She may greet a reluctant child by saying, "It looks like you didn't really want to come to school today." She might respond to an irate parent whose child has lost his third pair of mittens with, "It must be so frustrating to have to keep replacing things. It must feel like no one is keeping track of him." She might scold a child who is being disruptive because "it's boring" by saying, "I know you feel bored, but you can't disturb other people. You're going to have to think of a way to make it more interesting."

In each of these cases, the teacher could take an opposite approach. She might greet the child who is reluctant to enter by saying, "Now, let me see you smile. Don't you remember what a good time you had yesterday?" She might offer a defensive argument to the mother of the child with the lost mittens—after all, one teacher cannot keep track of 28 pairs of mittens. She might ignore the child's comment about boredom and just address the behavior. Teachers who have used reflective technique, however, have found it to be especially effective way to communicate because it seems to lessen the need for the other to be oppositional and helps heighten a feeling of connection on both sides.

Reflective technique can be verbal but is not limited to verbal interchange. For example, teachers whose rooms contain posters showing children with different affects are using reflective technique because they are offering children a mirror for their diverse feelings, positive and negative. This makes children feel that all feelings are acceptable and that they do not need to feel embarrassed about having feelings. A teacher whose pre-kindergarten or kindergarten classroom has a full-length mirror is practicing another level of reflective technique, giving her young students visual feedback about how affects express feeling and about self-constancy as they look at their mirror images.

Reflective techniques can also be used to address classroom dynamics that become difficult because the children involved lose perspective while the incidents are occurring. A teacher might use puppets to mirror an existing dynamic in the classroom, then invite the children to talk about what they have seen. For instance, the children in one second-grade class constantly complain about being hit, bumped, pushed, or squashed by their classmates. The teacher explains repeatedly that most of these encounters are unintentional but happen because there are a large number of children in a confined space. Yet day after day, she hears the same complaint. During a morning meeting, she may decide to put on a puppet show for the class, mirroring the situation that occurs daily. She then leaves the discussion of the puppet show open to the children: "Well, they keep bumping each other, and no one says, 'Excuse me,' so then everyone wants to fight"; "Well, it is really an accident, but then kids get mad with the other kid who bumped them and they fight on purpose"; "That reminds me of our class because of what happened yesterday with Renee and Pete." The teacher allows several more comments to be made, then invites a dialogue about what the children think would help prevent the bad feelings that occur because everyone assumes he or she is being hurt on purpose. One boy suggests, "You could ask if it was an accident, and then you could look at the other person's face to see if they're telling the truth." This leads to a discussion about how one can tell how someone feels by watching their expressions. The ongoing dialogue rich and valuable—more so than if this teacher had lectured the children one more time about being polite to one another and saying "excuse me."

Young children often benefit from the classroom teacher's use of drawing technique as a form of reflection that gives children perspective and insight without depending on a high level of verbal interchange. In this technique, the teacher draws an image of what the child is expressing instead of merely verbalizing it. For example, a child has a tantrum about a change in the schedule. He is nonverbal during the tantrum (except for screaming) and is essentially dragged from the room to the next activity. Later he allows the teacher to draw an image of what has happened. The teacher asks for his input. "This is Thomas, and this is me trying to bring Thomas to music. How should I make you?" Thomas thinks. "Mad and sad," he says. The teacher draws this. She then draws a thought bubble over Thomas's head and one over her own head.

"What were you thinking then?" she asks. Thomas shrugs. His teacher continues. "I was thinking, I wish there was someone to help me so I could find out what is making Thomas so upset about going to music class. But since there was no one but me, I just had to pull you." The teacher draws some symbols for her wish in the bubble. "Make my mommy in my bubble," Thomas instructs. "I'm sad to go to music class because my mommy might come, and she won't know where I am." The teacher does so and helps Thomas show his mother the music room when she comes later to pick him up. Drawing the event after it is over lets the child think about what has actually occurred and therefore can help to avoid a storm of emotion the next time the routine is disrupted.

Another form of reflective technique that has been used in classrooms with success is bibliotherapy—the practice of using literature to reflect issues that are salient for the group or individual to whom it is being read. A teacher who is concerned about the amount of fighting in her group might read a story about a group that fights a lot. A teacher dealing with the serious illness of one of her students might read a story about a child who becomes ill. When one of the children's parents is suddenly transferred out of state, the teacher might read a story about kids having to adjust to a move; she might also make a book for the child who is leaving, which allows the child to take something personal with her and to have her issues about the move reflected in a helpful way.

Because reading aloud is a common practice in the early grades, bibliotherapy is a highly accessible form of intervention. Teachers must be conscious of how certain books reflect social and emotional issues when they order books or use the library. Most important, teachers must achieve a level of comfort with the dialogue that ensues after a book has been read aloud. Bibliotherapy is essentially an inviting technique as well as a containing technique. It invites children to recognize an issue and to explore its meaning for them through open-ended discussion and follow-up projects. It provides the containing structure of the meeting and the reading aloud to hold what comes up for the children within the structure of the strong relationship that they enjoy with the classroom teacher. Teachers often need practice to allow the follow-up to the reading to unfold in a meaningful way. For instance, when Ms. S began using bibliotherapy as a reflective technique in her first-grade classroom, she was able to choose books that were emotionally relevant to the children but found it difficult to hear what the children had to say. Ms. S decided to address an issue of concern to her: When her class took trips, a few children became wild and did not stay with the group, and a few others wandered off without seeming to notice what they were doing. After reading a book that featured a child who got lost in a store, many children wanted to talk about their experience of getting lost. The teacher became anxious and began to ask specific questions about what children ought to do if they got lost, such as stay in one spot and look for a police officer. This kept the children's reaction from unfolding; thus, it was difficult for Ms. S to know where to go from there, because she did not give herself the chance to hear enough about what the story meant to the children.

Ms. W, who used bibliotherapy in her second-grade class frequently, advised Ms. S to read another story with a similar theme but this time to allow the dialogue to unfold without comment other than occasional reflective comments. Ms. S did this, saying only, "That must have been scary" occasionally when children talked about being lost. Finally, a boy said, "No one ever looked for me. The police brought me back, but no one cared that I was gone." Ms. S was silent and felt panicked for a moment. Then she said, "How can we make sure that no one in our class feels the way Martin felt that time? When we go on trips, kids sometimes wander away. How can we make sure we will notice when that happens and that we can communicate with one another and eventually with the lost kids so everyone knows that we care about them?" The kids had many ideas about this. They suggested a buddy system and talked about making complementary pairs for buddies, because it would do no good if the both of the pair wandered away. They talked about what they would tell wandering children when they returned so that kids knew that they had been missed. Ms. S was reassured by the exchange and planned another field trip, although she had sworn that the previous trip the class had taken would be the last.

Bibliotherapy and the interchanges that follow often give teachers a deeper understanding of the meaning of children's behavior and the connections between their experience and emotional life. The understanding that the teacher gains can inform her curricular agenda so that it becomes emotionally responsive curriculum and heightens the children's interest in, and their attentiveness to, learning. Ms. S's class became aware of a library book about a lost dog taken to a shelter. They were so interested in the book and had so many questions about what happened to lost animals that Ms. S began a study of pets, including the fate of lost pets. The children took a trip to a shelter that did not euthanize unwanted animals. They saw how the pets were cared for and wrote stories about what they thought the animals' lives were like before they went to the shelter and what their lives would be like when the pets were adopted. The curriculum was rich; the was writing highly motivated and expressive; and the children's involvement in their learning was obviously enhanced—as was their physical safety on trips and their emotional safety in the classroom.

Chapter 7, on staff development, gives considerable attention to training teachers to become involved in taking psychosocial histories and using these histories to inform their practice in the classroom. The training suggests using coverage by substitutes to give each student's family a 30-minute period in which to talk with their child's teacher about the important stories in the child's life. These story-gathering days provide a structure for parents and teachers to interact around the important stories in a young child's life and emphasize the need to bring teachers into the covenant of confidentiality by which clinicians must abide to ensure that the stories will be used in the children's best interest. When teachers meet with parents with no other agenda except to understand the child's life story, they communicate an openness and message of interest and acceptance that can form the basis of parent–teacher communication for a long time to come.

The story-gathering format offered in chapter 7 encourages teachers to ask a series of questions and record the answers while they are with the parent. Teachers often initially feel uncomfortable doing this and must, of course, begin with their comfort level in order to proceed with confidence. Teachers are often astounded by parents' readiness to talk and by their appreciation for the teacher's interest. That gives teachers a greater comfort level while interviewing parents. The process has something in common with the bibliotherapy process, because the teacher needs to listen to what the parent is saying without judgment or pressure to find immediate solutions. The important part is the listening and the feeling of connection during the interview and the subsequent consideration of how this knowledge can inform classroom practice. A kindergarten teacher who is appalled to hear that one of her students is in her aunt's custody because of repeated sexual abuse by her mother's boyfriend while the mother was working at night cannot change this child's past, but she can make sure rest time at school feels safe and comfortable, and she can express empathy to the aunt, whose challenges in raising the little girl are enormous. A third-grade teacher who becomes aware that several of her students witnessed a terrifying event during a field trip the previous year may listen for that subject if it comes up among the children and will make careful plans for field trips. She will realize that the memory is likely to be reinvoked when the group leaves the building together, and she may invite discussion about it some days before the trip so the children can tell her what happen and she can talk about their being safe during the trip to come. A second-grade teacher who learns that the fathers of five of her students work as building superintendents might decide to embark on a study of apartment buildings and how they stay in good repair. None of this important information is likely to surface without the opportunity for story gathering, although it may well be expressed through children's confusing behavior.

Imagining the Possibilities

Teachers who are committed to the emotional well-being of their students will have ideas about the techniques that will be useful, and those that will be not well suited, for their particular group of children. This chapter does not, of course, cover every possible tool that can enable teachers to promote emotional well-being among their early-grade students. However, it does offer a menu of techniques and practice models and encourages teachers to imagine the possibilities for responsive practice in their own settings. It is the power of the teacher's connection to her group that ultimately brings these technique to life and gives them the personal context necessary to become meaningful and effective.

CHAPTER 10

A Room with a View

Preventive Practice in the Early-Grade Classroom

An Agenda for Morning Meeting

THE CHILDREN in Ms. T's kindergarten classroom were a diverse bunch economically and developmentally. They had become deeply attached to Ms. T over time and were usually able to use her to organize themselves and to be a source of calm when they were excited or anxious. But this morning was different. This morning almost every child who arrived at this neighborhood school was buzzing about a fire that had broken out overnight on a street close to the school. The apartment in which one of the kindergartners, Dahlia, lived had burned down. The children were racing around the room, charged with the excitement of having seen the fire trucks and preoccupied with the trauma of having seen Dahlia and her family wrapped in blankets and taken into the waiting ambulances. Much to Ms. T's surprise, Dahlia arrived just as she was calling the children together for morning meeting. She looked tired and haunted.

Ms. T had planned to use the meeting to talk about a playwriting project that the class was going to begin. However, she knew from experience that trying to distract the children from what they had seen would be counterproductive. Reassuring them would be empty and ineffective, because she had no real information about the fire. They needed to talk about what had happened before they could move on and attend to more neutral matters. She started the meeting by acknowledging this.

Ms. T: Good morning! Before we sing our morning songs and talk about our classroom plans, let's talk about what happened last night.

Several children: There was a fire at Dahlia's house!

Ms. T *(addressing Dahlia, who has said nothing):* Was there?

Dahlia nods.

Ms. T: Do you want to tell us about it?

Dahlia shakes her head.

Ms. T: O.K. You tell me if you want to tell us how it was. Maybe some other children would like to tell us what they saw.

Anthony *(holding up his hand):* Me! I saw a lot of fire trucks! And the firemans got out and shooted water at Dahlia's house!

Anna: I saw the firefighter grab Dahlia from the window and her sister. And they was coughing and the fireman broke down the door and the cat ran down the street.

Mat: I saw smoke, and it made big black clouds in the air, and it made me cough.

At this point, all the children begin to giggle and to pretend to cough.

Ms. T: Alright. I wonder whether Dahlia is ready to talk. I'm thinking that the children saw a lot of what happened, but not everything, and they might have some questions to ask you about the fire. If you come here and sit with me, can you be the one to answer the questions, because I don't really know what happened?

Dahlia nods and sits on Ms. T's lap.

Ms. T: You may each ask Dahlia a question about the fire if you want to, but you have to raise your hand.

Jonathan: Did you go to the hospital?

Dahlia nods.

Amy: Why?

Dahlia *(whispering):* Because I got too much smoke in my body.

Ms. T: Did the doctors give you and your sister oxygen? Did they put a mask over your face to help you breathe better?

Dahlia: Yes.

Tatiana: Who started the fire?

Dahlia: The clothes dryer. It exploded, and fire came out.

Ms. T: Was it on when that happened?

Dahlia shakes her head.

Ms T: Probably gas was leaking from the pipe to the dryer, and that exploded and made the fire start. Then someone called the fire department. . . .

Dahlia *(speaking in a normal tone):* My mama.

Ms. T: Then Dahlia's mommy called the fire department; they rescued Dahlia and her sister and her mom from the building, and they had an ambulance take them to the hospital to give them oxygen so that they could breathe better, and at the same time the firefighters were spraying water on the fire to put it out.

Pierre: Where will Dahlia live now? Where will her toys be?

Dahlia *(with concern and sadness):* At my Nana's house. My toys got burned. I need new ones now.

Tatiana: You can play with my toys. I'll bring a dolly for you.

Several children also raise their hands to volunteer toys.

Ms. T: Is there anything else anyone wants to say about fires?

Several children: I saw a fire before!

My uncle's factory had a fire!

My car had a fire once!

My cousin started a fire by accident because he was playing with matches.

Ms. T and the children listen to the fire stories that the children tell.

Ms. T: A lot of children have seen fires before. The fire that happened at Dahlia's house made many children remember about other fires. Fires can be very scary, and they are always dangerous. We're so happy that Dahlia and her family are safe. *(Everyone claps, and Dahlia smiles broadly.)* But Dahlia might worry about the fire sometimes and think about it, and you might, too. I'm going to make a book with nothing inside yet for everybody's stories and drawings about fires. If you find yourself thinking about fire, you can come over and draw or write in the book.

Peter: I know an idea. Let's make our new play be about a fire!

Several children: Yes! Yes! Dahlia can be the star!

Dahlia again smiles broadly and nods in agreement.

Bibliotherapy in the Classroom

Ms. C teaches a second-grade class in a large city in the U.S. Southeast. Ms. C's class has 27 children who are well described as being at risk from poverty, drug use in the community, and exposure to adult violence and sexuality. Ms. C lived in the same community when she was a child and knows all of the children's extended families. She has strong relationships with the children in her classroom, and this familiarity has helped them to bridge the worlds of home and school. She is a clear and effective limit setter, and when she finds herself being a policewoman instead of a teacher for most of the day, she is wise enough to ask herself and her students what is going on. She is impressed with the fact that, much of the time, the children have something to say, and even when what they say does not reveal the source of their distress, just being asked seems to have a calming effect. Ms. C decides to do two things: First, she will use morning meeting as an open forum for discussion about experience that might be preoccupying the children and making them inattentive and likely to act out; and second, she will engage the services of a mental-health consultant who works in the school so she will have help in addressing what comes out of the open discussions.

Ms. C meets with the consultant before the consultant develops a plan. "I talk to the children every morning, and they have a lot to say," Ms. C. says. "So much happens in their lives between one school day and the next. And so much happened in their lives before they got to me, and it's all just sitting there waiting to come out in one way or another."

Ms. C describes some of the topics that arise in the morning meetings. They include seeing grownups die, being afraid of parental or sibling violence, seeing adults use drugs and experiencing neglect, and going to jail.

The consultant and Ms. C decide to do a collaborative project with the second-graders. The consultant will come to class to read a book about one of the subjects the class has been talking about with Ms. C. If the students want her to continue to read to them about important topics, they can write their names and topic of choice on a list that will be posted in the classroom. The consultant will come by weekly to check the list and will then find books to read to the group addressing these topics.

Ms. C introduces the consultant as a friend, which helps the children feel safe with her. She explains the collaborative plan to the second-graders and tells them that after the day's reading and follow-up session, it will be up to them to decide whether they want to continue and, if they do, what the reading should be about. The consultant posts the list. She then reads a book about having a parent in jail. The children are wide-eyed and attentive. They is no need to ask for quiet or to stop for behavioral intervention.

Consultant: Well, what did you think about that story?

Several children *(with hands waving):* My uncle went to jail and I saw the cops arrest him!

I went to see my daddy in jail, too.

I was in the back yard, and my neighbor Timothy, he ran in and said, "Hide me!" and then he dived into the bushes. Then the cops came, and they was asking me where he be at, and I started crying.

I was visiting my aunt, and then this man came in and they started fighting, and then he shot her in the stomach and then I called 911 and the cops came, and now he's in jail.

The consultant and Ms. C both comment on how scary some of the children's experiences were and how they must think about them a lot.

Kierr: I think about my daddy in jail every day.

Consultant: Maybe during the week you'll think of some more things that the book reminded you of, and you can talk to Ms. C about them at meeting time, or you can write down your stories and draw some illustrations, and we'll make our own book about adults in jail. I'll bring special notebook rings and cardboard for the cover.

Several children: Yeah! We can make our own book.

Consultant: Meanwhile, you might think of other topics that you think about a lot or that make you feel worried. Then you can write those down on this list, and I'll come back and bring a book about it, and we can listen and talk and make some more of our own books.

The children seem enthusiastic. When the consultant checks back at the end of the week, seven suggested topics are on the list: AIDS, death, guns, drugs, scary movies, being left alone, and being in the hospital. The consultant looks for and finds books on each of these topics to read to the group, who talk about their own experiences and feelings and then write and illustrate their collective stories in return.

A Proper Goodbye

When Ms. S found out that she was pregnant, she was ecstatic—until she thought about the possible impact her leaving would have on her classroom of at-risk 6-year-olds. The baby was expected in early May, and Ms. S was advised to work until the beginning of April. That meant leaving the children long before the school year was over. Ms. S had spent September and October building solid relationships with her children, getting to know their stories and attuning herself to their individual developmental levels. She finally felt as if she had the basis for a successful year with them, and knowing how many abandonments they had experienced in their histories, she began to feel increasingly guilty about the pregnancy. She finally spoke to the mental-health consultant in her school building.

> **Ms. S:** What am I doing to them? Can they deal with this? Can they recover from this? I don't know what to do. I'm so happy, but I feel so guilty!
>
> **Consultant:** You can help them deal with it. They've had so many abandonments, but no proper goodbyes. Separation for them has often happened abruptly, tragically, without regard for their feelings. We can do this one differently.
>
> **Ms. S:** But how? When? I can't tell them now, can I? I'm afraid someone will overhear one of the teachers talking, and when I start to show, they'll all figure it out. They know everything about the adult world.
>
> **Consultant:** No, you can't tell them now, for developmental reasons. Before age 7, their sense of time is nonexistent, so it will seem like tomorrow. You have to ask the teachers to be careful about casual references. When you're showing and they notice,

then it's a different story. You'll have to acknowledge their perceptions. But we have a long time before that to start to help with with it.

Ms. S: Good. How?

Consultant: When the time is right, you can talk to them about the baby coming, what babies need, where you will be and what you will be doing when the baby comes, and who will be with them when the baby comes and throughout the last months of the year. But before all that, we have to keep the relationships strong, and we have to help them acquire the developmental tools they need for a meaningful goodbye.

Ms. S: I lost you. What do you mean?

Consultant: How solid is their object constancy, on the whole? Can they think about you when they don't see you? Can they hold your image when they're apart from you?

Ms. S: I don't know. I would think so.

Consultant: Try something with them. Ask them where they think you are when then don't see you. See if they can come up with some imagery.

Ms.S: Alright. But why does that matter?

Consultant: Because if they become attached to you, which they already have, and they have trouble imagining you when you're out of sight, they'll be anxious when they're not with you. If you leave for good, they'll feel bereft. If they can still think about you and feel your connection to them, they'll feel better and do better.

Ms. S: I think you're crazy, but I'll try it, because I can't live with this guilt.

Consultant: Good. Try it.

Ms. S asks the children a question during the next day's morning meeting: "Where do you think I am when you can't see me?" The children look blank. She tries again: "I come to school to see you almost every day. But I don't see you when you're at home, and you don't see me. Every now and then, I miss school. Where do you think I could be when you don't see me?"

The children are silent and thoughtful for a long time. Finally, Gerad responds, "At a funeral." Ms. S was absent once to attend a relative's funeral, and he remembers that.

"Does anyone else have thoughts?" she asks. No one does. "How about Ms. Q?" (Ms. Q is the classroom's assistant teacher.) No one responds.

Ms. S returns to the mental-health consultant. "I was amazed. They couldn't come up with anything. I at least expected someone to say that we lived here at school. Nothing!"

Ms. S and the mental-health consultant decide to use emotionally responsive curriculum to try to help the children with the object-constancy issues that have been compromised by their experiences during developmentally critical periods. Ms. S starts with a curriculum that she calls, "Where Are People When You Don't See Them?" She make a book for the children about all the things she does all day long and all the places she goes, including her home, using photographs for illustrations. Ms. Q, the assistant teacher, does the same. The children are fascinated. They ask many questions about their teachers' lives and experiences and read the books during free periods many times over. Ms. S then invites parents to come in and talk to the children about what they do after they drop the children off at school. The children are also attentive and inquisitive. Even children whose parents work as police officers or school-bus aides appear to have little information about what their parents actually do at work and where they go during the day. The curriculum then focuses on where people are when they leave their classrooms during the school day. The whole class takes a tour of the school building to where their teachers go when they leave the room—the office, the teachers' lounge. They also find where the school custodians go when they are not fixing something in the classroom; where children go when they leave the classroom because they are not feeling well; and where children go when they are taken from the classroom for individual help. The class uses a digital camera to photograph these places and create a book about their discoveries, with the children dictating the captions for each page. Three weeks into the curriculum, the school lunch aide is absent one day. After lunch, Ms. S asks the children where they think Ms. T could be. Several children hold up their hands. "She went to the doctor!" "She ran out of milk for us and had to go to the grocery store." "She got runned over."

Ms. S: Why do you think she got run over?

Devon: Once, my uncle didn't come over for so many days, and then we found out he got runned over.

Ms. S: I don't think Ms. T got run over, but it sounds like what happened with your uncle makes you worry when you don't see people. Does anyone else worry about bad things then they don't see people they expect to see?

Again, many children respond. "I thought you died when you went away before. But then when you came back you said you went to a meeting," says one. "I saw the cops take my auntie away, so when I don't see someone, I think maybe the cops came and took them," says another. A third says, "When I was a baby, they took me away and brought me to the hospital, so when I don't see someone I think maybe they at the hospital."

Ms. S returns to see the mental-health consultant. "This is unbelievable," she says. "Now they have imagery, the kind that we gave them from the curriculum experience and the kind of imagery that has haunted them in a feeling way from their life experience. Maybe this is the reason they have always been impossible at rest time. The lights go out, and they have all this scary imagery. And what about their behavior with substitutes? Horrendous, right? Now I know why."

Ms. S and the consultant decide to proceed with a new version of the curriculum—one that fosters the use of transitional objects to help children feel connected to her and to school, that helps them comfort themselves when they feel overwhelmed by negative imagery, and that encourages them to nurture the baby selves that experienced so much grief and abandonment. They obtain 26 teddy bears, one for each of Ms. S's students. Ms. S distributes the bears, much to the children's amazement. "These are our bears," she says. "We're going to keep them here at school. We're going to take good care of them and make sure they feel safe and comfortable at school. We're going to have them with us at center time and at rest time and sometimes at meeting. But before we can do that, we have to give each bear a name, so we can tell who he is and he knows he belongs to someone. We have to decide how old each one is. We have to make each one a special bed to sleep in, and a special blanket to cover himself with so he's nice and warm."

The children sit cuddling their bears, looking into their faces and bursting with ideas about names and identifying features.

Ms. S begins the curriculum with the naming of the bears, sitting with each child during work time and talking with him or her about choosing a name. She records each child's choice and the child's personal association to the name. At the same time, she gives each child a ribbon to decorate with marker designs to tie around the bear's neck so it will be identifiable. Ms. S then makes a chart with each child's name, his or her bear's name, and a tiny piece of the ribbon that each bear wears around its neck. This leads to a study of the children's names. What do their names mean? How were they chosen? Ms. S invites parents to write the story of choosing their children's names or to come to class to tell the story. Ms. S and Ms. Q themselves research the meaning of the names of the children who are in foster care and have no source of information about how they were named.

The bears sleep with the children at nap time, and the room is calmer than it has ever been. They are part of invited dramatic play in which their caregiving needs, super powers, and adventures are acted out according to the needs of their owners. Each child has a bear diary to record his or her bear's feelings and adventures. Ms. S reads many books that feature bears, such as *Teddy bear tears* and *Good night baby bear,* but reflect children's affects and developmental issues. She also reads *Ira sleeps over* and *My brown bear Barney,* which deal with making transitions. The children are attentive and involved in the discussions that follow.

One morning in January, the children enter as usual and pass Ms. S, who stands at the door as they file in. Tanisha looks at Ms. S for a long time, then says, "Hi. You'll be having a baby soon. You got a baby in there."

Ms. S. gulps. "Yes," she says. "We'll talk about that at meeting time."

The moment of truth has come. Ms. S tells the class that Tanisha is right: There is a baby in there, and it is supposed to be born in May. She wonders what the kids know about babies.

They know a lot: "Babies come from in your body." "I was in my mama's tummy." "Babies grow inside you and then the doctor takes them out." They have a lot of questions: "Is it a boy or a girl?" "What will the baby's name be?" "How did the baby get into your tummy?" "Will it come to school every day?" Ms. S tells the children what she knows and invites them to hypothesize about what she does not know or does not want to answer directly. She promises to bring a book about babies while they are inside and when they were born. She tells them the baby will be too small to come to school every day. It will need a lot of care. She asks, "Does anyone know what babies need once they're born?"

The children verbalize what they know, and Ms. S records their responses on easel paper: "They need bottles." "They need their diapers changed." "They need naps." "They need a special kind of bathtub." "They need baby food." Ms. S suggests that, while they are waiting for her baby to come, they can study babies and what they need, and they can use their teddy bears to play about taking care of babies.

In the months before Ms. S's maternity leave, the class learns about taking care of babies. They make baby food by smashing bananas and pureeing carrots. They bring in disposable diapers and clothing for children who are interested in trying them out with their bears. They made books about what they could do when they were each babies and what they can do now that they are 6 years old. In March, four weeks before Ms. S's leave is scheduled to begin, she tells the class something that they had not assumed: "When the baby is born, I will need to stay home and take care of it. I won't be able to come to school. Ms. Q will still come to be with you every day, and Ms. T will come, too, and they will be your teachers until school is finished." The children looked at Ms. S in astonishment. "But you can get a babysitter!" Michael finally blurts out. Ms. S feels tears coming to her eyes, and she struggles to fight her guilt. "When the baby is a little older, in the fall, I will get a babysitter and come back to work at school. You will be in the second grade already, but you will be able to come in and visit with me and tell me how things are. But we will be together until March is over. Look. I'll write on the calendar when we need to say goodbye. Now, I'll write here on the calendar when the baby is supposed to be born. Then I'll write here on the calendar a week when I will bring the baby in to see you. On this day, when you have your moving-up ceremony, the baby and I will come to watch."

Adriana *(with certainty):* You and the baby will be home, like in our picture book, right? We know where the baby will live.

Ms. S: You do. You and I know a lot of important things about each other. We have to keep thinking about that, even when we don't see each other, and you and Ms. Q and Ms. T have to keep learning more and more important things.

Gerad: But Ms. T don't know what the important things are. She might be mean.

Ms. S: I was worried about you getting a mean teacher, so I talked a lot to our principal, Ms. L, and she let me help choose Ms. T for you, and she's not mean. Ms. Q knows the important things, and she can tell Ms. T some of them, but maybe you'd like us to make a list of the things you'd like Ms. T to know while I'm still here. We still have a lot of days to be together.

Everyone likes this idea, and during meeting for the next couple of weeks, the children add items to the list. Some of them are: "We don't like the dark. We like nightlights at nap time." "We like our bears." "We use a block at meeting to tell whose turn it is to talk." "We celebrate our birthdays with goodies." "We always have center time." "Even though Ms. S is at home, we love her." "We know about babies."

When Ms. S finally says goodbye to the class on her last day, they are able to say goodbye back. She cries, and many of them cry, and she promises to send them a letter from home at the end of the following week. Ms. Q and Ms. T wisely support the children's attachment to Ms. S and do not try to compete with her. Ms. T refrains from saying things such as, "Well, I don't care how Ms. S did it. This is how I do it." Instead, she says, "Am I doing it differently from Ms. S? How did she do it?" The children respond well. They often use center time to write letters to Ms. S or to have their bears draw pictures for her.

The day that Ms. S's daughter is born, the staff is excited, and the children are wild and regressed for the first time since Ms. S's departure. Finally, two days after the news, Ms. Q gets the mental-health consultant. She joins the group's meeting time. "Ms. S's baby came, and everyone is excited," the consultant says. "But maybe you have some worries about it. What do children worry about when a new baby comes?"

"No one takes no more care of you," Reshawn responds matter-of-factly. Many children nod. The mental-health consultant assures them that Ms. Q and Ms. T will keep taking good care of them, and that Ms. S will write or call when she is strong and rested. She points to the week at the beginning of June that Ms. S has marked to come with the baby to visit them. She invites them to write and draw stories about new babies coming in a special blank book she has brought and will leave in the classroom.

The class calms down. Relief is in the air as the children see symbolic ways to express their concerns and interests.

As the school year comes to a close, the consultant checks in on Ms. S's class at intervals. One girl with an extremely troubled history has regressed significantly and is becoming increasingly difficult to contain at school. The other children, all of whom had many risk factors, are thriving. They had said a proper goodbye.

Building a Room with a View

The three teachers discussed in this chapter were able to create classrooms that gave them a view into children's actual life experiences and into their inner lives. These teachers also incorporated therapeutic techniques that facilitated age-appropriate learning in at-risk children by heightening teacher–child attachment relationships and providing children with the symbolic tools that they need to integrate their emotional and actual experiences. Without timely intervention, Dahlia and her classmates might have been preoccupied with experiencing a fire for some time. The preoccupation would have distracted them at school and become an oppressive force contraindicated for emotional wellness. Certainly Ms. C's children would have been increasingly debilitated if they had been left isolated with the traumas that were part of their lives. Most often, traumatized children fail to retain information in a school setting and are often extremely difficult to contain. The teacher's ability to integrate therapeutic technique with sound early-grade use of emergent curriculum gave the children a window that illuminated developmental conflicts and prevented developmental arrest in the face of these difficult experiences. Ms. S's children would have been emotionally wounded by her departure without proper intervention, and, as a result, probably would have declined academically during the second half of the school year, when they needed to be consolidating their gains. Children who felt empowered by the responsive environment in Ms. S's class were attentive, active learners who tapped into their own potential to develop age-appropriate skills to express their feelings about their teacher's impending motherhood.

Many early-grade public-school children who are preoccupied with the kinds of problems and issues that troubled the children in the three classrooms described here are not able to concentrate on schoolwork and fall farther and farther behind as curricular content becomes more and more abstract. Motivation for connection and participation generally diminishes in tandem. Ms. T, Ms. C, and Ms. S knew that drilling children on material that eventually would be included on standardized tests would not prevent this kind of overall deterioration in learning potential and motivation. Investing in the emotional well-being of students and acting to diminish their isolation by addressing their concerns through relationship and curriculum was a more promising avenue of educational practice. Expanding on and generalizing the techniques used by these three teachers may be helpful for many early-grade teachers; these stories, however, by no means provide the only examples of emotionally responsive practice. The possibilities are endless for the teacher who is committed to the emotional health of her students and has administrative support for her progressive practice.

PART IV

A Challenge for Policymakers

TEACHERS AND ADMINISTRATORS *ultimately will not be able to devote energy to promoting schoolchildren's emotional well-being if policymakers support policies that undermine children's mental health. If the pressure continues to abandon mental-health issues in public elementary school in order to focus solely on academics, few schools will be able to stay true to their convictions about the need to focus on emotional well-being as a precursor to academic success. The social and emotional needs of thousands of young children will be neglected at a critical time in their development. These children may become adolescents whose needs will express themselves in potentially dangerous ways that cannot be ignored.*

Schools that are able to maintain their convictions about the primacy of emotional health need to be able to be articulate the connection between well-being and learning so that parents understand the benefits of responsive practice. Part IV illustrates both the benefits of responsive practice and the danger of false advertising on the part of schools whose rhetoric leads parents to believe that they value emotional life when they do not. For children who depend on a supportive school environment, the stakes are too high.

The terrorist attacks on New York City and Washington, DC, on September 11, 2001, taught us that schools that engage continually

in emotionally responsive practice are in a better position to respond to
a community crisis than are schools that are unfamiliar with the lan-
guage of emotional life within the classroom. Schools that have been
affected by disaster can help restore a sense of well-being in the com-
munity by addressing the experiences that children have had and mak-
ing young children's school routines comfortable and developmentally
appropriate. Curriculum in schools that heal does not need to circum-
vent children's reactions to bad things that happen, but can support
children's ability to articulate their reactions and to engage in prosocial
behavior. Many examples of this kind of responsive school practice are
given in Part IV.

Finally, there has been a strong emphasis on the need for more
rigorous standards in public schools as a remedy for a myriad of com-
plex educational problems. Part IV questions both the definition of
appropriate standards and the formulation that standards automati-
cally result in educational practices that benefit children in the early
grades.

CHAPTER 11

The Danger of Institutional Denial

The "As If" School in the Community

The "As If" Concept in Schools

IT IS ALWAYS IMPORTANT to look at how a school describes its educational philosophy on paper and to compare that description with actual observations of school processes. A school that wants to institute emotionally responsive practice must be true to its own ideals; it must look like what it identifies itself to be if it is to be an effective learning environment. If a school is committed to helping children grow and learn but is having trouble accomplishing those goals because it finds itself working with an unfamiliar population, has high turnover in staff, or has suffered from budget cuts that have eliminated effective programs, the responsible administrator will look for additional sources of support. If the school functioned well at one time, its prognosis for doing so again is positive, because the administration has a vision and seeks the wherewithal to realize that vision. However, if the school's description of its educational philosophy is quite different from its actual practice, but this difference is unacknowledged, the disparity between how the school thinks of itself and how it feels to the students will create a gap between truth and falsehood that many children fall into, with tragic results. In this chapter, such schools are considered "as if" schools.

The phrase "as if" was adopted for use in psychoanalysis initially by Alfred Adler, a disciple of Sigmund Freud. "As if" as a psychological concept is defined as "the tendency for a person to act as though he were genuinely superior to others when he is not" (Sutherland, 1989). Many psychoanalysts who followed Adler used "as if personality" to describe very disturbed people who acted as if they were doing what was expected of them but were unable to do these things with genuine feeling (Goldenson, 1984). When schools become "as if" environments, the actual needs of children are rarely acknowledged. The energy of the staff often goes into maintaining the "as if" identity, and when the validity of this identity is challenged by children, parents, or new staff members who need something that they are not getting, the motivation is to get rid of the source of the conflict as opposed to carrying out the written philosophy. "As if" schools are dangerous to the community, because unless they are exposed, no one is motivated for change and the children become the victims of the institutional denial.

A False Start

School X, a public school in a relatively high-need area of a Midwestern city, attracted Ms. K's attention at a public-school employment fair. Ms. K had just earned her master's in education from a prestigious program in the area that was known for devotion to the whole child and for innovative, progressive approaches in the classroom. She wanted to work with children who needed her, and when she picked up a brochure at the fair describing School X as an innovative program with a commitment to each child's well-being, she called for an interview appointment.

The principal of School X welcomed Ms. K after she had done the necessary paperwork. The principal talked at length about what a special place School X was and how fortunate it was to attract a person such as Ms. K who was well educated and had a lot of energy to give the children. She asked Ms. K about her student-teaching experiences and her goals for young children. She said she hoped Ms. K would be interested in a second-grade class. She offered Ms. K the school's mission statement, policy and procedure manual, and other literature describing School X's values, which seemed quite similar to Ms. K's own educational philosophy and values. Ms. K eagerly agreed to a position at School X.

Ms. K got permission to enter the building the week before school began so she could familiarize herself with her room and set it up the way she wanted. She spent a few days sorting through boxes of material, most of which was not in good shape. She made lists of things she needed to order and lists of things she had and could bring in. She organized bulletin boards to post children's work and arranged desks in groups so that children could collaborate on projects and get to know one another. The day before the school officially opened for staff, Ms. K was surprised by a visit from a fellow staff member. She rose to introduce herself but was addressed curtly before she had a chance. The other teacher was angry that Ms. K had requested permission to begin working early. Ms. K tried to explain her motivation, but the other teacher left. Ms. K became anxious and distracted and decided to quit for the day.

On the first staff day, Ms. K was introduced to her colleagues at a staff meeting. She was warmly welcomed by some teachers and felt slighted by others. Ms. K was a racial minority in that particular school, and she wondered whether that was a factor in the reception she felt. She sat anxiously, trying to listen to the many beginning-of-the-year rituals and paperwork requirements that the principal was explaining. She heard nothing about the kind of commitment to children that she had heard about in the interview. She wished the children would come in right away, because she felt that once the children were present, the staff politics would take a back seat.

The children finally arrived on Thursday. Ms. K met the children as they came in and spoke briefly with the parents who accompanied them. As the children took their seats, Ms. K began to feel overwhelmed by the little bit of information that she had taken in from her brief introductions. Her class contained three boys who had been held back and were huge compared with the other children. One mother spoke critically about her son's teacher the previous year, who had called her at work nearly every day because she could not control the boy. A foster parent pulled Ms. K aside to explain that her foster daughter sometimes wet her pants, and they believed this was related to seizures or to the sexual abuse that she had suffered in her biological parents' home.

As the day progressed, Ms. K's head began to throb. Five children in the class were impossible to contain and required constant attention; without it, they endangered themselves and other children. The girl with the foster mother wet her pants and the floor twice and became tearful and terrified when ridiculed by the other children. Ms. K used all of her skills to proceed through the day in a way that would help set the tone for the year to come and focus the children on their initial class project. She dismissed the children at 3 P.M., relieved that they were gone so she could talk to the administration about her experience and the children's needs and strategize about staffing and support services. Ms. K knocked on the principal's door, but the office staff told her that the principal was unavailable—and would be unavailable for the rest of the afternoon. Ms. K persistently asked to see the assistant principal and finally was allowed to go to her office after waiting for 45 minutes. The assistant principal listened to Ms. K's description of her class for a few minutes. "Close your door," the assistant principal said finally.

Ms. K stared at her in disbelief. "We have to figure out what to do with this group," she said. "These kids shouldn't all be together. There's no balance. It's not in their best interest. Weren't most of them known to the school from first grade? Only Tina is listed as being new. Who is in charge of grouping?" The assistant principal responded: "Now, Ms. K, relax. It's only your first day, and you're a new teacher. It takes a while to get things together. You'll do just fine with them. Why don't you use your prep to watch Ms. R, one of the the other second-grade teachers who has been here for a while?" Ms. K agreed to do that and left, incredulous at the administrative response. Was it only her anxiety and her imagination? Or had she been given a classroom with children whose needs were impossible to meet in a group of this size?

The second day was also hellish. The boys escalated their aggressive, provocative behavior, which might have been designed to test Ms. K's ability to survive them. She decided to use the school counselor and filled out referral forms for three of the boys. Tina's wetting accidents continued, and Ms. K took her to the nurse after the first one so she would be well attended. During the prep period, Ms. K stepped into Ms. R's second-grade class. She was amazed to see a group of relatively well-functioning children attending to Ms. R's lesson. She was also amazed to see that Ms. R was drilling the children as a whole group and had nothing at all that seemed innovative or child-centered in her room, in spite of School X's claim that is was known as an innovative school.

Ms. K wandered into the office to look in her box. She noticed Martha, one of the secretaries. "Who places children?" she asked Martha quietly. Martha gestured toward the assistant principal's door. Ms. K looked at her wide-eyed."Why would she put all the needy children together?" Ms. K asked. "The manual says you don't do tracking here." Martha responded simply, "Oh, well, you know that Ms. I [the assistant principal] and Ms. R are best friends, so she gets all the good kids." "*What?*" said Ms. K, gasping with disbelief. "Shush," said Martha, who had returned to her computer.

Ms. K went home feeling dizzy and confused. She felt as if she had been had. She had been courted and wooed, and now she was stuck. She did want to do right by this classroom of difficult children, but it seemed impossible. Maybe a more experienced teacher could manage it, but she was not sure that she could. She was pretty sure none of the friends she had made in graduate school had chosen public school for their first jobs. Maybe this was why. She fell asleep exhausted and troubled. She dreamed about the children.

The next day Ms. K woke up with a sore throat and a fever. She reluctantly called in for a substitute, worried about the state her classroom would be in when she returned. After being diagnosed with strep throat and starting antibiotics, Ms. K was well enough to return to school. She was shocked when she entered her classroom. She walked out to look at the room number to make sure that it really was her classroom. It had been entirely rearranged. The desks were in traditional classroom rows; the bulletin boards were void of students' work and full of pre-made slogans and calendars; and the material that she had brought in had been taken off the shelves and stored in a box under her desk. Ms. K stormed into the office and happened to catch the principal while her secretary was out of the office. "What happened to my room?" Ms. K demanded. The principal looked up from her paperwork. "We rearranged it for parent night," she said calmly. Ms. K looked at her, not understanding. "Why?" she persisted. "Our parents like a more traditional approach," the principal responded.

"You told me you wanted me because I could offer a different approach," Ms. K answered. "You told me that School X was known for innovation and for being committed to every child. And yet you let the assistant principal place the kids according to the preference of a teacher who is her best friend instead of according to the needs of the kids. I don't understand."

The principal glanced at Ms. K and returned to her paperwork. Finally, she said, "You're overwrought. We couldn't ask you about the room arrangement because you were out."

"I was out sick. I'm well now. I want my room the way it was."

"Rearrange it after tonight then," replied the principal.

"But that would give the parents the impression that that's the way I teach. It's not true," Ms. K replied in exasperation.

"I have to make a call," said the principal, returning to her inner office.

Ms. K stood there for a moment. Then she borrowed a pen and a piece of paper from Martha and wrote her letter of resignation.

False Hope

Annique was a 7-year-old girl in Ms. K's class. She had been so happy to find that Ms. K was her teacher. Ms. K seemed nice. She let Annique sit with her best friend, Monica, and she let Annique write stories. Annique loved to write. What Annique did not like to do was talk. She rarely spoke in school, and she never spoke to teachers. This pattern had begun in kindergarten at Annique's old school, and Annique's mother had had her transferred partly in the hope that a fresh start in a new place might make it easier for Annique to start speaking at school. That is what a school psychologist had recommended. The school psychologist had also asked Annique's mother a lot of questions about Annique's early experiences, but Annique's mother did not know all of the details, because Annique had been in the South for the first few years of her life, living with her grandparents and uncles while her mother was working in the city.

Annique's mother had toured a few schools in the neighborhood and had chosen this school because it seemed to care about the children. The other schools had been alright, but this one had a cheerfully painted mission statement hanging over the front entrance that read, "School X Is Committed to Every Child Achieving" All of the bulletin boards in the hallways and in the classrooms were decorated with printed slogans such as, "Children Are Our Best Hope for the Future," "Each Child Has Special Gifts," "Every Child Can Learn," and "We Believe in Children!" The other schools did not communicate as much about their values.

Annique came home energetic and content after the first few days of school. Then something changed. She seemed depressed and apathetic. Her mother asked what had happened. "Ms. K was out today," Annique answered. Her mother assumed that Ms. K was sick. She did not receive a note indicating that Ms. K had resigned. She assured Annique that Ms. K would be back soon.

The string of substitutes who covered Ms. K's class had difficulty maintaining any kind of order. They soon resorted to repressive tactics to contain the children, including screaming in their faces, demeaning them, banging rulers on their desks, and grabbing the children and throwing them into the hallway. On one particularly difficult afternoon, following a confrontation with one of the aggressive boys, the substitute demanded that Annique answer a question about the reading. Annique stood up to answer. She knew the answer, but she could not make the words come out of her mouth. She felt terrified. "Do you know?" the substitute demanded. Annique nodded. "Then tell us. You are wasting time," said the substitute. Annique stood silent and motionless. The substitute, whose patience had been exhausted much earlier in the day, slapped Annique in the face. The other children shouted. Annique stood still and silent as if nothing had happened. She had already removed herself from the situation psychologically and was only partly present. Her lack of response further enraged the substitute, who shouted, "Do you want more?" The principal, who happened to be passing by, opened the door. "What is happening here?" she asked. All the children started talking at once. "She hit Annique across the face, and Annique didn't do nothing." The principal dismissed the substitute at once and took over the class for the rest of the day. She settled Annique near her desk and gave her a connect-the-dots book that she had in her bag. She told the children that the substitute would not be back. They would have a new teacher who would start the next day. Ms. K was not coming back, either.

Annique worked on each page of the connect-the-dots book carefully until the pictures emerged clearly. She did not look up. She did not register affect when she heard that Ms. K would not be returning. She sat in a dissociated state, removed from her inner world and the world around her. She was surprised when she was dismissed to the nurse's office because she had defecated in her pants. "You tell the nurse what you did, a big girl like you!" chastised the principal. The other children laughed. Annique went to the nurse, who called her mother to come and pick her up, after threatening to put a diaper on her. "Ms. K's not coming back," she told her mother flatly. She never mentioned that the substitute had slapped her. The principal never called about the incident. Annique's mother did not find out for weeks.

Annique had a tantrum when it was time to go back to school the next day. Her mother requested permission to go into the classroom with her and stay for the morning. She was told that this would be too disruptive, but she could stay for the first half-hour. The new teacher, Ms. M, seemed pleasant enough. She gave the children a schedule of the day in case it differed from what they had done with their old teacher. She seemed organized, somewhat experienced, and familiar with second-grade curriculum. Annique's mother decided to try to talk with to Ms. M about Annique's sensitivity and her difficulty with speaking in school. She approached the teacher during the children's seat work. The teacher stopped her. "Don't worry about Annique in my room," Ms. M said. "I treat every child exactly the same. And I'm fair. She'll have the same chances as everyone else." Annique's mother tried again: "Yes, I know, and that's good. But Annique has special needs that most people don't notice right away, and . . ." Ms. M reassured Annique's mother: "I've been a teacher for 22 years. I know what to do with all kinds of children. Now, go on to work, and don't worry. Annique will be fine in here." Annique's mother reluctantly went to work.

The new teacher sat Annique next to Tina and put them both in the back of the room. "That way you'll be close to the hallway, near the bathroom," she told them. Annique did not respond. She missed sitting near Monica. She did not like Tina. She decided to write a story. While the new teacher was in front of the room talking about something, she got her pad of paper out and wrote about a girl who was in the jungle and who feared that a tiger might pounce on her. She sat writing furiously, absorbed and productive, until the teacher suddenly grabbed the pad of paper, startling Annique. "What are you doing, Annique? This is not time to write; it's time to listen." Annique sat silently, looking straight ahead. "Annique, you have to answer me when I talk to you. It's not polite to ignore someone." Annique could not respond. The teacher angrily tore up Annique's story and put it in the garbage. Then she took Annique out of her seat and stood her in the front of the room. "You can sit down when you decide to answer me," Ms. M said calmly. Annique stood silently, staring at the board. She was looking at the shadows that the erased chalk had made. She was vaguely aware of the hot mess flowing into her underwear, then dripping down her legs. The other children taunted and teased; the teacher called the office for the nurse to come and remove Annique and took the other children out of the room to the library.

Annique's mother was called and informed that Annique was being put on home instruction pending an evaluation for special education. Children had to be toilet trained to attend School X or had to have a special paraprofessional attending her. Annique's mother protested that Annique certainly was toilet trained, and that something must be happening to cause her to react this way. She had tried to talk to the teacher, who had not wanted to listen. The principal responded, "School X is not the place for a child like Annique."

False Promises

School X's false promises were destructive to the teachers, parents, and children. The false promises created a mask for the actual emotional climate at School X, which certainly was organized not for the well-being of the children, or even of the teachers, but apparently for the well-being of those in the school who were powerful or had special privilege because of their connections to those with the power. Although all schools have a number of children with recognized special needs and with challenging behavioral problems, there are many more children in every classroom who have less overt needs and for whom the school experience determines the level at which they are able to function. For these children, making a good match between school and child and teacher and child is critical. A solid match may affect a child's outcome not only in terms of academic learning, but also in terms of overall functioning and emotional well-being. Sometimes parents know this and attempt to sort out what is available to their children within the public-school system that can support their children. Sometimes teachers know this and look for a fellow teacher at the next grade level who can receive the emotionally fragile children in the classrooms and do well by him or her. Thus, it is extremely important for schools to represent themselves accurately.

"As if school" can have extremely debilitating effects for those who survive them and who remain part of them, not only on those like Ms. K and Annique, who could not survive and left. An "as if school" teaches more than academics. It teaches children that what adults say is not necessarily what they mean. It teaches them that external presentation does not necessarily convey real feeling. It teaches them to mistrust adults, to be suspicious of their environment, and to hide their real feelings so that they can fit into the acceptable structure. It provides an atmosphere that can make both children and teachers anxious by simultaneously telling them that they are valued and acting to devalue them. Teachers may or may not be able to survive this kind of environment with a sense of self-worth and personal mission. Children cannot survive this kind of environment without injury, because their evolving self-image and powers of personal initiative are still developing. The combination of being told that they are valued while they are being demeaned will have the insidious effect of making them feel that they are bad and worthless, because if they were "good enough" they would become valued, as the posters promise.

The children at School X deserved and required a teacher like Ms. K, who had energy, initiative, education, and commitment. But School X's false promises make it unlikely that any teacher with Ms. K's qualifications and commitment will want to stay. Yet teachers may initially be attracted to School X and have a false start, as Ms. K did. Ms. K's personal strengths allowed her to pursue her desire to teach in the public sector, and after a few weeks of feeling depressed and angry, she carefully sought a position in a school whose values were similar to her own. No slogans, store-bought posters, or statements adorned this school's halls. Instead, the school had administrators who articulated their missions, teachers who demonstrated the mission every day in the classroom, and children who thrived on the mission and showed the results in the work hanging on each of the school's bulletin boards. Ms. K learned how to look for truth in public schools. Annique's mother is still searching.

CHAPTER 12

The Responsive School During Crisis

What We Are Learning from September 11

WHEN THREATS to the well-being of children and families comes from an external source and is visited on society without warning and with devastating results, as occurred in New York City on September 11, 2001, the school faces a great challenge to protect and respond to its children and families. At the time of this writing, the horrifying consequences of the terrorist attack in New York City were only beginning to unfold. The role of schools on that terrible day, and the role of schools on each day that has followed, has been significant and has had the potential to ameliorate the long-term effects of the event for thousands of early-grade schoolchildren and their families.

The September 11 attack shook our deepest beliefs about the strength and security of our nation, overwhelmed us with the realization of our own vulnerability, and in an instant shattered our trust in our ability to keep our children safe. Many Americans who do not live in urban areas may imagine that New York City is a dangerous place and one that is not healthy for raising children, but most city residents do not hold those views and do not generally feel that they or their children are endangered in their own home town. In fact, the part of the city most directly affected by the attack was an affluent neighborhood in which the local public schools are considered safe, secure learning environments with excellence academic records and developmentally appropriate teaching practices. Many parents were just delivering their children to school when the first plane crashed into the World Trade Towers and rushed back to school to retrieve them, only to take them out into streets that became a scene of trauma and panic when the second plane hit.

When New Yorkers tells their stories about that horrifying event, they often refer to their children's school: "Thank God for my son's school"; "We went back into the school and stayed all together"; "Thank God, my daughter's school stayed open all day and all night for parents who couldn't get over the bridge to come to pick their children up." For many families, the school became a refuge on that terrible day.

Educators talk about the overwhelming responsibility they felt toward the children and families on that day, and the terrible conflict they felt as spouses, parents, and grandparents who were unsure of the whereabouts of their own family members but could not leave the children in their care to find out what was happening. Because most public schools have only one or two phone lines, and many cell phones were not working that day, they could not get access to the vital information they needed without leaving the school. Yet few educators, administrators, or clinicians left their buildings on September 11. The schools needed to function as ports in the storm for young children and their families, and the people who work in the schools knew it. Attentive principals and clinicians all over the city met distraught parents at schools' front doors and discouraged them from entering classrooms in panic and fleeing with their children. Instead, some principals provided coffee and doughnuts, encouraged parents to talk with one another, and invited the families to stay at the school with the children, where they would be safe and could feel relatively calm.

Among the heroic stories that have emerged from this tragedy are those of educators who were taking care of our children during the crisis. But apart from parents who experienced the power of the schools' embrace on September 11, few Americans recognize the rescue efforts carried out by teachers, administrators, and clinicians or acknowledge their personal sacrifices as people who had to make the well-being of the children in their care their priority, even as they longed to be reunited with their own families or be reassured of their safety.

What Comes Next

The day after the attack, all of New York City's schools were closed. The schools in direct proximity to the World Trade Center site have remained closed, and the children have been reassigned to other buildings. Children who went to school in other parts of downtown Manhattan could not attend school for a week because only rescue vehicles were allowed. Therefore, the beginning of the school year was disrupted for every schoolchild in New York City, and for some, the disruptions were extreme. On September 11 and on the following days that schools were closed, young children most often encountered adult affects of fear, sadness, worry, and shock.

As buildings began to reopen and children and teachers returned to school, they brought with them issues that would affect their functioning for many months and years to come. In some neighborhoods, children, parents, and teachers had watched the planes hit the towers, had seen people jumping to their deaths, and had run to escape falling debris as the buildings collapsed. Many of those traumatized children found themselves with their classmates but in different school buildings, often doubled up with other classes in the same grade. In other neighborhoods, scores of firefighters and police officers were missing and presumed dead. Some schools had bereaved children. Others had bereaved teachers. Still other children were not touched personally but began reacting to the grim mood that had come over the city and to the signs from adults that all was not well and perhaps never would be well again. Parents who had already helped their children to separate and feel comfortable in the school setting were unwilling to leave their children. Children who had been willing to separate became unwilling to leave frantic parents whose livelihood had been affected by the tragedy and were desperate to get to work. School-based clinicians held workshops and informal groups for parents to advise them on anticipating changes in their children's behavior, to provide reassurance, to decrease their exposure to the media, and to give them opportunities to talk about their experiences and worries. Many school-based clinicians met within their districts while the schools were closed to organize a response in the schools once they reopened. Thus, almost all of New York City's schools planned to address the aftermath of the crisis within their buildings, yet the way that these plans were carried out with early-grade children were as varied as the schools themselves.

Almost everyone agreed from the outset that older children needed a forum to discuss what had happened. But soon after the tragedy, many parents, teachers, and administrators began denying that the events had affected very young children. Even administrators who had been the most active about making their building into shelters on September 11 had difficulty acknowledging the ongoing effects of the tragedy on young children. Many teachers were told not to talk about September 11 in pre-kindergarten and kindergarten unless the children themselves brought up the subject. Children in first, second, and third grade were dealt with using a wide variety of techniques that ranged from allowing one discussion on the day after the events, then forbidding further dialogue, to creating classrooms that integrated writing, drawing, and fund raising into the curriculum and helped children feel that they were part of the support network for rescue efforts.

The crisis in New York brought out many myths about trauma that are pervasive in our society, even among those who are educated to work with children. One such myth is that trauma has a greater impact on older children and adults than on young children or infants and toddlers. Another myth is that young children will forget such an event easily if they are not reminded of it. In reality, such events have an insidious effect on society's youngest members when they experience the trauma firsthand (Terr, 1992). Although children younger than 28 months may not have verbal memories of a traumatic event, evidence of the event will be present in their dreams, play content, and behavioral reenactments (Terr, 1992). Children older than 28 months may have verbal memories, and if they felt helpless and endangered during the event, they are likely to stay preoccupied with it in a way that consumes their mental space and decreases their attention to other input. Single-incident trauma may cause children to remain so preoccupied that they will not concentrate well and therefore will not retain in school. These children may also show other symptoms of post-traumatic stress disorder, such as hyperarousal, hypervigilance, flashbacks, panic attacks, and traumatic play. Thus, these children may well bring the trauma into the classroom, regardless of whether it is invited and of whether it is recognized by staff members.

For many children who had traumatic histories before September 11, the World Trade Center attack brought back feelings from prior traumas and may have left them overwhelmed, vulnerable, and driven to talk about other disturbing events. Therefore, it is likely that early-grade teachers will be confronted with the ripples of this disaster in their students for a long time, and it is incumbent on early-grade teachers, administrators, and clinicians to plan a response that is well suited developmentally to their young students. Without a planned response that invites children to be expressive, children who have been negatively affected are likely to escalate their acting out or show diminished capacity to pay attention in school. Even more troubling is the possibility that, in the absence of adult acknowledgment and support, children will remain frightened and worried but become isolated with their fears.

Unfortunately, the World Trade Center attacks were of such magnitude that they traumatized the young children who observed them but also resulted in traumatic loss on a large scale for many families. Many schools in New York City had grieving children, teachers, or other staff members. Bereaved teachers struggle over the degree to which they should make their losses public; classmates of bereaved students struggle to show compassion toward their peers while trying to maintain their own fragile sense of security. Teachers struggle to address death in the classroom in a way that they find comfortable and the children find meaningful. Everywhere in the schools the disaster's ripples widen as the days go by, as they do in the broader society.

Actualizing Our Commitment to Well-Being in School

The horror of what happened on September 11 will force us to respond to children's emotional needs at school. It will also force us to address and invest in the emotional well-being of teachers as they struggle to continue their mission while feeling sadness, depression, and fear. In this chapter, I will explore a continuum of responses for addressing the essential well-being of both teachers and children in New York City and beyond. These responses will include arenas for dialogue about the event and its aftermath, assessment for risk, community building, emotionally responsive routines, proactive responses directly related to the disaster and its victims, and life-affirming curriculum. These responses will have to unfold on parallel tracks so they can be made available to staff members as well as to the children and parents who make up the school community.

Business as Usual

One possible response to the aftermath of the World Trade Center disaster that many schools are likely to adopt is to proceed with a business-as-usual approach. Surely, there is some comfort in returning to what is felt to be normal and usual during a traumatic and tumultuous time. Many children were relieved to be able to go back to school. Although separation anxiety may have been heightened for the youngest children, older children felt reassured by the familiarity of school routines and some level of activity that did not focus on the tragedy. Parents who were almost desperate to believe that they had been able to shelter their children from most of the impact of September 11 also felt comfortable with having the children return to an environment that was untouched by what had happened.

Schools that choose the business-as-usual approach must be mindful of the need to make sure that the "usual" structure is adhered to but also used as a strategy for containing the anxiety that children, parents, and especially staff members are likely to bring with them into the building. The existing structures and routines should be thought about carefully to consider which have comforting and containing value and which have potential to invite children and others in the school community to express themselves in a comfortable and appropriate way. For example, School Y holds a monthly assembly for the entire lower school and wants to keep this routine going, perhaps to use this arena to address the events of September 11 in some way. The first assembly following the tragedy might focus on the topic of heroes and how much we need heroes in our everyday lives. The special teacher who teaches art to each group in the school may want to postpone her usual fall agenda to allow art to become a medium for children who want to express their feelings about what happened. The social worker who usually holds a parent seminar about separation anxiety in the early grades in the fall might want to expand her topic to focus on separation anxiety in the aftermath of September 11. Thus, School Y can proceed with its usual rhythms, routines, and structures, but also use these structures to support people's coming to terms with what has happened instead of using these structures to deny that there is an aftermath.

Schools seeking a business-as-usual approach will find a balance between including new and timely themes and enhancing usual topics and curricula for their life-affirming value. Carving a pumpkin, harvesting its seeds for cooking and planting, and making pumpkin pie for a classroom celebration are all energy-giving, life-affirming activities that should not be surrendered to terrorism. Cutting jack-o'-lantern faces out of paper that all have the same happy smile denies the variation of affects that children carry and that they need to project, especially in times of crisis. Cutting out jack-o'-lantern faces with varied affects chosen by individual artists preserves the tradition and simultaneously supports the emotional life of the child.

Like all schools, schools that choose a business-as-usual approach will have certain daily routines that do not vary, such as lunch time, rest time for the youngest children, and yard time. These routines should remain intact but will need to take a softer tone to be calming to the children and to the teachers and paraprofessionals who are participating in them. Administrators should be mindful that everyone in their school buildings will feel some nervousness for some time. These feelings will be made worse by loud sounds, abrupt physical activity, and so on. Existing routines can be made more intimate and calmer by adding homelike features. Rest time can be accompanied by soft music, nightlights, and teddy bears. Cafeteria time can be enhanced through stable seating locations, seating adults at tables with young children, family-style decorations for young children or a restaurant motif for older children, classical music, and an age-appropriate plan to engage children who are finished eating before their peers (see chapter 5). For the business-as-usual approach to be viable during a tumultuous and potentially dangerous time, administrators and teachers will have to give the routines and structures that they seek to preserve careful attention in order to enhance their strength and value. The rhythms and routines of the school will survive the uncertainty of the world outside the building if they can serve a reassuring and protective function. If the usual rhythms and routines of the school produce anxiety in children, and they continue as usual in an unstable environment, they will further aggravate post-traumatic phenomena and create an untenable situation for children and staff members

Expanded Mental-Health Services

Another possible response to the disaster is to expand the role of mental-health professionals in the school and increase the school population's access to mental-health professionals in the community. Schools may want to put various services in place, including preventive services for teachers, parents, and children and clinical services for those staff members, children, and families who have been the most profoundly affected. For instance, the school social worker might hold an evening meeting for parents about dealing with the tragedy and invite those who are interested to participate in an ongoing group. An outside agency might run a support group for teachers who are interested in attending. A school might decide to use bibliotherapy in all classrooms to invite children to express their feelings, thoughts, and worries about the tragedy as a form of preventive intervention. They might follow up the bibliotherapy sessions by implementing emotionally responsive Curricula that help children integrate their experience further and feel safer in the school environment. These projects might bring out reactions indicating that some children are at risk and would benefit from more intensive clinical attention. Those children could be referred to on-site clinicians, who would contact their families to get consent and connect to parents as a foundation for their intervention.

Administrators who know that their school population is characterized by many risk factors should expect a community tragedy to remind children and families of prior traumas and other losses. Teachers who might not expect their particular classes to be profoundly affected because no one suffered direct losses or connections should be aware that the tragedy and exposure to the imagery of the event might elicit overwhelming feelings of insecurity as well as connections to feelings about more personal losses and tragedies. Thus, a class of urban second-graders invited to discuss their reactions to the World Trade Center tragedy with an on-site therapist might spend 5 minutes talking about the event and 40 minutes recalling shootings and car crashes in their families and community. The clinician should understand that many of the children in that classroom have experienced multiple traumas and allow them to talk about those experiences, which are so readily accessible in the aftermath of terror.

Take, for example, the Head Start director in a Hispanic neighborhood who notes that many of her staff members in apparent distress after September 11 are Hispanic mothers of young children. The women seem to be experiencing extreme anxiety over separation from their children and are distracted at work. She engages a mental-health provider to offer a group in Spanish and English for that contingent of her staff, as well as for single staff members who, she perceives to be at risk because their support networks may be more fragile than those of staff members who live in family households.

Schools that choose to expand the clinician's role in response to community crisis will need the school administrator to articulate her vision concerning educational–clinical collaboration. If there is no clear administrative vision, teachers may feel intruded on and undervalued at a time that it is important for everyone to understand their professional potential and feel their personal worth. If clinicians are to take on an expanded role in the school community in response to the community's mental-health needs after a tragedy, time must be set aside for teachers and clinicians to communicate during the school day. If clinicians are to serve children well, they will need teachers' valuable perceptions and group-management skills. To provide an emotionally responsive environment during tragic times, teachers will need to consult clinicians about the meaning of the behavior, drawings, narratives, and play that they are seeing in the classroom. If necessary, administrators can devote meeting time that is usually used to address grade-level or curricular issues to teacher–clinician communication until the need diminishes.

Emotionally Responsive Curriculum

Teachers may want to use curricular avenues to help children process what has happened while they are in school. The curricular approach guarantees that children will be less distracted in the aftermath of crisis because the crisis itself will become part of the curricular focus. Thus, the teacher will not be attempting to compete for the attention of children whose internal preoccupations diminish their capacity to take in external input. Because a curricular focus allows the teacher's agenda to mirror the children's agendas, both learning and emotional resilience are likely to be enhanced.

Teachers may doubt the feasibility of addressing such a profoundly tragic event as the World Trade Center attacks with early-grade children. Some may not know how to go about it, while others may feel anxious about what the curriculum will bring up for the children. Still others may feel an obligation to make the tragic event understandable to the children or to enhance feelings of patriotism in the classroom.

Teachers who want to use a curricular approach to deal with a community tragedy can use the principles of inviting and containing that were introduced in chapter 7. They must find a way to invite dialogue about what happened within the containing structure of the group. The invitation is easier to extend than most teachers imagine and can be extended at all developmental levels. While a third-grade teacher can say, "I know everyone has been seeing the news and hearing their parents talk about what happened in our city. I wonder if anyone has anything they'd like to say about it?" a kindergarten teacher might say. "I remember Tuesday, when parents were coming to pick children up early, and everyone looked upset and worried. Does anyone want to say more about what happened on that day?" A pre-kindergarten teacher whose children started school just a day before September 11 waited until the children had been in school long enough to feel grounded. He then brought the matter up in a morning meeting, saying, "A lot has been going on for kids these days. Some of you are new to our school. Some of you went on vacation during the summer. Some of you know about things that have been happening in our city and have been on the news. Does anyone have anything to say about any of that?" Although the invitation was global, every single child responded in terms of the World Trade Center. By extending these kinds of invitations in school, the teacher gives the message that the meeting can contain the responses that the children give.

Readers may wonder what pre-kindergarten children actually had to say about the tragedy. Many of their responses included direct statements of fact, such as, "An airplane flew into the World Trade Center, and it fell down." Some were attempts to integrate explanations given to them by adults: "Bad guys who live in another country and are jealous of our country did that." And some showed the children's own process of perceptual intelligence at work as they try to integrate what they are taking in: "Everyone was so sad, and they put the flag out and sang America's favorite song." Some children's responses indicated that they had not taken the event in as a real, as opposed to a fictional, occurrence: "I saw that movie! My sister was scared of that movie, but I wasn't."

The teacher said very little during the discussion, except to refer occasionally to the possibility that these events were scary. He listened to how the children understood what had happened and how they might be feeling about what happened, but he did not attempt to give them information. After all of the children had had a chance to say what they wanted to say, he told them that they would stop talking for now but that they might want to talk again later or on another day.

A kindergarten teacher whose class had received teddy bears from an organization that was distributing bears to New York City public-school children in the aftermath of the attack introduced the bears at a morning meeting. As it happened, the meeting was held the day after an American Airlines plane crashed into a neighborhood in the New York City borough of Queens. The teacher said, "Some people who live far away were thinking about the scary thing that happened in our city and were thinking about what they could do to help New York City children feel safer, and. . . ." Several children held up their hands, and when the teacher continued to speak, some blurted out: "A plane to the Dominican Republic crashed!" "A lot of people got hurt or died." "My papi was going to take that plane but he decided not to." "I saw the planes that knocked the buildings down." "I remember the day that the planes knocked the buildings down and there were bad guys flying the planes, and now the police put them in jail." The teacher intervened here to confirm that the World Trade Center disaster was caused by bad guys but that the plane to the Dominican Republic had crashed by accident. She then continued by explaining that the children had been sent bears, by distributing the bears, and by introducing a curriculum for their use (see p. 185).

Many teachers were not prepared to invite discussion about the events surrounding their classes and were indeed advised to leave the subject alone unless the children brought it up. They then found themselves at a loss when the children did bring the subject up spontaneously. For example, a classroom that had suffered the loss of a first-grade child in the American Airlines crash was lining up to go to the library. "Everyone find their partner," advised the teacher. "I can't find my partner," a boy replied. "She was killed in a plane crash." The teacher burst into tears and left the room, and the school social worker was sent for to help the children, who were able to use drawing and writing to express their feelings about their loss and about their personal safety.

Because emotionally responsive curriculum practice often incorporates the use of transitional objects in early-grade classrooms to help children with unresolved developmental issues, it can be adapted easily for use in a tragedy. Curricula developed for the New York City Board of Education on the use of teddy bears in pre-kindergarten through eighth grade classrooms are included later in this chapter as examples for teachers and administrators who are interested in helping schoolchildren who have experienced an overwhelming event.

Enhanced School Community

The school community in itself may become a heightened focus in the aftermath of tragedy because it is an important constant in what feels like a shaken world. Efforts to build community in the aftermath of a tragedy that has political implications may feel more problematic for a diverse school population than community building following a flood, earthquake, or other natural disaster. Indeed, members of the student body or staff members may identify with the culture of those who committed the terrorist acts and experience conflict or discrimination due to their cultural identification. Therefore, it is essential for diverse school communities to teach tolerance in the classroom and to articulate the vision of tolerance and unity to the parent population (Morris, 2001; Seikaly, 2001)

In addition, community-building events that are not necessarily related to the disaster can help people feel less isolated and more reassured that life can still be joyful and connections can remain strong, even during stressful times. Parent, child, and staff singalongs; potluck dinners; quilting bees; outings; and retreats can be enormously powerful during times of stress. Administrators, teachers, and school-based clinicians who want to enhance community building as a response to tragedy may want to consider starting a small committee of staff members who are interested in planning events and structuring their implementation. This may be necessary because it is difficult to rely on voluntary participation from the parents and staff members who are usually active when everyone is feeling stressed and experiencing difficulty meeting their day-to-day obligations. Once an event has been held and is successful in heightening the school community's feeling of connection, momentum for planning and participation in implementation may grow.

Discrete events can be energizing and reassuring to a school community in times of crisis, but they need to complement an increased commitment to providing children, parents, and staff with an emotionally safe school environment. Teaching tolerance is one way to enhance emotional safety of people who may belong to minority groups within the school community. Many other avenues are also available for supporting emotional safety throughout a school building that can help protect a school community during trying times. These include the many staff-focused interventions elaborated in earlier chapters that allow staff members to be reflective about their practice and about the quality of their interactions with children. They also include administrative attention to the staff's well-being and administrative implementation of policies and routines that support staff as well as children. Although we may be motivated to give more attention to fostering emotionally safe school environments in response to crisis, enhancing the capacity of staff to create such an environment is in reality a long-term project that cannot be implemented on the spur of the moment. A core principle of the emotionally safe school environment is a commitment to supporting emotional reality and to promoting emotional truth. Therefore, if a teacher extends an invitation to children to talk about crisis but does so under pressure and really cannot tolerate the discussion, the milieu becomes emotionally unsafe, and the discussion is likely to be inhibited or to go out of control. The schools that will be in the best position to be responsive in a time of crisis, therefore, are the ones that have taken a preventive approach and have invested in developing their capacity for supporting emotional well-being in the best, as well as the worst, of times. These are the schools that have the courage to invest resources in the mental health of their population, even when it is not a popular focus. These are the schools that our nation can be proud of.

Guidelines for Using Teddy Bears in Emotionally Responsive Classroom Practice

Many charitable organizations across the United States responded to the September 11 tragedy by sending teddy bears to New York City's children. In addition, children in Oklahoma City sent teddy bears, books, and cards empathizing with the children and sharing their experiences as residents of a city that had been harmed by terrorist activity.

Teddy bears can be very useful to young, traumatized children as comfort objects and as objects that stimulate symbolic processes that enhance early learning. Many early-grade teachers, however, may be unfamiliar with the potential uses of teddy bears in school and may appreciate guidelines for emotionally responsive practice featuring the bears.

All of New York City's children were affected to some degree by the terrorist attack. Many children who live and attend school in downtown Manhattan witnessed the attack, were trapped inside their homes, or had to run to escape falling debris. Children around the city suffered primary losses of family members who died in the assault. All of the city's young children saw adults express horror, alarm, fear, sadness, and despair. Their world was transformed from a safe place into an unsafe place in a matter of minutes. Many had too much access to television and other media that portrayed the terrible event over and over again.

Children who feel endangered do not learn well. They tend to be preoccupied and inattentive or to experience extreme separation anxiety when separated from their parents and during classroom transitions. Children who were actually traumatized by proximity to the event may experience panic, hyperarousal, or other symptoms of posttraumatic stress disorder. The energy of bereaved children will be taken up with grieving. The need to help these children build a bridge back to experiencing school as a safe environment where they can focus on learning must include a clear focus on their emotional well-being and an acknowledgment of any traumatic experiences that they have had. The curricular use of the teddy bears that New York City's children so generously have been given can offer the opportunity to build such a bridge.

Guidelines for Pre-Kindergarten

1. Introduce the bears in the context of a meeting: "Some people who live in other places heard about the scary thing that happened here when the World Trade Towers were knocked down. They wanted to do something to make New York City children feel better, so they sent us these bears."
2. Allow the children to respond to what you have said through open-ended dialogue. If this includes a retelling of the original events, listen and affirm their experiences. If it includes comments about the bears or their ideas for use, or their prior experiences with stuffed animals, listen. When they finish talking, say that one of the things that makes these bears special is that they will live in the classroom for the whole school year. The children will have to find ways to make the classroom be a safe place for the bears to live.
3. Again, allow the children to respond to what you have said through open-ended dialogue. How do they think they can help to make the classroom feel like a safe place for the bears? Listen to and record the children's responses.
4. Acknowledge how many good ideas the children have come up with to make the bears feel safe and talk about how hard they

will all have to work to put those ideas into practice. Meanwhile, even though they will work very hard to make the classroom a safe place for the bears, some of the bears might think about scary things that they saw before they came to live in the classroom. Sometimes the bears might remember something sad, or they might become sad or worried while they are in the classroom.

5. Ask what the bears can do if they are feeling sad or worried in the classroom. Listen to and record the children's responses. When the children are unable to think of more, add suggestions that have not already been made, such as drawing about what worries them; painting about their feelings; creating with clay; playing about the things they are remembering; telling you a story to tell the teacher so she can write it down. Tell the children that the next time the class goes to the library, everyone can look for books that the teddy bears might like us to read about coming to a new school, feeling safe, and having all kinds of feelings.

6. Follow through on all collective suggestions, including providing time for using creative-arts material, symbolic play, and choosing books related to issues of well-being. Read the books aloud to the group and keep them available on the shelves for individual viewing. Create safe spaces such as beds or houses from shoe boxes if these were ideas presented. Give each child a blank book titled *My teddy bear*, and allow her to draw and dictate stories that come to mind. This project should also include ways to differentiate the bears, including a name and a distinguishing feature, which can lead to open-ended discussions and creative play.

7. Make sure to have the bears available for rest time, free play and work time, and meetings that involve bear topics in stories. (As noted earlier, rest time can be an especially difficult time for children who are experiencing severe separation anxiety or who have been traumatized.) Bears can be incorporated into other times of the day if the teacher finds it useful. Children who form deep attachments to the bears as comfort objects should be allowed either to hold them or to make a safe space for them. Letting the bears go home with children and return the next day might work for some families, but it will not for others. Teachers should know their population before making a policy about this. Keeping the

bears in school until the end of the year will probably diminish confusion and ensure that the children have bears with them when they need them. Meeting time should always include an invitation to express concerns or thoughts.

Guidelines for Kindergarten

The guidelines for kindergarten are virtually the same as those for prekindergarten, with a few additions:

1. Introduce the bears in context of meeting: "Some people who live in other places heard about the scary thing that happened here when the World Trade Towers were knocked down. They wanted to do something to make New York City children feel better, so they sent us these bears."
2. Allow the children to respond to what you have said through open-ended dialogue. Be prepared for some children to share information not only about September 11, but also about the larger context, such as the ongoing war. Listen. When the children finish talking, bring them back to the idea that the bears will live with them in the classroom all year and that they will need a way to help the bears feel safe within the classroom environment.
3. Allow the children to respond to what you have said through open-ended dialogue. How do they think they can help to make the classroom a safe place for the bears? Listen to and record the children's responses.
4. Acknowledge how many good ideas the children have come up with to make the bears feel safe, and talk about how hard they will have to work to put those ideas into practice. Meanwhile, even though they will work very hard to make the classroom a safe place for bears, some of the bears might still think about scary things that they saw before they came to live in the classroom. Sometimes the bears might remember something sad, or they might become sad or worried when they are in the classroom.
5. Ask the children what the bears can do if they are feeling sad or worried in the classroom. Listen to and record children's suggestions. When the children are unable to think of more, add ideas that have not already been raised, such as drawing, paint-

ing, working with clay, playing, and telling stories that the teacher can write down. Include writing stories with inventive spelling as well as dictating for those children comfortable using writing as a means of expression. Tell the children that the next time they go to the library, they can look for books that the teddy bears might like to hear.

6. Follow through on the collective suggestions. Also provide an option for the children to write in teddy bear books directly with inventive spelling, if that is a comfortable medium. Children can take some responsibility for seeking out the story of their name or inviting adult an to tell the story.

7. Make sure to have the bears available for rest time; free play and work time; and meetings that involve relevant topics. See the pre-kindergarten guidelines.

Guidelines for First Grade

1. Introduce the bears in morning meeting: "People all over the country have been sending teddy bears to New York City school-children to try to make them feel safer. Can anyone think of a reason why?" Listen to the children's theories, which will probably include the World Trade Center disaster, the war, terrorists, and so on.

2. Introduce the idea that the bears will be staying in the classroom with the children for the year. Ask the children how they think the bears might be helpful to them. Listen to and record their comments.

3. Tell the children that the bears are there to help them feel safer, but that it is their responsibility to make the classroom a safe environment for the bears. How can the children help the bears to feel safe in the classroom environment? How can they make sure that each bear is recognizable and will not get lost? Listen to and record their responses.

4. Ask what the can children do to help the teddy bears respect one another and get along well together. Ask them to think about this during the day and at home in the evening and to come back to meeting the next day with some plans.

5. Give each child responsibility for choosing a name for his or her bear and for deciding when the bear's birthday will be and how

old the bear is. Each child can record this information on the front cover of his or her bear book and write the story of the name he or she has chosen and what kinds of things the bear knows how to do in the book. Each child should decorate his or her bear by making a distinctive beaded collar for it.

6. Record the bears' birthdays on the annual calendar and give each child responsibility for planning his or her bear's birthday party, including a cooking activity, and letting other children know what kind of presents they can make for their bear that will help it feel safe and comfortable at school.

7. Give children responsibility during weekly library time for choosing a book for themselves and a book that would be interesting or comforting to their bear. During reading time, the children can read to themselves or to their bears. If a child chooses a book that he or she thinks will be of interest to all the bears, he or she may request permission to read it or have it read to the whole group.

8. Make bear books available so the children can write about their bears'—and their own—worries and other feelings.

9. Make sure the bears are available to the children during free reading time, meeting time, and center time, if appropriate. They should also be available as comfort objects for children in distress. Teachers may decide to invite the bears to participate in other parts of the day, as well. Some time should always be set aside during meetings for open-ended discussion or for children to discuss concerns.

Guidelines for Second Grade

1. Introduce the bears in morning meeting, according to the guidelines for first grade.

2. Introduce the idea that the bears will spend the year in the classroom with the children, according to the guidelines for first grade. Add that, even though teddy bears are not real, they can feel real to the children who own them. Ask how this happens. Listen to and record the children's ideas.

3. Tell the children that the bears are there to help them feel safer, but that they are responsible for making the classroom a safe environment for the bears. Proceed according to the guidelines for first grade.

4. Ask what the children can do to help the teddy bears respect one another and get along well together, as per the guidelines for first grade. Add: What if the bears feel that there is not enough room for all of them in the classroom, or that there will not be enough food or toys for them each to have enough? What if some of them feel excluded because they are different in some way? Let children talk about these things in a group and come prepared to revisit the topic the next day with suggestions that they can put into practice in the room.

5. Give each child a blank book to record his or her bear's name and age and a story about the things he can do and likes to do, given his age. Also, invite the children to write stories about things that happened in bear's life before he came to live at the school. These can include happy as well as sad and scary things. Things that the child or the bear worries about can also be recorded in the books.

6. Have each child decorates his or her bear in some way that makes it distinctive as his or her own. This might involve a collar or felt clothing.

7. Choose relevant books for read-alouds, such as *The velveteen rabbit*. The children should be invited to choose books for their bears as well as for themselves at library time, to look for titles that would be interesting or comforting to their bears or that they would like to read to the class to address concerns that other bear have.

8. Bears should be present at meeting; at center time, when appropriate; and whenever children are in distress. Meetings should always have a certain amount of time allotted for open-ended discussions of for children to express concerns.

Guidelines for Third and Fourth Grade

1. Tell the children that people all over the country have been sending Teddy Bears to New York City schoolchildren to help make them feel safe after the World Trade Center tragedy. Add that the bears were not sent only for the youngest children in the school building. They were sent for children of all ages, because what happened affected everyone in a powerful way, and everyone needs comfort, no matter their age. Ask the children to respond

with their own thoughts about this. Listen and allow all children who want to speak to express themselves fully.

2. Schools that received bears from Oklahoma City should distribute them along with the letters, drawings, books, and cards that Oklahoma schoolchildren sent to New York City children to express empathy. In a group meeting, allow the children to hold and get to know their bears and to read the material attached or that arrived in the box. While they are holding their bears, allow for comments on and discussion of the material they have read.

3. One of the items included with the bears is a large book by Oklahoma City children about what happened there. If your school did not receive Oklahoma City bears, it is worthwhile to try to find a copy of the book. Read the book to the group with the bears present. Invite comment and discussion.

4. Propose that the children form several committees. One will be responsible for corresponding with the Oklahoma City children who sent the materials. Another can work on making a book about what happened in New York City to keep in the classroom, share with others in the school, and photocopy for the Oklahoma City children. Another third committee can be in charge of organizing a crafts table so the children can create identifying features for their bears. The children on this committee can also be responsible for planning and organizing events involving the bears, such as ceremonies, celebrations, and expressive-arts workshops, that will help them and their classmates feel safe at school and hopeful about their future.

5. Give each child ongoing assignments that involve the bears. Give each child a bear journal along with his or her bear. Have each will give his or her bear a name and write about the meaning of the name chosen. Children who know the origin or their own names can be asked to write about it; those who do not can be asked to research it. Each child will be responsible for writing a story about his or her bear's history. How old is the bear? How much of the world has it seen? Does the bear still worry things that happened in its life before it came to live at school? At the end of each day, each child can write a journal entry about the bear's thoughts on classroom dynamics that day. Did the bears feel included? What were the interactions among the children in the classroom like?

Guidelines for Fifth and Sixth Grade

1. Tell the children that people all over the country have been sending teddy bears to New York City schoolchildren, following to the guidelines for third and fourth grade.

2. Schools that received bears from Oklahoma City should distribute them along with the letters, drawings, books, and cards from Oklahoma City schoolchildren. Allow the children to read the material and to discuss their reactions in a group meeting.

3. Read the book but the Oklahoma City children to the group at the next meeting. Invite comment and discussion. Have the children compare and contrast what the Oklahoma City children say in the book with what happened in New York City and with their own thoughts and feelings about it. Some schools have received mail and drawings from children in other states, and even in other countries. This material can also be adapted to these guidelines.)

4. All of the children have heard words of comfort from adults during the crisis; now they are hearing words of comfort from other children. Ask them what has been the most helpful to them. How have they felt about adults during this crisis, particularly about adults in charge (that is, adults in charge of them, in charge of the city, and so on)? Has the crisis affected how they feel about adults and about other children in the city?

5. Keep the bears for upper-grade children in the classroom for a few months. The children will be in charge of

   a) making sure that the bears are comfortable and feel safe;
   b) making sure that the bears know their own histories and will be accepted, regardless of their origins;
   c) making sure the bears are always available to comfort classmates in need; and
   d) making sure that the group can organize itself to meet the needs of the bears.

6. To accomplish these goals, children will have to talk in a group about how best to be in charge of the bears. Distribute one bear to each child, and assign each the job of giving the bear an identity and a history. (This will happen in written form as well as using creative arts to make the bear identifiable). Items a, c, and d, will

have to be worked out by the group through discussion. Teachers may suggest forming committees to address community building, issues of inclusion and exclusion, defining and addressing needs of new participants in a community, and being attuned to their own needs and the needs of their fellow classmates since September 11.

Guidelines for Seventh and Eighth Grade

1. Tell the children that people all over the country have been sending Teddy Bears to New York City schoolchildren to help make them feel safe after the World Trade Center tragedy, as per the guidelines for third–sixth grade. Depending on the school's structure, the bear-centered discussions and curricula can be carried out during the homeroom, English, or social-studies period.
2. School that receive bears from Oklahoma City should distribute them along with the letters, drawings, books, and cards from Oklahoma City schoolchildren. Follow the guidelines for third–sixth grade.
3. Obtain a copy of the book by the Oklahoma City children and read it aloud to the group. Invite comment and discussion.
4. Ask the children to write, design, and print a book about their experience of the World Trade Center disaster using narrative, poetry, drawing, photography, and computer technology. The Oklahoma City book is written for a young audience; books created by seventh- and eighth-graders should be written for middle-school kids. One copy of the book can be sent to Oklahoma City; other copies can be made for classrooms and library use. Children can volunteer for the editorial team that puts the book together, but everyone must make a contribution. The time line for the project should be one month.
5. During the month that the book is being written, the teddy bears can remain in school to remind kids that they are not alone and that other children and adults across the country are thinking about them. The children can keep the bears in their lockers or backpacks if they desire, or they can make displays in the classrooms to help other kids focus on their symbolic value. Children who feel that they have more to say should be given journals as

an invitation for ongoing expression. A "Teddy Bear Group" should be made available for kids who want continue to meet to talk about what has happened, with the school guidance counselor or social worker present as a facilitator.

6. Teachers should set behavioral parameters before they distribute bears to help the children understand their symbolic value.

Note to Upper-Grade Teachers

Feel free to use suggestions made at lower or higher grade levels than the ones indicated, depending on the maturity of your particular group and the developmental and experiential challenges that the children are facing during this difficult time.

CHAPTER 13

A Question of Standards

IN RECENT YEARS, early-grade classrooms have become increasingly organized around demonstrating that they uphold state and city standards set for each public-school grade. Teachers are advised to become well versed in the standards so they can justify each of their classroom projects and curricula. Teachers are often required to post standards, by narrative and number, under displays of student work to show the value of the work undertaken. Administrators often feel that it is helpful for teachers, parents, and children to have a framework for understanding what a certain grade level aspires to teach. Therefore, standards can fulfill an important function if they are well thought out, developmentally appropriate, and clearly stated.

Why, then, would a book concerned with the mental health of public-school children address the issue of standards at all? What do standards have to do with children's mental health? The answer is, perhaps, nothing and everything. It can be said that, in many cases, standards have nothing to do with children's mental health, because standards rarely address mental-health issues directly. When they do, they are rarely enforced. One may find references to children's social adjustment and emotional well-being in public schools' standards manuals; at the same time, however, one can observe school policies and routines that undermine social adjustment and emotional well-being on a daily basis.

Standards have everything to do with the emotional well-being of children when they are *interpreted* in a way that actively interferes with the emotional health of children. The word "interpreted" is important, because the standards themselves most often are written by people who have expertise in the education of early-grade children, are reasonable, and can be translated into sound classroom practices. However, the standards are frequently used by practitioners concerned about their schools' performance levels to justify unsound practices.

For instance, the literacy standards for kindergarten children in New York City, which are published for parents in a pamphlet titled "What Did You Learn in School Today?" are age-appropriate and sound. They include, among others, developing an understanding of the meaning of stories read aloud, beginning to read common words around the classroom and at home, and understanding the idea that letters stand for sounds that form words when put together (Rizzo, 2001). Experienced early-grade teachers will tell you about countless ways in which these standards can be addressed within developmentally appropriate kindergartens. Yet many kindergarten children are suddenly being deprived of recess and rest time. Ask about the changes in policy and routine and you will be told that this is necessary in order to uphold the standards for literacy. Because each class must have a 90-minute literacy block each morning, no time is available to address other academic subjects unless rest and recess are eliminated.

We are left with many questions about how standards translate into actual practice in public schools. How is it that reasonable, age-appropriate standards are used to justify unreasonable practice? How is it that standards in one area take priority over standards in other areas? What is driving the current emphasis on standards, and are the standards being implemented to benefit public-school children?

In the example given earlier, 5-year-olds are being deprived of gross motor activity as well as an opportunity to rest and regroup before beginning their afternoon. Most 5-year- olds need to expend energy during the day, and many still fall asleep when rest time is available. Emotionally fragile and highly stressed children tend to need motoric outlets and opportunities to rest in a quiet and protected atmosphere the most. When they are deprived of both during the kindergarten day, these children are more likely to fall apart, become a drain on the teacher's time and energy, and disrupt the other children. They are less likely to be able to employ successful defenses or use their ego strengths, and they are more likely to become overwhelmed by negative effects as the day goes on. Yet it becomes difficult for teachers to adjust their practices to meet the needs of the particular children in their classes when all practices are framed in terms of compliance with standards. It is easy to see how fanatic adherence to the school's individual interpretation of standards can conflict with emotionally responsive practice and may constitute a threat to the emotional well-being of many young children in the public-school system.

Evaluating Performance—but Whose?

Few educators would argue with the thesis that fanatic adherence to standards is driven by concern about students' performance on standardized tests, particularly in the area of reading. Urban children have not performed as well as their suburban counterparts on standardized reading tests, and this has raised a great deal of concern about the quality of the education urban children are receiving. The concerns of parents and politicians has translated into enormous pressure for urban schools to invest in helping children to perform better on the tests—"as if," all things being equal, urban children simply are being taught in a deficient manner and are not performing well as a result. In reality, all things have never been equal between poor urban students and higher-income suburban students. Yet the concern about test scores does not seem to translate into city, state, or federal action designed to even the playing field.

In her book *A teacher's guide to standardized reading tests,* Lucy Calkins addresses the issue of "accountability" in a new light. She notes that, although testing is thought to hold educators accountable, low scores indicate the need to hold communities accountable by giving their children small classes, access to literate mentors, and equal access to books and opportunities to hear and tell stories (Calkins, 1998). Instead of focusing federal resources on giving children the kind of experiences that are precursors to literacy in the early grades, the United States is using its resources to implement annual testing for children in grades three and higher. It is "as if" more frequent testing will somehow result in higher student achievement. In reality, more frequent testing is likely to result in an increasingly narrow educational focus as districts strive to tailor their curricula more closely to skills that are likely to be called on during standardized-test taking. Research has shown that teaching to the tests can produce higher test scores, but it does not necessarily bring about greater proficiency in reading. Test-score gains disappear when a different test is used (Calkins, 1998). An overemphasis on drilling and answering multiple-choice questions has allowed less time to focus on more critical areas of learning, such as self-expression through oration and writing, the development of analytic skills, and creative problem solving (Darling-Hammond and Wise, 1985).

If children are not performing well on standardized tests, who is responsible? Are communities to blame for not offering the support necessary for emergent literacy? Are schools to blame for not engaging in sound educational practices? Are the tests themselves responsible for not testing those skills required by the grade-level standards set by the city or state? Calkins refers to the paradoxical situation in which many states that use standardized tests do not test the skills included in their own grade-level standards, and refers readers who want to explore advocacy issues on testing concerns to the National Center for Fair and Open Testing (Calkins, 1998). She also notes that Vermont and Rhode Island have adopted standards developed by the New Standards Project in Pittsburgh, and that they use standards-based assessments that are based on a deep understanding of what is needed to be a thoughtful reader (Calkins, 1998). Although multiple factors contribute to poor performance on standardized tests, the blame is most frequently placed on teachers and administrators. It is the teachers, administrators, and the children themselves who pay the highest price for the notion that standardized testing is the only valid measure of a school's success.

Under Siege

Low-performing schools are schools under siege these days. They hear: "If the test scores don't go up, the school may close"; "If the test scores don't go up, the principal may be reassigned"; "If the test scores don't go up, teachers won't be eligible for merit pay"; "If your children's test scores don't go up, you'll be assigned to pre-kindergarten in the fall." Schools whose test scores are high may enjoy a relatively warm and supportive educational climate; the ever-present threat of poor testing outcomes, however, creates enormous stress in low-performing schools. This stressful atmosphere is severely undermining to emotionally responsive practice. Because the children in low-performing schools are likely to have the most risk factors for mental-health difficulties, and the fewest resources to compensate for the risks, they may be especially dependent on their teachers to enhance their emotional well-being and, thus, their receptivity to learning. Although research has shown that at-risk children's ability to achieve positive outcomes can be correlated with their opportunities for strong and supportive relationships with adults outside their own families (Edwards, 2001), the emphasis on testing often minimizes the interpersonal potential of the teacher–child relationship as teachers become focused on outcomes instead of personal meaning and process. This diminishes the power of the teacher to become a midwife for the birth of symbolic processes in at-risk children (see chapter 4), which may in turn result in the children's being less invested in classroom process and less able to use language, drawing, and writing as avenues for personal expression. Deprived of these avenues of expression, at-risk children are more likely to become behavior problems in the classroom.

Teachers in low-performing schools are likely to require the highest energy levels and the deepest level of commitment to children to do their jobs well. They must have conviction about their ability to make a difference in the lives of young children in need. They often feel dependent on positive feedback from their building administrator in order to be persistent and have confidence in their ability to prevail with struggling children. When building administrators experience persistent pressure to evaluate teachers based primarily on testing outcomes, they may feel the need to detach themselves from personal connections that they feel to the teachers in question, making them distant and less available. Certain teachers may not be able to sustain their confidence in the face of administrative detachment. They may become less effective and more tense in the classroom. They may also feel depressed or anxious or become more susceptible to illness and miss more school days as the workplace ceases to be a source of support or self-esteem.

Teachers who take jobs in low-performing schools because they want to work with children in need are frequently people who are exhilarated by creative challenges and are ingenious and inventive in their practice. However, schools under siege often require teachers to use prescriptive curricula that they hope will prepare children to be successful test takers. Teachers may need to devote all of their staff-development time to learning these prescriptive methods. Competent, creative teachers who know what works for their students are unlikely to remain in a building under siege if they are not allowed to use teaching methods that work for them. They are likely to request transfers to more successful districts, leaving in the low-performing schools less experienced teachers, many of whom were placed there because they lacked seniority, to teach at-risk children.

The Day of the Test

Ms. M's third-grade class was three days away from a scheduled two-day standardized test. Ms. H, the mental-health consultant in Ms. M's school, was surprised to find Ms. M sitting on her desk in tears after school. Ms. M was usually authoritative and powerful in her presence and extremely devoted to her students. She always came to school early in the morning and stayed after hours. She frequently went home with children to make sure they were safe or to check in with a worrisome parent. "They can't do it," she said, crying. "They'll fail."

"What happened?" Ms. H asked with concern.

"Nothing. And nothing is going to happen in the next three days that is going to let those children succeed on that test. There's nothing I can do to help them with it."

Ms. M continued to cry, and Ms. H looked at the 27 drawings on the bulletin board, each created by one of Ms. M's students. The children's personal stories jumped off the paper and brought Ms. H back to the reality of what it was like for Ms. M to teach these children. Jarad had just joined the class, having been placed by child-protective services in a foster home in the school's catchment area. He had never attended a school for any length of time and did not read or write. Fernando had entered in October and spoke little English. Rhonda had come to school three days in a row with suspicious bruises, and Ms. M had reported the family after going to the home herself and being refused entry. Rhonda had been absent today. Anis was a brilliant artist and a great writer but could not seem to keep her mind on external stimuli for more than a few minutes. She seemed to be in her own world a lot of the time. Jackson was a great reader, but he was continually distracted by sounds such as the steam heat and outside traffic, which made him so anxious that he had panic attacks. The twins Rebecca and Ramona trailed after Ms. M all day and were functional learners only when they were sitting right next to her. Keith read well and had a wealth of information but could not stay in his seat for more than three minutes at a time. Ms. H was allowed to see children individually when they were in crisis, but she was not allowed to do ongoing work with the children. Instead, she was advised to refer their families to community agencies, but the families rarely followed through with the referrals.

"I know what to do on a regular day," Ms. M continued. "I know what will bring them out and calm them down and be interesting enough to keep their attention. But two days of testing is two days of hell. There's nothing I can do but tell them to begin. There's nothing I can do to help them, and I know they will fail."

Ms. H agreed with Ms. M that her class was unlikely to do well on the test as a group, for obvious reasons. She reminded Ms. M of the academic and social levels of functioning that characterized the children when they came in at the beginning of the year. Ms. M had succeeded in getting the children to function as a group. She had been able to read their strengths and weaknesses, to develop relationships with their families, and to learn their personal stories. She had found ways to get them to tune in to the curriculum and experience learning as an avenue of growth and personal expression. But the children needed to interact with Ms. M in order to do that. They needed the material to be meaningful. Maybe they would not test well, but they were doing well, all things considered.

Ms. M dried her tears and thought about what Ms. H said for a while. "You and I know that that's true," said Ms. M. "But no one else knows or cares."

Ms. H agreed. "The most important thing is that you know, and the children know, that they are learning." Ms. M gathered her things to leave and thanked Ms. H for being there at the right moment.

On the first day of the test, Rhonda came back to school accompanied by her mother and a case worker. She had dark circles under her eyes from fatigue. She lay her head on the desk on top of the test pamphlet. The caseworker took Ms. M aside and told her that Rhonda had been in the emergency room most of the night to be evaluated for sexual abuse. The results were inconclusive. Rhonda's mother whispered a threat to Ms. M as she left Rhonda in the classroom. Ms. M's heart pounded with distress and fear. She started to approach Rhonda but thought better of it, because the testing would not allow her to sustain the kind of attention Rhonda might need. Ms. M advised the children to remove everything from their desks except a pencil and the test pamphlet. Anis started talking loudly to herself in an agitated way, because the testing rules precluded having her drawing notebook on the desk, and she felt upset if she could not see it. The kids began to laugh and get unruly. Ms. M tried to calm Anis so she could finish giving the testing directions, but she could not, so she took Anis to the office. When Ms. M returned, she fished a pair of foam earplugs out of her purse for Jackson. She seated Rebecca and Ramona near her desk. "Alright, class," she said in a strong voice. "You may begin."

When the test results came in, they showed that Ms. M's class had scored well below the national average in reading and math. Ms. M's school came under review, and Ms. M and all the other teachers were interviewed individually and asked how they planned to improve the testing outcomes. No social services were added to Ms. M's school, and no considerations for improving the emotional climate in the class-rooms were noted in the recommendation report that the school eventually received.

Standards for Well-being

Standardized tests have been around for a long time, but they have not always been used the way they are used now. Standardized tests used to be used to measure children's status compared with that of other children of the same age nationwide. If the tests revealed a large discrepancy between a child's functional level and his or her testing level, teachers made note of it, discussed it with parents, and spoke about how to enhance the child's classroom performance. Increasingly, standardized tests seem to be understood as evaluations of schools or school districts as opposed to evaluations of children. If a school does not perform well, it is considered "sick" and is ordered to "get well," most frequently by following a certain prescription designed to produce higher test results. The prescription rarely includes treating the many stressors that distract and preoccupy children and make their prognosis as learners poor. Indeed, the prescriptions themselves often deprive children of needed avenues of expression and add to the stress that they and their teachers feel.

Existing standards commonly refer to social and emotional health in terms of children's becoming "good citizens" or showing that they are of "good character." Considerable energy is spent in the early grades discussing good citizenship with groups of children, most often approaching the development of good citizenship from an educative perspective. But to become good citizens, children have to have their emotional needs met. When they are not burdened by an overwhelming sense of deprivation, they can be part of community and consider the needs of others. Teaching good citizenship is rarely successful unless the children are well cared for and well protected, because even if they learn to recite the requirements for a "good citizen," they cannot fulfill the requirements without a partner who is attuned to their emotional status.

Many studies correlate social and emotional competence with success in school (see, e.g.,. Ladd et al., 1999; Raver, 2001). Cybele Raver of the University of Chicago has documented the connection between emotional well-being and learning in early childhood and recommends including emotional and behavior-adjustment goals along with academic goals in performance standards (Raver, 2001). To take these new standards seriously, school districts would have to make emotional well-being a priority on par with literacy, math, science, and social studies. Practices that undermine emotional well-being would be considered contrary to the school's performance standards. Teachers, paraprofessional staff, and administrators would need to receive staff development on emotional and developmental issues for children in each grade, precursors for emotional well-being in children, and the connection between emotional well-being and learning potential. Administrators would have to have a clear basis for intervention when staff members act in ways that undermine children's well-being. Emotional well-being would become an administrative priority as well as a priority for school-based clinicians and early-grade teachers. Because this would require an interdisciplinary approach to achieving the standards of emotional well-being, the potential for positive outcomes would be greatly enhanced. Ms. M's talent as a teacher would be recognized, and more of her students probably would become empowered learners.

There are several ways to construct standards for emotional well-being that are appropriate for early grade children. The framework that follows can serve as one model for educators who are interested in pursuing a standards-based approach to emotional health in early elementary school.

Pre-Kindergarten Standards for Emotional Well-being

1. The child will show the capacity to think about important people when they are out of sight.
2. The child will be able to separate from important people without too much distress after the first months of school, and he or she will use the teacher as a resource when he or she feels needy in school.
3. The child will be able to identify and name emotions (positive and negative affects) in photographs and in peers.
4. The child will be able to express his or her own affects verbally—that is, he or she will be able to say, "I feel angry."
5. The child will find pleasure in relating to other children. He or she will become motivated to have friends and will express concern about other children's rejection.

6. The child will anticipate and participate in routines, activities, and transitions most of the time.
7. The child will negotiate routines that include lunch, toileting, rest, and outdoor play with adult support.
8. The child will use pretend play, drawing, paint, and clay to process experiences and express thoughts and feelings.
9. The child will attend to stories that reflect developmental issues and emotional status.
10. The child will begin to appreciate and articulate social and emotional cause and effect—saying, for example, "I feel sad when mommy leaves" or "Michael gets angry when someone grabs his toy."
11. The child will move toward representational drawings and eventually draw a face with affect.

Kindergarten Standards for Emotional Well-being

1. The child will use symbolic play, storytelling, drama, drawing, and physical activity to work out age-appropriate conflicts, such as issues surrounding competition, authority, and identity.
2. The child will become increasingly connected to other children and form more stable friendships during the school year.
3. The child will begin to anticipate social and emotional causes and effects—saying, for example, "If I take Ana's toy, she will get mad" or "If I lose my teddy bear, I'll feel sad, so I'd better put it in my cubby."
4. The child will anticipate and participate in routines, activities, and transitions most of the time.
5. The child will be increasingly motivated toward independent mastery and will take pride in that mastery, but will ask for adult support when he or she feels the need.
6. The child will become more accepting of limits set by adults and will try to internalize classroom rules. (This is often demonstrated by tattling.)
7. The child will use adults to assist with reality testing and with open-ended interaction with materials in the classroom environment.
8. The child will engage in group dialogues related to collective experiences. For example, the child will participate in and or

attend to group discussions about a fire or other event in the neighborhood.

9. The child will be engaged in group discussion about what to do when he or she feels angry, sad, scared, excited, or worried.

First-Grade Standards for Emotional Well-being

1. The child will have stable relationships with peers, often including a best friend or friendship group.
2. The child will begin spontaneously to use a problem-solving approach to negotiate peer conflicts, as modeled by classroom adults.
3. The child will begin to use writing, as well as drawing and play, to express thoughts, concerns, and feelings and to process experiences.
4. The child will become increasingly capable of expressing distress verbally and will become less dependent on acting things out.
5. The child will begin to pursue interests and talents with adult support. The child will take pride in his or her accomplishments.
6. The child will take more ownership of the classroom, participating in such activities as planning and cleanup in a responsible fashion. The child will be protective of his or her schoolwork.
7. The child will be able to find meaning in stories, plays, poems, and other media that reflect age-appropriate social and emotional issues and conflicts and elaborate themes in response.
8. The child will be able to regulate emotional responses according to the severity of the stressor.
9. The child will follow classroom rules most of the time.
10. The child will continue to use adults to support reality testing and interaction with materials in the classroom environment.

Second-Grade Standards for Emotional Well-being

1. The child will begin to show capacity to draw accurate lines between fantasy and reality.
2. The child will have a best friend or a secure place in a friendship group.

3. The child will use teachers to help regulate self-esteem and value his or her uniqueness at a time that the developmental pull is to be the same as peers.
4. The child will participate in group projects with energy, excitement, and eagerness to contribute, and with the ability to follow through on his or her contribution.
5. The child will use writing, as well as language, art, and movement activities, as primary forms of expression.
6. The child will internalize a problem-solving approach to peer conflicts.
7. The child will verbalize distress, including social and emotional cause and effect, ambivalence, and complex or multiple emotions. He or she will be able to say, for example, "I'm glad that Peter moved to a new school because he used to hit me on the playground, but I miss how funny he used to be in the lunchroom" or "I'm excited about the spelling bee, but I'm scared I might not remember my words."
8. The child will be motivated toward mastery without becoming immobilized by perfectionistic standards for his or her performance. For example, he or she will attempt to draw from observation without crumpling the paper because outcome is not what he or she envisioned.
9. The child will have developed his or her own repertoire of expressing feelings constructively in the school situation and will be able to engage in constructive expression in emotional situations.

Third-Grade Standards for Emotional Well-being

1. The child will be able to argue a position coherently, without becoming overly distraught.
2. The child will be able to look at the past, present, and future on a new level and express thoughts and concerns verbally or via creative symbolic processes, such as writing, dance, art, poetry, and other projects.
3. The child will find meaning in what he or she reads and use reading to expand the universe, strengthen identity, and feed interests.
4. The child's place in the peer group will be secure.

5. The child will resolve peer conflicts verbally most of the time.
6. The child will maintain a positive self-image that includes dreams of the future.
7. The child will find meaning in his or her experience and use writing and other forms of creative expression to explore and communicate what is important.
8. The child will accept limits set by adults and respect boundaries in peer relationships.
9. The child will feel confident about his or her abilities and will be comfortable exploring new experiences and discovering new talents.
10. The child will present himself or herself with genuine affect and will be able to perceive accurately the affects of others.

The Potential for School Environments That Heal

When teachers, administrators, and clinicians organize around a school's priorities, those priorities flourish. If a school takes pride in the quality of its band, buys ornate uniforms, and finds a talented conductor to work diligently with the children, the band is likely to sound better and better. If a school takes pride in its baseball team, its science fair, or its reading levels, energy will be committed to those endeavors, and they are likely to improve or even to shine. Our standards for supporting the emotional health of children in public schools have been low, but the stakes for supporting emotional health have never been higher. Unless a commitment is made nationwide to the emotional health of young schoolchildren, we are likely to continue to witness the tragedy of violence in middle-school and high-school populations. Unless a commitment is made nationwide to the emotional health of young children, too many children will be preoccupied by emotional issues to concentrate on learning, and too many children will not reach their potential to become intelligent, curious learners and social, stable citizens. The potential to create healing school environments is there. Will we accept the challenge?

Inviting and Containing Workshop

Inviting Techniques

- Inviting techniques invite expression and exploration of thoughts or feelings.
- Inviting techniques encourage activity (talking, singing, movement, drawing, etc.).
- Inviting techniques tap into children's energy in the service of expression or exploration.
- Inviting techniques act to decrease isolation in children.

Containing Techniques

- Containing techniques provide form, boundaries, and structure for children's energy.
- Containing techniques help children feel safe and secure.
- Containing techniques address collective energy so that it does not become overwhelming.
- Containing techniques "hold" the material that has been invited.

Inviting Techniques + Containing Techniques = A Holding Environment for Children

Inviting and Containing Workshop: Which Is Which?

- Classroom routines
- Making the whisper sign
- Songs with fill-in lyrics
- Use of transitional objects
- Blank books in which children may write
- Books read to children about the end of the year
- Reflective technique
- Curriculum on going away and coming back
- Water table with soap added
- Singing a cleanup song at cleanup time
- Singing "If You're Sad and You Know It . . ."
- Morning-meeting conversation about a fire in the neighborhood
- Saying "No!" in a stern voice when a child is intruding on others
- Holding a child who is crying during separation
- Holding a child who is out of control and kicking other children
- Making "yucky soup" (soup that looks or tastes bad) at cooking time
- Providing cookie cutters at the play dough table
- Doing affect dances

Inviting and Containing:
A Menu of Interventions

Teacher–Child Interactions

- Use of reflective language, such as, "You seem upset about being in school today."
- Use of instructive language, such as, "You can tell Alicia that you need more space."
- Use of drawing technique. For example, the teacher draws a picture of a conflict that occurred in the cafeteria and asks the children involved to help clarify events and feelings.
- Use of blank books that invite children to express complex issues. For example, the teacher gives the child a book about feeling worried so he can draw in it when he feels worried at school.
- Use of structured check-in. For example, the teacher invites or instructs a disorganized or demanding child to check in with her after he or she is finished and before moving on.

Environment and Routines

- Environment is made warm and inviting.
- Environment is more clearly defined and thus more containing (e.g., by moving the furniture).
- Children's work is displayed in a careful way that shows the content but is not overwhelming.
- Child population is reflected in photos, drawings, and book illustrations about children of their own cultural backgrounds, as well as others, and by representing a range of affects.
- Routines are made more predictable and developmentally appropriate by heightening adult–child intimacy and adding homelike features.
- Teachers or other adults to whom the children are attached are involved in caregiving routines such as lunch and rest time.
- Routines include opportunities for dialogue and genuine expression. (For example, meeting goes beyond ritual and allows children to be involved in the content.)

(continued)

Curriculum

- Curriculum emerges as a reflection of the social and emotional agenda of the children.
- Curriculum offers children opportunities to use symbols and metaphor to express their inner life and to convey the nature of actual experience.
- Curriculum gives children opportunities to process actual experiences by increasing their understanding of cause and effect and placing them within a social context—for example, a study of firefighters following a school fire.
- Curriculum projects encourage group interaction as well as individual pursuits that best serve the group dynamic.
- Curriculum includes literature that invites children to explore further their own interests and concerns.
- Curriculum includes teacher-made and child-made books that represent important experience.

Why Gather Stories?

Why do we need to know where children are coming from, developmentally and historically? Why is it important to ask parents for history, even though they may initially feel that questions intrude on their privacy? Why is developmental history any of the teacher's business to begin with?

Children's backgrounds historically have been regarded as something that might prejudice teachers. If teachers know that children are at risk, they may not expect them to be able to learn. For this reason, history has been considered potentially dangerous—something that the social worker has to keep in a file, where it can do no harm.

Programs that embrace emotionally responsive practice can use history to enhance a teacher's ability to facilitate development. Instead of keeping teachers from investing in children's potential, knowledge of developmental history can help teachers assess children's confusing behavior in new ways.

For example, one child in the classroom becomes disruptive whenever the lights are turned off, including during rest time and birthday parties. The teacher makes many attempts to reassure the child and correct his disruptive behavior, yet it continues. While taking a developmental history at a parent conference, the teacher learns that the child was present one night while a visiting relative molested his sibling and has been very anxious in the dark ever since. The next day, the teacher takes the child aside and says, "Mommy said that when the lights go out, it might remind you of something scary that happened. I know that sometimes we turn the lights off in our class. So if the lights get turned off, and you start feeling scared, come over and sit by me." The boy is able to do this, and the disruptive behavior diminishes. Because of the disturbing nature of the child's experience, the teacher calls in the school social worker, who refers the family for counseling.

A girl in the same classroom never pays attention when books are read aloud to the group. She looks around the room constantly and seems focused on the area of the classroom near the door. It is hard to help her attend to her own activity unless the teacher stays by her side. A conference with the girl's mother reveals that she began speaking very late: She did not start using words until she was almost 3. She has extreme reactions to separation and screams hysterically when her mother leaves her with anyone. Each morning before she leaves for

(continued)

pre-kindergarten, she whimpers and cries but stops crying as she gets closer to the school building. Then she becomes "spaced out."

After the conference, the teacher takes a picture of the child and her mother and puts it in the girl's cubby, inviting her to get it whenever she wants. The teacher chooses to read a book to the group titled *You go away*, which portrays children separating from and reuniting with their parents (Corey, 1999). The girl is fascinated. After the teacher finishes reading to the group, the child spends several minutes deeply focused on the book on her own. Later in the year, the vocabulary in this book becomes her sight vocabulary and the basis for her feeling empowered as a reader.

Why gather children's personal stories? Because experience and development proceed hand in hand. If parents feel trusting enough to put their children's stories in the teacher's capable hands, they can become tools to increase the educational potential of every child.

Story-Gathering Day

This year, we're going to use our parent conferences to get to know each of our children better. We're meeting them as ___-year-olds, but we missed knowing them when they were babies, toddlers, and pre-schoolers. We're going to try to get to know the important stories of each child's development and life experiences so we can help our children understand their experiences and feel good about themselves as learners.

Here are some questions that will help us to know your child better. If you feel uncomfortable with any question, we can skip to the next one.

1. The first question is about the beginning of your child's life. Was there anything significant about the way he or she came into your family? Were there birth complications? Has your child ever had to be in the hospital, apart from his or her birth experience? What was it like for him or her?

_____

_____

_____

2. How did you choose your child's name? What made that name special to you? Does your child know the story of how his or her name was chosen?

_____

_____

_____

3. When did your child begin to crawl? Walk? Was he or she adventurous or cautious? When did your child begin to talk? What were his or her first words?

_____

_____

_____

(continued)

4. Did your child ever have to be separated from you for a long period of time? What happened? Did he or she ever have to be separated from another important adult? How did it effect him or her? If your child attended preschool or day care, how did the separation go? Was there anything that he or she especially liked or disliked?

_____

_____

_____

5. Who are the important people in your child's life? Who are the people in your child's home life?

_____

_____

_____

6. Did anything ever happen that you felt was very frightening or upsetting for your child? How did it effect your child at the time? How does it affect your child at this time?

_____

_____

_____

7. What are the most important things for us to know about your child?

_____

_____

_____

Confidentiality Statement, Story-Gathering Information

I understand that stories shared on Story-Gathering Day are personal and confidential and may not be shared outside the educational team working with the children in my classroom. These stories will be used for the sole purpose of enhancing each child's emotional well-being and learning and will inform my teacher–child interactions and curriculum planning.

_____   _____
Teacher's Signature   Date

Guide to Creating
Emotionally Responsive Books

1. Define the parameters of your topic based on the child's issues or on common-ground issues of the group. Do not include extraneous material.

2. Assess the developmental and language levels of your audience and reflect that level in your choice of words.

3. Content should address developmental reality, experiential reality, or both.

4. Content may be reflective of affects or experiences on which you are focusing or may invite exploration of that topic. Emphasize process in resolution. No "shoulds."

5. Consider addressing the topic directly or using metaphor to address your topic. Given your intended audience, choose the format that is likely to be better received.

6. Use illustrations and photographs that correspond to content.

7. Draw figures using the Drawing Technique guide (Handout 8), or use pre-cut paper dolls to trace and fill in to reflect affects, features, and cultural identities of your population.

8. Listen to the children's responses to inform your practice. Responses may be immediate, or they may be forthcoming over time. Children may respond differently each time the book is read.

Drawing Technique

Drawing Technique is a form of reflective technique. The teacher or clinician using Drawing Technique represents a child's experience and affects through drawing as a way of clarifying and affirming her social and emotional reality. As she draws, the adult invites input from the child concerning the events being portrayed in the drawing and the ways that he or she wants them represented. The adult may say, "Let's draw about what happened when it was time to clean up. I'll make you first. How should I make your face?" The child may reply, "Sad." The teacher then represents the affect. "Then I will make myself. I came over to you. Then what happened?" etc.

Indications for Use

Drawing Technique can be useful as a means of processing and clarifying a situation that has caused emotional upheaval for a child or group of children, and has caused them to lose perspective about the event, or left them unable to articulate their feelings about it. It is especially helpful when teachers see a problematic pattern in children's emotional reactions to classroom routines and interactions. (For examples, a child always has difficulty in the cafeteria, gets into fights on the playground, is fearful at rest time, becomes distraught when the teacher leaves the room, etc.) Other indications for use of Drawing Technique include the following: the teacher perceives that a child is confused about social and emotional cause and effect; the child is having trouble staying focused on his or her own issues or experiences; the child is having difficulty expressing affect appropriate to the situation or reading affects in others; or the child is having difficulty spontaneously using symbols to represent thoughts and feelings and behaves in an infantile manner.

How To Draw People

1. Draw bodies with form and substance—No Stick people! Teachers and clinicians who have difficulty drawing can use paper dolls to make body outlines.
2. Represent affects.
3. "Fill in" figure with matching skin tones, hairstyles, colors of clothing, and other realistic details to facilitate the child's identification with the figure.

(continued)

4. Provide a recognizable context for the events portrayed by including a symbolic feature of the actual context. For example, if the event happened in the play yard, make a slide.

5. Incorporate children's verbal responses and direction but don't depend on them. Proceed by portraying the affects and events as you see them if there is no verbal participation. Allow children to keep drawings, or create a folder to keep an ongoing record of the drawings that the child can access when needed.

References

Administration for Children and Families, Office of the Assistant Secretary for Planning and Evaluation, Substance Abuse and Mental Health Services Administration. (1999). *Blending perspectives and building common ground: A report to Congress on substance abuse and child protection.* Washington, DC, and Rockville, MD.

Allard, Henry. (1977). *Miss Nelson is missing.* Boston: Houghton Mifflin.

Arnold, D. H., Ortiz, C., Curry, J. C., Stowe, R. M., Goldstein, N. E., Fisher, P. H., Yershova, K., & Zeljoja, A. (1999). Promoting academic success and preventing disruptive behavior disorder thorough community partnership. *Journal of Community Psychology, 5,* 589–598.

Bowlby, J. (2000). *Loss: Sadness and depression (attachment and loss).* New York: Basic Books.

Bronson, M. B. (2001). *Self-regulation in early childhood.* New York: Guilford Press.

Calkins, L. (1998). *A teacher's guide to standardized reading tests.* Portsmouth, MA: Heinemann.

Calkins, L. (2000). *The art of teaching reading.* New York: Longman.

Clarke, L. (1985). *Principal stress.* Paper presented at annual fall conference of the Arkansas Association of Elementary School Principals, Nov. 10–12. Little Rock, AR.

Corey, D. (1999). *You go away.* Morton Grove, IL: Albert Whitman.

Council on Children and Families, New York State Division of Criminal Justice Services, New York State Education Department, New York State Office of Alcoholism and Substance Abuse Services, New York State Office of Children and Family Services, New York State Office of Mental Health, and New York State Police. (2000). *Prevention: Creating safer schools in New York State.* Albany, NY.

Currie, J. (1988). Affect in the schools: A return to the most basic of basics. *Childhood Education,* Winter, 83–87.

Darling-Hammond, L., and Wise, A. (1985). Beyond standardization: State standards and school improvement. *Elementary School Journal, 85*(3), 315–336.

Dyson, A., and Genishi, C. (1994). *The need for story: Cultural diversity in classroom and community.* Urbana, IL: National Council of Teachers of English.

Edwards, C. (2001). Moral classroom communities for student resiliency. *Education Digest, 67*(2), 15–20.

Erikson, E. (1963). *Childhood and society.* New York: W. W. Norton.

Figuerido, B. (1996). *Postpartum depression: Is it a condition affecting mother–infant interaction and the development of the child across the first year of life?* Paper presented at the biennial meeting of the International Society for the Study of Behavioural Development, Quebec City.

Fox, M. (1994). *Sophie*. New York: Harcourt Brace.

Fraiberg, S. (1980). *Clinical studies in infant mental health: The first year of life.* New York: Basic Books.

Fraiberg, S. (1984). *The magic years: Understanding and handling the problems of early childhood.* New York: Fireside.

Goldenson, R. (1984). *Longman dictionary of psychology and psychiatry.* New York: Longman.

Havill, J. (1999). *Jamaica and the substitute teacher.* Boston: Houghton Mifflin.

Hazler, R. (1994). Bullying breeds violence: You can stop it! *Learning, 22*(6), 38–41.

Ivey, A. (1974). Microcounseling: Teacher training as facilitation of pupil growth. *British Journal of Educational Technology, 5*(2), 16–21.

Karen, R. (1998). *Becoming attached: First relationships and how they shape our capacity to love.* New York: Oxford University Press.

Karr-Morse, R., & Wiley, M. (1997). *Ghosts from the nursery: Tracing the roots of violence.* New York: Atlantic Monthly Press.

Katz, L. (1993). *Dispositions: Definitions and implications for early childhood practices.* Urbana, IL: ERIC Clearinghouse on Elementary and Early Childhood Education.

Katz, L. (1995). *Talks with teachers of young children.* Norwood, NJ: Abley Publishing.

Katz, L. (1999). International perspectives on early childhood education: Lessons from my travel. *Early Childhood Research and Practice, 6*(1).

Kopacsi, R., & Onsongo, E. (2001). *1999–2000 evaluation update: New beginnings student outcomes—Cohort and non-cohort comparison.* Newark, NJ: Newark Public Schools, Office of Planning, Evaluation, and Testing.

Koplow, L., ed. (1996). *Unsmiling faces: How preschools can heal.* New York: Teacher's College Press.

Koplow, L. (2001). *Emotionally responsive early childhood programs.* Presentation to the New York City Office of Early Childhood, New York.

Koralek, D. (1999). *Classroom strategies promote children's social and emotional development.* Villanova, PA: Devereau Foundation.

Ladd, G., Birch, S., & Buhs, E. (1999). Children's social and scholastic lives in kindergarten: Related spheres of influence? *Child Development, 70*(6), 1373–1400.

Lifton, R. J., & Lindy, J. D. (2001). *Beyond invisible walls: The psychological legacy of Soviet trauma.* New York: Brunner-Routledge.

Mack, F. (1995). *Preschool teacher attitude and knowledge regarding fetal alcohol syndrome and fetal alcohol effects.* Paper presented at the Annual Conference of the National Association of Early Childhood Teacher Educators, Washington, DC.

Mahler, M., Pine, F., & Bergman, A. (2000). *The psychological birth of the human infant: Symbiosis and individuation.* New York: Basic Books.

Morris, J. (2001, December 31). Teaching for tolerance: Jenny Penado. *U.S. News and World Report, 131*(27), 45.

National Institute of Mental Health. (2000). *Child and adolescent violence research at the National Institute of Mental Health.* Bethesda, MD.

Paley, V. (1993). *You can't say you can't play.* Cambridge, MA: Harvard University Press.

Phelps, L., Wallace, N., & Bontrager, A. (1997). Risk factors in early childhood development: Is prenatal cocaine/polydrug exposure a key variable? *Psychology in the Schools, 34*(3), 245–252.

Pickens, J., & Fields, T. (1993). Facial expressivity in infants of depressed mothers. *Developmental Psychology, 29*(6), 986–988.

Raphael, R. (1985). *The teacher's voice: A sense of who we are.* Portsmouth, NH: Heinemann.

Raver, C. (2001, October 24). *Promoting emotional health in pre-school children: Research findings.* New York University Center for Children and Families.

Reiser, L. (1998). *Cherry pies and lullabies.* New York: Green Willow Books.

Rizzo, J. (2000). *What did you learn at school today? What every student should know and be able to do.* Pamphlet, Board of Education, City of New York.

Rohner, R. P. (1986). *The warmth dimension.* Beverly Hills: Sage.

Schonkoff, J. P., & Phillips, D. A. (2000). *From neurons to neighborhoods.* Washington, DC: National Academy Press.

Seikaly, Z. (2001, October). At risk of prejudice: The Arab American community. *Social Education, 65*(6), 349–351.

Sheridan, M., Radlinski, S., & Foley, G. (1995). *Using the supportive play model: Individualized interaction in early childhood practice.* New York: Teacher's College Press.

Siegler, A. (1998). *The essential guide to the new adolescence.* New York: Plume.

Starky, D. L. (1980). The relationship between parental acceptance, rejection, and the academic performance of 4th and 5th graders. *Behavior Science Research, 15,* 67–80.

Stern, D. (1985). *The interpersonal world of the infant: A view from psychoanalysis and developmental psychology.* New York: Basic Books.

Sutherland, N. S. (1989). *The international dictionary of psychology.* New York: Continuum Press.

Terr, L. (1992). *Too scared to cry—Psychic trauma in childhood.* New York: HarperCollins.

U.S. Department of Commerce, Bureau of the Census. (1999). *Digest of education statistics* (Historical Statistics of the United States, Current Population Reports, Series P-20, Current Population Survey). Washington, DC.

U.S. Department of Health and Human Services, Center for Disease Control and Prevention, National Center for Health Statistics. (1998). *Suicide Fast Stats.* Hyattsville, MD.

U.S. Public Health Service. (2000). *Report of the surgeon general's conference on children's mental health: A national action agenda.* Washington, DC.

Winnicott, D. W., & Winnicott, C. (1982). *Playing and reality.* New York: Routledge.

Index

Italic letter *t* following a page number indicates a table.

About the Author

LESLEY KOPLOW, C.S.W., is the Director of the Center for Emotionally Responsive Practice at Bank Street College. The Center does staff development training and consultation on Emotionally Responsive Practice in the school setting. Ms. Koplow is also a psychotherapist in private practice, and the author of books on child mental health including *Where Rag Dolls Hide Their Faces; The Way Home; Tanya and the Tobo Man;* and *Unsmiling Faces: How Preschool Can Heal.* She lives in New York City with her young daughter.